D0425136

Praise for *Right Away and All At Once*

"Greg applies straightforward learnings from his considerable experience running complex global companies and boils them down into a playbook that can help any business leader be more effective and successful. He challenges the reader by explaining how these concepts can also be applied to our personal lives to achieve the meaning and purpose we all desire."

—Martin Craighead,
Chairman and CEO, Baker Hughes

"Business growth requires the ability to both advance what is working, and turn around what is not. Leaders need a clear path for doing both. Greg Brenneman's competence and character come through in a book that will catalyze your organization, no matter what state it's in."

—John Townsend,
New York Times bestselling author of *Boundaries*,
Leadership Expert and Psychologist, Founder, the Townsend
Institute of Leadership

"It is rare that a book offers such sound business advice coupled with insightful spiritual guidance. Whether your pursuit is the secular or the sacred, *Right Away and All At Once* is a must read."

—Kyle Vann,
Chairman, Generous Giving

"Insightful, practical, and powerfully effective. Greg Brenneman has distilled the key steps to turn around your business and your life!"

—Vinh Chung,

Member, World Vision Board, author of *Where the Wind Leads*

"In *Right Away and All At Once*, Greg Brenneman has provided a framework and methodology for looking at our businesses with fresh eyes, but more importantly he's provided a roadmap for integrating our personal and professional lives with incredible clarity."

—Les Brun,

Chairman, ADP

"*Right Away and All At Once* reveals an ancient secret. God's ways are excellent, which should surprise no one but will actually surprise many. When things need to happen anywhere, everyone is better off when God's man shows up. This book shows why."

—Britt Harris,

Chief Investment Officer, Teacher Retirement System of Texas

"The principles outlined by Greg Brenneman can have a profound impact on you personally as you wrestle through some of the most important questions about life, family success and beyond. I encourage you to read this book...it is excellent!"

—Mario Zandstra,

Former President & CEO, Pine Cove Regional Director,

Redeemer City to City

"Through many examples, *Right Away and All At Once* shows us how we need both mentors and close friends to reach our full potential. The importance of generosity as it relates to developing leaders, serving friends, and giving back to others less fortunate is apparent throughout each chapter. It will serve as a great reference for business leaders, management teams, and individuals wanting to make a difference in this world."

—Waters Davis,

President, National Christian Foundation, Houston

"Greg Brenneman's personal and professional story is compelling, and the invaluable life lessons drawn from his extensive CEO experience are insightful and clear. This is a must read for anyone who is engaged in the daily battle of the marketplace. I wish this book had been available at the front end of my career. Buy it!"

—Jim Lane,

Founder, New Canaan Society, Former General Partner, Goldman, Sachs & Co.

Right Away
&
All At Once

Five Steps to Transform Your
Business and Enrich Your Life

By Greg Brenneman

NEW YORK 2016

RIGHT AWAY AND ALL AT ONCE
Five Steps to Transform Your Business and Enrich Your Life

RosettaBooks editions are available to the trade through Ingram distribution services, ipage.ingramcontent.com or (844) 749-4857. For special orders, catalogues, events, or other information, please write to production@rosettabooks.com.

For information, please contact RosettaBooks at production@rosettabooks.com, or by mail at One Exchange Plaza, Suite 2002, 55 Broadway, New York, NY 10006.

First edition published 2016 by RosettaBooks

Cover design by Peter Clark
Interior design by Corina Lupp

Library of Congress Control Number: 2015949098

ISBN-13: 978-0-7953-4748-1

RosettaBooks®

www.RosettaBooks.com

Printed in the United States of America

For Ronda,
Andrew, Nina, Bethany and Aaron
My Life Team, The Inner Circle

Contents

Step Five

Acknowledgments

It turns out that writing a book is a humbling experience. It takes both a lot of time and mountains of mental energy. Writing a book in your personal time while running a private equity firm and serving on several large corporate and nonprofit boards borders on foolish. I was blessed to have the support and contributions of many people who guided me through the process and made the impossible seem possible.

My partners at CCMP—Chris Behrens, Doug Cahill, Jon Lynch, Kevin O'Brien, Joe Scharfenberger, Tom Walker, Tim Walsh, and Rich Zannino—are simply amazing. Their diligence in serving our firm and investors every day with equal displays of intelligence and integrity makes coming to work fun.

Much of the material in *Right Away and All At Once* exists only because of the hard work and accomplishments of the hundreds of thousands of coworkers who have labored alongside me at CCMP, Bain, Continental Airlines, PricewaterhouseCoopers Consulting, Burger King, ADP, The Home Depot, Baker Hughes, Francesca's, Generac, Milacron and many other organizations. Thank you for the contributions you have made to my career, my life, and to this book.

To the boards, CEOs, and management teams of those organizations, I tried my best to represent our joint stories in a manner that honors you. I remembered the facts to the best of my ability. Any lessons, suggestions, positions or conclusions in this book are mine alone and do not represent any of the organizations or individuals I have worked with in the past or present. Likewise, any errors or omissions are mine too.

Much of the content developed for the life lessons in this book has come out of a great partnership with an exceptional couple, Britt and Julia Harris. My wife, Ronda, and I have the annual privilege of mentoring younger couples with Britt and Julia. A special thanks to them for their friendship and ongoing contribution to our lives.

There is no such thing as a self-made man. I highlight more than a dozen of my mentors, who informed the five steps, both business and personal, of *Right Away and All At Once*. In some small way, I hope this book serves as my tribute to you.

I felt honored to have the critical feedback of three CEOs, Hal Chappelle, Bill Nath, and Kyle Vann, who I consider both trusted external colleagues and dear friends. They read an early draft and provided me with valuable feedback. Thank you, guys.

I began the book writing journey in late 2014, not even sure I *could* write a book. John Townsend provided the initial encouragement by convincing me that not only could I, but that I should. He then shepherded me through the early part of the process and introduced me to Steve Halliday. Steve came alongside me as a co-collaborator. This book would not be what it is today without his extraordinary guidance, patience, and skill.

A chance breakfast in New York City with a longtime friend, Chuck Lisberger, led me to the wonderful folks at RosettaBooks. Chuck introduced me to his friend, uber-editor and publishing icon Roger Cooper. Roger motivated me to take the time to express my thoughts in this form, served as the editor, and made immeasurable contributions to the final product. Roger brought along his RosettaBooks partner, Arthur Klebanoff, agent extraordinaire and publishing world innovator, who served as an encouraging realist throughout the project. The Rosetta team, especially Peter Clark, Navjot Khalsa, Hannah Bennett, Michelle Weyenberg, and Corina Lupp, is incredible. They are like an invisible force that effortlessly shepherded the book to production.

Finally, I can't fully express the support and love I have received from my wonderful wife, Ronda, and our energetic adult children, Andrew, Nina, Bethany, and Aaron. Ronda's willingness to serve as the CEO of our home over our thirty-one years of marriage has fully enabled my career. She is equal parts spouse, mother, business partner, and best friend. Ronda also served as a terrific editor. This book would not have been possible without her.

Introduction: Looking for Results

F OR ALMOST TWENTY YEARS, friends and associates have been hounding me to write a book about how to successfully turn around a company. "You've been at the center of some of the highest profile turnarounds in American business history," they'd tell me. "The five steps you've developed to turn around and grow companies really *work*. You need to put them in writing!"

But until recently, I refused.

Now I'd like to tell you why.

Much of my hesitation relates to a helpful distinction David Brooks makes in his book *The Road to Character*. Brooks says that while "résumé virtues" wind up on a list of one's accomplishments and achievements, "eulogy virtues" are the ones that get recalled at funeral services. Strong moral qualities have a profound and lasting impact on others.

Until very recently, writing *Right Away and All At Once* seemed like résumé fodder to me. Even though I know the five steps detailed in this book will help you become a better leader and enable your company to perform much better, writing about it violated my core DNA, for three reasons.

First, I don't want this book to be about me. I grew up in

a small Mennonite farm town in Kansas where strong, faith-based values taught me early on that there is no such thing as a self-made man. My success and the discovery of these five steps happened in large part because of the efforts of my mentors, along with the great management teams with whom I had the privilege of working. Many folks intervened at key moments in my life and helped me learn and grow. Some of them you have heard of, such as the late Senator Lloyd Bentsen, President George H.W. Bush, Governor Mitt Romney, Jamie Dimon (chairman and CEO of JPMC) and the founders of Home Depot (Bernie Marcus, Arthur Blank, and Ken Langone). Others you will learn about for the first time in this book. Really, this is *their* book, and I have included their stories at intervals throughout, between the formal chapters. I hope that the insights in this book give full credit to them, worthy of their legacy.

Second, the power and effectiveness of the five steps in this book, whether applied to business or life, comes from their simplicity. I worried that describing them in a book would make them appear too complicated, when in fact, anyone can quickly grasp them and apply them fairly rapidly. Brevity is a real key, perhaps *the* real key, to effective leadership. Blaise Pascal wrote in 1657, "I would have written you a short letter, but I did not have enough time, so I wrote you a long one." I have tried to perfect the "short letter" over time as it relates to business. I have worked very hard to make *Right Away and All At Once* easy to read, understand, and apply.

Third, the five steps I offer are equally applicable to both your business and your life. Stephen Covey's *The 7 Habits of Highly Effective People* became a best seller because it captures easy-to-understand concepts that readers can apply to both business and life. If this book were only about business, I never would have felt motivated to write it. I got interested, however, once I applied these five steps to turn around my own life, to move from what the author of *Halftime*, Bob Buford, calls "success to significance." I have seen many others do the same, with terrific results. It is this life change—embracing the virtues that lead to a moral legacy—that really motivates me.

While the concepts in *Right Away and All At Once* have a foundation in strong moral values, they are agnostic to any specific set of beliefs. Where your beliefs differ from my own, just accept the five steps for whatever value they bring you.

Getting Those 10,000 Hours

Before we launch into the core content, let me tell you a bit about my background and explain how I finally decided to write *Right Away and All At Once*. Maybe the best place to start is by reflecting on a key concept that Malcolm Gladwell popularized in his influential book *Outliers*.

Gladwell claimed that a great deal of success comes not

merely from innate talent, but from accumulating about 10,000 hours of concentrated practice. He cited a variety of examples, but the one that stuck in my mind concerned the legendary British pop group the Beatles. How did the Beatles become so skilled as a rock band that they first became a sensation in England, then conquered America, and finally took over the world? The answer is that they spent many arduous weeks playing from twelve to fourteen hours each day in German bars. They spent a whole summer in Germany, in fact, perfecting both their songs and their act. They got extremely proficient at what they did by putting in the time... and the rest, as they say, is history.

It really does matter how much in-depth experience you accumulate! And that fact helps to explain why I held off writing this book for so many years. I needed to put in my 10,000 hours, and then some.

Early in my career, right after earning my MBA from Harvard Business School, I worked at Bain & Company during Mitt Romney's tenure. Yes, *that* Mitt Romney. During an economic crisis at Bain, Mitt supported three of us young guys as we took a risk and moved to Texas to start Bain's Dallas office. We very quickly took that office from three professionals to about one hundred twenty, primarily by focusing on corporate turnarounds. That's where the five steps began to take root. Our success there led to my becoming a partner at Bain at age thirty, and soon afterward I joined Bain's board (its youngest member by about a decade). So began my rapid career advancement.

Not long afterward, David Bonderman, now the founder of the private equity firm TPG but then the new owner of Continental Airlines, asked me to leave Bain to become, at age thirty-three, Continental's president and chief operating officer. He needed us to turn around what may have been one of the worst companies in corporate America.

When we arrived, Continental was a terrible company. We called it the tenth-place airline: tenth out of ten in on-time performance, tenth out of ten in baggage handling, tenth out of ten in customer complaints. It had suffered through ten presidents in ten years and had gone bankrupt twice in ten years.

A total mess, in other words.

Along with CEO Gordon Bethune, a sharp management team, and an amazing workforce, we quickly led the airline from "worst to first." We pulled it off, together, by applying the five basic steps:

Have a plan and track your progress

Identify the three to five actions that, if executed, will fundamentally improve your business. Write them in a one-page plan, communicate them to your organization in an understandable way, and relentlessly measure your progress.

Build a fortress balance sheet
Make sure you have adequate time to execute your plan by having plenty of liquidity (cash), along with debt covenants and maturity that match your company's needs.

Think money in, not money out
Profitably grow your business to optimize returns for your shareholders and employment opportunities for your coworkers.

Build a team (clean house if necessary)
Build a board and organization capable of executing your plan and then properly motivate everyone involved.

Let the inmates run the asylum
Empower, motivate, and encourage your coworkers to make decisions consistent with your plan.

By executing these five steps, we took the airline from number 499 of the Fortune 500 to number 18 of the best places to work in America. Continental went from a $640 million annual loss to a $770 million annual profit. The company's stock shot from $6 to about $120 a share, and we won the J.D. Power Award as the Best Airline in the United States, five years in a row. Once again, I saw that these five steps *work*.

Our dramatic turnaround sparked a ton of speaking requests. People clamored to know how we did it. Gordon wrote a book titled *From Worst to First*, and I wrote an article for the

Harvard Business Review, reprinted in the appendix. But I was still in my thirties and didn't think I had the experience to write a worthwhile book.

After spending seven years at Continental, I left to run several other companies. The great management team we built at PricewaterhouseCoopers Consulting used the five steps to turn around that struggling firm. I then ran Burger King, also using the five steps, and our management team got that turned around as well. Along the way, I learned a lesson or two about how failing to *fully* execute on the five steps can lead to disaster.

As we completed these turnarounds, I got a lot of great experience as a board member at big firms such as Home Depot, ADP, Baker Hughes, J. Crew, and many others where I saw other CEOs take their own versions of these five steps and use them to grow and prosper their own companies.

For the last several years, I've done the same at a large private equity firm called CCMP, where I serve as chairman and CEO. We apply the five steps to the companies we own, helping them to grow and give their employees rewarding pay and work while striving to earn significant financial rewards for our limited partners. My dream job!

By now, my career has spanned four decades. Over that period, I've seen the five steps work in multiple environments. I saw them work as a consultant, as a president and CEO, as a board member, and now as a private equity owner. I've watched them create tremendous returns.

But even all of that was not enough to get me to write the book.

What finally *did* motivate me to write *Right Away and All At Once* happened eight years ago, when I was about forty-five and coming off of my time as chairman and CEO of Burger King. As I reflected back on my life, I told myself, "I've had a very successful career, by any measure. But something's not right. Something's missing."

Eventually I started wondering, *If my five steps really work in business, then what would happen if I took the same five steps and applied them to my life? Could I actually live a more significant, fulfilled life?*

Well, how would I know unless I tried it? So I wrote a one-page Go Forward plan for my life and applied these five steps—and the results, for me personally, have been dramatic. The exercise changed my life. More than any other reason, that is why I finally decided the time had come to write this book. I've amassed my 10,000 hours. I've seen the five steps work repeatedly in business. And now I've seen them work for me personally, as a man, and for many other people I know.

In the pages to come, you will hear some great business stories about several well-known companies—Continental Airlines, Burger King, Home Depot, PricewaterhouseCoopers

Consulting, etc.—as well as some stories about businesses you've probably never heard of. You will see how the five steps can transform your company, whether it needs a dramatic turnaround or is satisfactorily underperforming and needs to be tuned up. You will also read about the mentors who have inspired me and helped to shape both my business outlook and personal values.

Even more important, however, you will learn how applying the five steps can take you from where you are today to having a truly rewarding and significant life.

I think you'll like the business lessons, but I hope your biggest takeaway is personal.

And ultimately, that's why I wrote this book.

Who Needs a Turnaround?

> *The greatest pleasure in life is doing what people say you cannot do.*
> WALTER BAGEHOT

WHENEVER SOMEONE ASKS ME, "Who needs a turnaround?" two kinds of companies quickly come to mind:

⇨ Companies in serious trouble that require a radical overhaul even to survive.

⇨ Companies seemingly doing just fine, even though they should be doing far better. We call these "satisfactorily underperforming" businesses.

Change tends to come much more easily for businesses in real trouble, since crisis makes it obvious to everyone that *some* radical change must take place for the business even to survive. But change is equally important for businesses just going through the motions, although it is much harder to accomplish. While everyone inside a failing company at least knows that change must occur, in satisfactorily underperforming companies, people tend to resist change.

Let's see why.

Deeply Troubled Companies Need Turnarounds

Big companies in need of major turnarounds tend to grab the headlines. You know by name many of the businesses, and the CEOs, that pulled off such turnarounds: Chrysler under Lee Iacocca, IBM under Lew Gerstner, Ford under my friend Alan Mulally, and Continental Airlines under Gordon Bethune and me. The headlines tell the tale.

That certainly was true of Burger King. In 2004, shortly before I arrived at the company, Bloomberg Business proclaimed in an unflattering headline, "Burger King's Whopper-Size Woes." The accompanying story spoke of the company "gagging on sales and management turmoil" and ended by saying, "It's tough having it your way at Burger King these days."[1]

The crisis at Burger King had played out over a long period of time. This proud American brand had languished for about a decade under the ownership of a British spirits company named Diageo, primarily because the restaurant chain had become part of the corporate family only as part of a larger acquisition. Burger King, therefore, was an afterthought. Since it didn't represent part of the parent company's core business, it didn't get much attention. CEO after CEO rolled into Burger King's Miami headquarters, year after year (nine in fifteen years), creating enormous instability and leaving BK's franchisees angry and frustrated. Sales nosedived.

Burger King needed a major change in direction, a complete turnaround.

By applying the five steps, we gave it one. Sales at the restaurant level increased about 20 percent on average, while profits at the restaurant level went up about five times. The private equity owners of the business generated a huge return, receiving many times the money they had invested.

Even as the changes began happening, the headlines also changed. "Flipping Burger King," proclaimed one headline from the *Wall Street Journal* in April 2005. The article noted, "Burger King now has posted 14 consecutive months of sales growth in stores open more than a year. Customer traffic is up 7% since the fiscal year began July 1, for the first time since 1997."

We'll revisit the Burger King story as we move along, but the kind of thing that happened there naturally grabs headlines. When these big, brand-name businesses get into deep trouble, the entire world *knows* they need a radical change.

Their fortunes have dipped so low that the vast majority of the men and women inside the companies welcome whatever changes might have the power to help them survive. When most of us think about turnarounds, these are the kind of stories we have in mind.

Satisfactorily Underperforming Companies Need Turnarounds

The second type of company needs to apply the five steps just as much as the firms in deep trouble—and there are far more of them.

They just don't know it.

Let's be honest here. Which of our businesses *don't* land in this second category, at least sometimes? We think they are doing just fine. But because we've never subjected them to a complete checkup, we don't realize they have seriously clogged arteries. Call them a corporate heart attack just waiting to happen. From the outside, all seems well.

Until it isn't.

A large number of American companies, perhaps the majority, are satisfactorily underperforming. They live from quarterly earnings report to quarterly earnings report. Although their performance, revenues and profits all appear tolerable, even adequate, in reality they are performing at levels far below their full capabilities.

Their boards are not properly pushing them to do better. They suffer from corporate arterial sclerosis, and unless they do something to get healthy again, they will end up in serious trouble or, at the very least, face attack by dissatisfied shareholders lobbying for change.

Let me cite three examples.

In 2007, The Home Depot was generating more than five billion dollars of free cash flow per year. Earnings per share looked respectable. By every financial metric, in fact, the company seemed to be doing well. Even Wall Street had judged the company a decent performer. Few outsiders suspected that The Home Depot needed a turnaround.

As my fellow board members and I evaluated the company through the grid of the five steps, however, it became clear that we were seriously underperforming. If you carefully compared our performance against our biggest competitor, Lowe's, you could see serious trouble bubbling just below the surface. Even though sales in the stores had risen slightly, foot traffic (the lifeblood of any retailer) had dropped for four straight years.

What had happened? In an effort to save money, the company had moved away from staffing the stores with skilled associates—craftsmen like plumbers and electricians, capable of truly helping customers—to more part-time employees. Store managers had to operate their stores using dozens of financial metrics that took time away from associates, and store associates were required to spend most of their time on tasks like inventory and restocking, leaving little time to spend with customers. New stores failed to generate good returns, leading to even further reductions in staffing. As a result, both customer satisfaction and employee satisfaction plummeted.

It didn't take a rocket scientist to figure out that Home Depot had navigated into very rough and dangerous waters. Despite its fine-looking financial metrics, a large crack had opened up in its foundation. And that crack was growing.

Once the board agreed that the company needed a turn-around, we elevated Frank Blake to CEO. Frank expertly led the company through an amazing transformation in its day-to-day operations, applying his own version of the five steps. He took the firm from satisfactorily underperforming to firing on all cylinders. As a result, the company's stock soared. It had bottomed out at $18 per share, and by the time Frank retired as chairman in early 2015, the stock had risen to more than $105 per share.

A similar story unfolded at ADP, another proud American company. The late Henry Taub founded the business, and a talented team of managers had grown it from a small payroll accounting firm to a huge enterprise that provided paychecks for about 16 percent of the US workforce. Payroll is very complicated, given the differing tax regulations in each jurisdiction, and many companies both large and small feel quite happy to outsource such a critical function to ADP.

In late 2012, when CEO Carlos Rodriguez took over, ADP was one of four companies in the nation with a triple-A rating—a higher credit rating than the US government. ADP also boasted a decent stock price and generated about a billion and a half dollars of free cash flow a year.

So who could complain?

Carlos painted a very different picture of the company's health to the ADP board. We had fallen significantly behind our competitors in many areas, especially in our core payroll products. We badly needed to change to the technology platforms that would enable us to compete into the future—a very large investment.

In other words, ADP was satisfactorily underperforming. Most outside observers would have seen no obvious need for change, but ADP absolutely needed to apply the five steps. Carlos and our board successfully led the company through that process, bringing ADP to a place of strength it had not enjoyed for years. Since then, the firm's stock price has soared from under $50 per share to over $80 per share.

The third example involves Baker Hughes, one of the world's largest oil field service companies. It found itself in a comparable place of mediocrity when Martin Craighead took over as CEO in 2012. As fracking—the process of forcing liquids into fractures in rock formations to increase the size of the cracks, which allows more oil and gas to be extracted—began to take off in the United States, Baker Hughes acquired a company in the fracking business called BJ Services. The merged company appeared to be doing just fine, but if you compared its margins and asset utilization in fracking to its largest competitor in the United States, Halliburton, it was seriously underperforming.

Because US fracking quickly became a big piece of its oil field services business, Baker Hughes decided it had to take some significant action and so chose to implement a process very similar to the five steps described in this book. Once it became obvious that Baker Hughes had improved its fracking margins and developed world-class technology in key parts of oil field services like chemicals and lift, it became a very attractive company. Halliburton recognized what Baker Hughes had done and made an offer to acquire the company at a record-setting premium of in the largest oil field services deal ever announced. By successfully setting the company on a proper course, Martin Craighead, our board, and management drove enormous shareholder value.

If these satisfactorily underperforming companies had not recognized their need for change and acted on it, eventually they would have needed more radical turnarounds at far greater cost. Frank, Carlos, Martin, and their boards managed to radically improve their respective companies, even though most outsiders saw little reason for any significant change.

What about your own company? In all likelihood, it's not on its deathbed. But I'll bet you could drive far better performance and create many more jobs if you applied the five steps to execute your own turnaround. You may not even think you need a turnaround, but wouldn't you like to know for sure?

An Activist Shareholder's Hunting Ground

In the last several years, activist shareholders in publicly held companies have increasingly made their presence and power felt. Almost every day, an article in the *Wall Street Journal* reports how some activist group of shareholders attempts to use its stock position in a company as leverage to force radical change.

Whenever activists sense that a business is satisfactorily underperforming, they buy up stock and agitate for the company to take action to become more profitable, sell itself, buy back stock, or increase dividends. They will propose everything from just meeting with management to replacing the entire board and management team. Essentially, they want the satisfactorily underperforming company to become as healthy and profitable as possible—exactly what the five steps in this book are designed to achieve.

The appearance of activists means that your board should take a good, hard look at itself. Activists are usually rational actors. If your board does not have the proper culture, board experience, and discipline to insist that your company identify the relevant issues and execute to drive shareholder value, then you may very well deserve the attention of activists. The best antidote to activists is a great board, supporting a talented CEO and management team.

Most people see activism as bad. They view activists as ego-maniacs, as vultures with short-term orientations. But the truth is like anything else: sometimes they're good for a company and sometimes they're not. Let me give a quick example of each.

When David Batchelder of Relational Investors recognized Home Depot as satisfactorily underperforming, he bought a small amount of stock. His group didn't present a real threat to the company, the way some activists do, because it lacked the resources to accumulate a large position. Nevertheless, they had the power of publicly agitating for their position in the press. David and his partner, Ralph Whitworth, asked to meet some members of the board. We scheduled the meeting and agreed with most of their thoughts around capital allocation. We liked David so much, in fact, that we asked him to join the board. For more than four years, David was a terrific director for us.

On the other end of the spectrum, activism sometimes comes with a short-term mindset that devastates the companies targeted. JCPenney is likely the most visible example of a recent activist disaster.

In response to some very vocal activist shareholders who took control of the board, the company hired an outsider with an incredible track record, Ron Johnson, who had made Target hip and launched the Apple stores, which were a runaway success. Johnson made a slew of huge changes at JCP without testing any of them. When I saw him eliminate the sales that longtime customers relied on, choosing instead to go cold turkey to "everyday low prices," I thought, *This turnaround is doomed. Selling apparel is a lot different from selling iPhones.* At both Home Depot and Walmart, it took more than five *years* to make such a change. Customer behavior can be altered only very gradually.

Predictably, sales tanked.

In the aftermath of the disaster, one expert thought Johnson had erred in at least five ways: by missing what shoppers wanted; by failing to test his ideas in advance; by alienating the company's core customers; by totally misreading the company brand; and by not seeming to like or even respect JCPenney itself.[2] Mark Cohen, former CEO of Sears Canada and currently a professor at Columbia University, wrote of Johnson that

21

"Penney had been run into a ditch when he took it over. But, rather than getting it back on the road, he's essentially set it on fire."[3] He was let go after a short period of time.

But what might have happened had Johnson applied something like the five steps to turn around the struggling company? How might things have turned out differently if he had taken the time to really understand JCPenney and its customers and identified a few key levers of value?

If your publicly held company is satisfactorily underperforming and your board is asleep, expect activists to buy your stock and start agitating for change. You might hope that their activism works out well. But recognize that it can also come with a very short-term mindset and a totally unworkable strategy that can sink your business.

Don't wait for activists to come in and drive your company! Use these five steps to continually think like an activist yourself. Always ask yourself, "How can I help my company reach its full potential? How can I help spur growth? How can we leave behind fat, dumb, and happy and move toward chiseled, smart, and successful?" If you do that, you will deliver great results.

But We're Not Publicly Held!

"Okay, Greg," someone objects. "I know what happens if a company in trouble really needs a turnaround and the CEO doesn't do something about it. I get it; it crashes and burns.

But do you really think the same thing can happen to my 'satisfactorily underperforming' company just because I don't take it through your five steps? *Really?* Listen, we're not a publicly held company. We don't have to worry about proxy advisors like ISS or Glass Lewis, unhappy investors, or activist shareholders. So how can your five steps help us?"

It's a fair question. I've worked with a lot of companies in many industries, from large to small, and *every* company that I know of needs to continually refresh itself. I can't think of a single company in any industry that wouldn't profit from applying these five steps. How would it ever be a *bad* idea?

Think of it as something like a complete health checkup for your company.

We get annual physicals for a reason. Things change. Our health can fluctuate from month to month, week to week, even day to day, but certainly from year to year. Most companies today require their senior executives to get an annual checkup for that very reason. They don't want to sink a lot of money into a key leader only to have that individual get sidelined by a lengthy hospital stay—or worse—shortly after becoming effective at some vital job. Preventive care is always better, more effective, and less expensive than emergency health care.

That goes for your business too.

To make the five steps work most effectively for you, don't just run through them once and expect the results to last for the life of your business. That doesn't work for your personal health any better than it works for your corporate health. Working through these five steps, at least on an annual basis, gives you the best chance to keep your company healthy over time.

The Key: Grow Your Company

The key to everything in this book is to *figure out how to grow your company*. Healthy growth is the crucial thing for all companies, and it's the primary reason for you to apply these five steps to your own business, whatever that business happens to be.

Although to this point I've referred mostly to large businesses and CEOs, it's important to note that growing revenue and providing great customer service is critical at *all* levels of the organization. Almost every company I know will thoughtfully reward employees and teams that drive great customer service and revenue growth—it's the fastest way to a promotion. It really doesn't matter whether you are a division manager, a department head, in a frontline customer-facing role, or even providing a support service to those dealing with customers. Make the choice every day to focus on what your customers want *and* will pay for.

Empirical evidence shows that you get at least *four times* the market value for a dollar of profit that comes from revenue growth versus a dollar of profit that comes from cost reduction. Four times! Of course, we all need to think about cost reduction and direct at least some of our energies to it. I'm the last person on the planet to advocate that we forget about cost reduction! We must take steps to ensure we're both efficient and effective. But if you *really* want to have a successful company, then you must focus on growth. We'll talk about how to how to grow revenue in chapter six.

Maybe you've heard the business saying "sales cures all ills." It simply means that if your company is growing and you're succeeding at your mission, the rest of your problems melt away. You create jobs for lots of people... and profits tend to follow.

If you're not growing as a company, however, you tend to stagnate—and that's when serious problems occur. Couch potato companies tend to fare no better than couch potato people. At CCMP, we built our private equity business by focusing strongly on growing companies as rapidly as we could. We do this because we know it's best for them and best for us. Everybody wins.

We therefore hunt for companies we believe we can grow. We also make sure we have the operating resources in place to grow the business. Our focus on growth has allowed our companies, on average, to have organic growth at a per annum rate substantially higher than the US economy as a whole. That kind of growth obviously creates a lot of value!

I also believe strong growth allows us to fulfill the mission that God has placed on all businesspeople, namely, to create jobs. That's one of the main reasons why He put us here on earth. Just imagine the benefit to society when everyone who wants to work, can work. God created all of us to work. I don't mean to be sacrilegious here, or to take my point too far, but even Jesus chose secular businessmen and not clergy to help him grow His organization. A full one-third of His disciples were fishermen, and they were the group's leaders, to boot: Peter, John, James, and Andrew. I like to joke that they were the oil and gas guys of biblical times—they dropped a line in, and then they prayed.

We all know what happens when a person has a job fully capable of supporting his or her family. That individual's self-esteem goes up, along with a strong sense of personal fulfillment. As businesspeople, it is a great honor to be able to create jobs for the men and women who want them. Not everyone can do that, but we can. And we must.

Can I Lead This Turnaround?

It's one thing to know that a specific company needs a turnaround, whether a radical one or a less drastic but equally necessary one. But how can you tell if you're the right person to lead it? Just because a company needs help doesn't mean you're the one to take the job.

In my CEO days, I had a very simple test I used to determine whether I should take any job offered to me. I asked myself, "Can I sit down and, on one piece of paper, write a plan to turn around this company and grow it?" That one-page plan is the subject of the next chapter. But for right now, let me give you a flyover of what I did.

I divided a single piece of paper into four columns. At the top, I wrote "Market," "Financial," "Product," and "People." Then, under each of those headings, I wrote down the key actions I thought the company had to take, either to go from a terrible situation to a complete turnaround, or more often, from satisfactorily underperforming to performing a whole lot better. If I could identify the key value drivers with 80 to 90 percent accuracy, then I would seriously consider taking the job (or today, buying the company). If I couldn't write that one-page plan or had trouble identifying the key value levers, then I knew pretty quickly that the company would be better off in someone else's hands. I'll explain what I mean by "value drivers" in the next chapter.

As a CEO, I accepted only about one of every fifteen jobs that I seriously considered. I had no idea what to do with most of the companies I looked at: Motorola, Compaq, Waste Management, you name it. People approached me about a bunch of companies. "Hey," someone would ask, "would this be interesting to you?" Many of them, frankly, sounded absolutely fascinating to me; but once I sat down and tried to write the one-page plan, I just couldn't do it. I had no idea. My inability didn't mean that no one could do the job. It meant only that *I* wasn't the right individual to help that company grow.

The test remains the same today at CCMP with the companies we investigate before buying. Can we grow the company? Can we write a one-page plan that outlines what we'd do differently? Do we have the necessary operating resources? And, of course, can we buy it at the right price? We call this having a view, a plan, and the resources to execute the plan. Ultimately, we don't buy a company unless we have all three. And about 95 percent of the time we walk away from the process.

Not a One-Time Event

We often talk about turnarounds as if they're a one-time event. I've heard individuals express great skepticism about the conclusions Jim Collins makes in his books. "Well," they'll say, "that principle didn't work for long in *that* company." In fact, however, it did work for twenty years—until somebody dropped the ball and forgot to do their annual corporate health checkup.

Just so you know, I also tend to be a bit of a skeptic. When I first read *Good to Great* and then *Built to Last*, I also noticed that many of the companies Collins featured were doing well when he wrote the books but sometime afterward had fallen on hard times. Similarly, take a look at the corporate leaders listed in the Fortune 500; note the significant changes that occur from decade to decade. Very few companies dominate the lists for more than just a few years. It's very, very difficult to sustain success over a long period of time.

So does this mean that Collins's principles were wrong? No. Does it mean that without knowing the value drivers and daily applying the five steps it's easy for any company to go off the rails over time? Absolutely.

The same principle holds true of companies featured in this book. They all got turned around and performed at high levels over a substantial period of time. But through mergers, changes in management or ownership, evolving marketplace forces, and other factors, some have lost their edge. That doesn't mean the five steps don't work; it just means those companies have to go back and apply the five steps all over again. Any of them really can become great once more.

Now think of your own company or business. It's not as though you can work throughout these five steps a single time and then say, "There! I'm done." To achieve sustained success, you have to repeatedly come back to the five steps and apply them to your company in its changing environment—like a doctor's checkup, at least once a year.

Challenge yourself to continually understand what is changing. That's really the only way you can sustain greatness in any company over time.

Life Goes Stale Too

All of us can name companies that went from terrible to excellent through a well-managed turnaround, only to get stale again over time. That happens in business… and it also happens in life. It happens to all of us.

So how do you know if *you* need a personal turnaround? Only you can answer that question; I certainly can't answer it for you. But as you honestly consider your life, you may decide that you need a radical turnaround. Perhaps you sense your life is about to come off the rails, or that something doesn't feel quite right. I've known a number of executives like that.

Much more common, however, are the execs who tell me that while their lives seem okay, they fear they're merely coasting along. I tell them, gently, that in order to find the fulfillment and satisfaction they sense they're missing, they need to make a few changes.

Does any of that sound familiar? Do you feel satisfied with your life? Do you like the direction it's headed? Do you feel great about the contribution you're making to society?

Based on conversations I've had with hundreds of CEOs and other managers, I'd guess that the most common answer to these questions is, "Things could get better." I'll talk about my own life a bit later, but I can say from personal experience that as you apply these five steps to your life, you *will* find greater significance and fulfillment.

I encourage you to take some time to seriously ponder the question, *Do I need a personal turnaround?* Don't shunt it to the side, as I did for many years. Pointedly ask yourself a few questions:

⇨"Am I performing in life to my full potential?"
⇨"Does my life feel fulfilling and significant, apart from my business?"
⇨"Are there any areas in my life where I need to change?"

I can't answer those questions for you, as I said. But I can help you to understand how the five steps apply to your life. So let's move along to the first of them, Have a Plan and Track Your Progress, which lays the groundwork for all turnarounds, whether in business or in life.

It all starts with that first step.

The Five Steps

Step One

(icon) **Have a Plan and Track Your Progress**

Identify the three to five actions that, if executed, will fundamentally improve your business. Write them in a one-page plan, communicate them to your organization in an understandable way and relentlessly measure your progress.

(icon) *Stay Focused with Some Simple Life Rules*

Develop a plan for your life around the things you consider most important so that you avoid getting sidetracked by less important activities. Make key decisions using a consistent framework.

Step Two

(icon) **Build a Fortress Balance Sheet**

Make sure you have adequate time to execute your plan by having plenty of liquidity (cash), as well as debt covenants and maturity that match your company's needs.

(icon) *Choose Freedom*

Manage your personal lifestyle and financial resources so that money becomes your faithful servant and not your relentless master, thus freeing you to focus on your life goals.

Think Money In, Not Money Out

Profitably grow your business to optimize returns for your shareholders and increase employment opportunities for your coworkers.

 Think Money Out, Not Money In

Provide for those in need. Generosity is the key to happiness and fulfillment and the only antidote to materialism.

Step Four

 Build a Team (Clean House If Necessary)

Build a board and organization capable of executing your plan and properly motivate everyone involved.

 Build Your Life Team: Align and Prune

Build a support structure of family, friends and coworkers who give you support and energy. Don't get bogged down by those who take lots of time but add limited value.

Step Five

 Let the Inmates Run the Asylum

Empower, motivate and encourage your coworkers to make decisions consistent with your plan.

 Invest in Family and Friends

Build eulogy virtues, not résumé virtues.

Have a Plan and Track Your Progress

> *Take the first step in faith. You don't have to see the whole staircase, just take the first step.*
> Dr. Martin Luther King Jr.

O NE OF MY GOOD FRIENDS, Erik Weihenmayer, often tells me, "Great plans allow you to accomplish difficult tasks with measured risk." He should know, because he's constantly off somewhere in the world on some amazing adventure—and without a plan, he probably would have crashed and burned a long time ago.

Erik has climbed all seven of the highest summits in the world, including Everest, Denali, and Kilimanjaro. He's climbed the rock wall of El Capitan in Yosemite National Park, one of the toughest in the world. He paraglides. Last fall he finished a 277-mile kayak voyage down the Grand Canyon, including all its dangerous rapids. He also climbs ice waterfalls while hanging hundreds of feet in the air.

And did I mention that Erik is blind?

Erik is now in his midforties and every year adds to his long list of adventures. That he's still alive is a testament to his superb planning.

Erik and I first met at a Pepsi CEO event in Venice, where I heard him speak along with a lot of other top-shelf communicators including Tony Blair, Deepak Chopra, and Newt Gingrich. Erik topped them all, by far. By the time he finished his talk, you could have heard a pin drop.

Erik had synced his speech with a video playing behind him. I'll never forget the scene shot in his own backyard in Golden, Colorado. He set up a ladder a foot above the ground and then practiced walking across it. He fell down a lot, got back up, and continued to practice. Suddenly the video switched to some dramatic footage of his climb over the Khumbu icefall on Mt. Everest. He had to walk on rickety ladders across deep crevasses plunging thousands of feet. I watched, almost breathless, as Erik slowly made his way across those shaking ladders, loaded down with his massive backpack. And I kept thinking, *he's blind!*

A short while later, at my invitation, he and his ski guide

came up to Beaver Creek and we skied together for a day, in the process becoming fast friends. Ever since, he and his family ski with us a few times a year.

Erik has been a huge inspiration to me. Not only does he humiliate me into embracing a no-barriers mindset—last summer we climbed *three* 14,000-foot peaks together in *one* day—but whether he's skiing, kayaking, or presenting, I've never seen a guy work harder on developing a sound, well-researched plan. And yes, that includes surrounding himself with great teammates and guides, such as Eric Alexander, who led him up Everest, and Jeff Ulrich, who guides him when skiing. Erik does this because he knows that if his plans fail, he may not make it. And so he *always* has a rigorous plan.

The same is true in business. If you want to make it, you *must* have a solid plan.

The Importance of a One-Page Plan

It's critical that you develop a very simple, one-page plan to help you reach whatever business destination you have in mind. This is the all-important Step One of my five-step process.

When I worked at Continental, we used to tell our pilots, "We are going east today. East is 090 on the compass. You could go 070 to 110 (directionally east) and I'd be okay with that. But if you decide to go 270, you'll have to turn your butt around."

Stephen Covey emphasized a similar principle in his book

The 7 Habits of Highly Effective People. He insisted on the importance of "beginning with the end in mind." The main point of developing a one-page plan is that it helps you to begin with the end in mind. It permits you to say with utter clarity, "This is where we want to be three years from now with our company." In a powerfully succinct way, it lays out how you intend to get "there."

Where to begin? First you need to identify the three to five critical levers that drive your business. (I'll talk more about this important concept in a bit.) If you require more than one page to lay out the key parts of your plan, then you'll have almost no chance of actually executing it. You *must* pinpoint the key activities that, once accomplished, will take you most of the way to becoming a great company. Many call this the 80/20 rule, where 20 percent of the identified actions yield 80 percent of the results. In most businesses, I think it's probably more like 90/10.

Every year, I sit down with CEOs of the new businesses we buy and ask them to bring me their strategic plans. Most of the time, they bring one of two things: either a huge, thick document with enormous detail that requires a forklift to move (which you know hasn't come off the shelf since it was written), or four to six pages of tiny script filled with long lists of to-do items. Neither is a strategic plan. Nobody in a company can communicate, action, or track that many items.

Studies show that our brains are pretty good at remembering three or four major categories and then recalling three to five elements categorized beneath each of those categories. If we try to remember fifteen to twenty strategic goals without any categories, or without subdividing them, we almost always fail. Your one-page plan should be so clear, so condensed, and so potent that everyone in your company can remember these key items and take appropriate action on them.

Let others help you develop your plan. Invite your board and management team to comment on it, discuss it, and change it. In the end, they need to own the plan too. Their input will make it better. I'd even encourage you to ask some of the younger, high-potential men and women in your company to give you feedback. You will be surprised by the fresh perspective that they bring. If you're not the CEO, no worries. A one-page plan can be applied to a division, department, or function to achieve similar results.

Once you finish, assign each item on the one-page plan to an executive or a team, who creates even more detailed plans about how to achieve that particular objective. They should also develop a target and a "stretch" goal so you can measure progress. I ask them to develop a plan for the first one hundred days to make sure they get off to a fast start. As Peter Drucker said, "what gets measured gets managed." Measurement is critical.

You'll see a good example of a one-page plan later in this

chapter for a company called Generac (and another in the appendix for Continental).

The Necessity of Identifying Value Drivers

The key to being able to get your plan on one page is to thoroughly understand the value drivers of your business. What is a value driver? You already know of about a million tasks you could pursue to improve your business. These are actually pretty easy to identify. It's difficult, however, to boil down that long list to the three or five actions that *really* matter, that really drive profitability. When I talk about value drivers, I'm talking about that short list.

Do you have businesses, for example, that are losing money? Stop doing that. That fastest way to make money is to stop doing things that lose it. Do you have businesses you should acquire, businesses that fit perfectly with yours? By all means, pursue them. Are you providing your customers with the type of service they want and will pay for? If not, figure out how to do so. You must be able to clearly identify the levers that, once pulled, will make your business hum. Sound easy? It really isn't.

To help you identify the correct value drivers, I'll recommend some strategic planning tools in a bit. If this reads too much like a trip back to business school, then just skim the material. But remember, your plan has to be right or you may end up destroying your company.

I began learning how to identify value drivers for businesses at Harvard Business School, where I pored over hundreds of business cases. I received seven additional years of excellent training at Bain, one of the top consulting firms in the world. I then spent several more years leading a succession of high-profile turnarounds and did a very similar thing on boards. My last seven years at a large private equity firm have further sharpened my proficiency at this skill—and yet I still struggle at times to identify this or that company's key value drivers.

Think of the Domino Theory you experimented with as a kid. The key value drivers are like the lead domino in a complicated design. When the lead domino falls, all the other dominos fall, in order. If you get the value drivers right in your company, it's like knocking over that lead domino and watching all the others fall. It's a beautiful thing. If you get them wrong, however, it's like having spent hours setting up the dominos individually and knocking them over one at a time. Not so beautiful.

Let's start by examining the value drivers of two very different companies: PricewaterhouseCoopers Consulting (PwCC) and Generac.

PwCC: Two Levers and a Quick Sale

PricewaterhouseCoopers Consulting found itself battling gale-force headwinds in 2002. As the information technology consulting industry contracted, three external factors caused the firm to lose a full third of its business in just a few months.

First, Y2K had ended (and the world did not come to an end, despite many projections to the contrary), and focus on the worrisome change from 1999 to 2000 was over.

Second, the original dot.com bubble burst.

And third, the implosion of companies like Enron, Global Crossing, WorldCom, and others prompted the SEC to require companies to get their consulting services from anyone but their auditor. That meant that the audit clients of PricewaterhouseCoopers had to stop using PwCC's consulting services—and almost half of PwCC's business came from those audit clients. Without a dramatic turnaround, the company's very survival seemed in doubt. Its dire situation became even more difficult when the SEC started breathing down the firm's neck, requiring it to fix the business in just three months.

I had been brought on as CEO to apply the five steps. We managed to do the heavy lifting in just a month. The process ended not in an IPO as planned, but in a very attractive $4 billion sale of the company to IBM. Ginni Rometty, the current chairman and CEO of IBM, did a great job navigating the deal and successfully integrating the two companies.

To get to that point, I had to sit down and very quickly figure out the key value drivers so I could write a one-page plan and lead the PwCC partners toward the planned IPO.

Almost immediately, I found two primary value drivers that would allow us to take the business from a 4 percent margin business to a 12 percent margin business (nearly matching the margins of Accenture, our largest competitor), which would allow the company to go public.

The first value driver allowed us to get PwCC to the appropriate number of partners it needed to support its smaller business. I looked at revenue per partner in 1999—right before Y2K, the dot.com boom, and the fraud that prompted the SEC changes—and then at revenue per partner in 2002. I found that we had about a third too many partners, some of whom were attached to business lines that were losing money.

I asked Tom O'Neill, a very senior partner at PwCC and my predecessor as CEO, to stay on as chairman.

"Tom," I said. "I have a job for you."

"What's that?" he asked.

"You're going to be a working chairman, not just a pretty face. We have a third too many partners here, judging by revenue per partner. The problem is, I don't know which third of the partners should go—but you do. You've been here a long time. I need you to identify that third and develop a process for how to reduce our number of partners. And we have to do it in a few weeks."

Tom was like everybody's grandfather. People widely respected whatever he said and would willingly work with him.

I had been there only a couple of weeks, and if *I* had let that many partners go, I would have sparked a revolt. Tom's word, however, was like gold. He did an amazing job, and we quickly removed a third of the partners, including those attached to money-losing businesses, taking care to treat them all with dignity and respect.

The second value driver involved reducing overhead costs, specifically advertising. We typically spent $80 million a year on advertising. "How much of this advertising brings us real value?" I asked myself. "How do I calculate its value to the company?" To make simple a very complicated story, I learned that every partner at PwCC had managed to squirrel away some marketing funds for his or her favorite golf tournament or charity outing. Our CFO, Frank Sowinski, and I went through the line items and asked, "What amount of this really adds value to our business? What part generates revenue?" It turned out only a quarter of it did. It took us about two days to make that determination. We removed $60 million in non-value-added marketing cost.

So in just two weeks, we had identified two key value drivers and pulled them. We pruned the organization so it could grow again. We reduced the marketing budget by three quarters, from $80 million to $20 million, and we let go a third of the partners, amounting to several hundred individuals. My good friend Frank Brown—at the time an audit partner in charge of the sale from the tax and audit side—agreed with these decisions, and together we took the necessary action to get us ready to go public.

Soon thereafter, I left for a partner meeting in Amsterdam to explain our Go Forward plan and how the IPO would work. I got a call from Sam Palmisano at IBM. "Greg," he said, "we really need to buy PwCC, but we need to do a lot of diligence."

"Sam," I replied, "we're going to start our IPO road show in a couple days. We're ten days from our financials going stale. We simply can't wait another quarter to separate from PwCC, because our revenues are dropping too quickly. We don't think we have time to sell it to you. Besides, we've already filed four S-1s with the SEC to take this public. You don't need to do much diligence. Every Wall Street proctologist in the world has peered at us."

"No," he said, "you don't understand. We really need to buy it."

"Okay," I said, "it's Friday. Why don't I put my guys on a plane and they'll meet with your guys over the weekend? They'll present a proposal to us on Monday and we'll see what they have to say."

The two groups did a magnificent job and gave a terrific presentation. I looked at the IBM team and said, "You're going to have to buy this thing."

"That's what we've been trying to tell you," they replied.

We settled on a price, got some accounting firms, lawyers,

and bankers together, and we all went to Armonk, New York, to IBM's training center to finalize the deal. The whole thing came together in three or four days, and we announced it in six: a $4 billion purchase of PwCC by IBM.

We never could have reached that place without first identifying the two key value drivers, completing our one-page Go Forward plan based on those value drivers, and then swiftly executing against it.

Generac: Four Levers and Tripled Profits

In 2006, CCMP bought a company called Generac, the market leader in the home standby generator business. The company enjoyed more than 70 percent market share.

We purchased Generac from the founder, Bob Kern. Bob was among the first inventors of both portable and home standby generators. He recognized the benefits of standby power for households and created the category.

When big storms hit and the power grid shuts down, your whole home goes dark. The air conditioning or heat quits working, your refrigerator stops, and you stub your toe on your way to the bathroom. It's miserable. As our CEO, Aaron Jagdfeld, says, "Life gets primitive real fast without power." Some homeowners put standby generators on the sides of their houses to quickly restore power as soon as it goes out. Generac had tremendous growth potential when we bought it, because only about 1 percent of the homes that really needed a home standby generator actually had one. Just growing penetration from 1 percent to 3 percent would make us very successful.

The year before we bought the company, the Western Hemisphere suffered through the most active Atlantic hurricane season in recorded history. Monster storms with names like Katrina, Rita, Wilma, Emily, and Dennis killed almost 4,000 people and caused nearly $160 billion in damage. Home generator sales went through the roof. The founder of the business, then in his eighties, said, "This is a perfect time to sell," and we bought it. While we knew the business had just enjoyed peak sales, we also knew it had tremendous growth potential. We promoted Aaron Jadgfeld, then in his late thirties, from CFO to CEO.

Boy, did we time the purchase poorly. Over the next three years, no big storms hit, which stifled normal growth. In addition, purchases of consumer durables plunged 30 percent because of the 2008 financial crisis, and consumer durables attached to housing dropped even more, a full 40 percent. Who buys an $8,000 standby generator when they owe more on their home than the home is worth? As a result, the company's earnings took a huge dip, and Generac soon found itself in very serious trouble. So how did we respond?

First, given the new realities, we had to go back and reunderwrite our plan for the business. Was it still reasonable to assume that we could drive penetration from 1 percent to 3 percent? If so, how long would it take, and could we survive long enough to make it happen? What else could we do in the meantime to adapt our plans and programs to conform to the new economic environment?

Standby generators had many challenges, but two stood out. First, as a new category, they weren't widely available. Who would you contact if you wanted one? Second, they were expensive. A standby generator installed could easily cost $10,000 or more. If we were to succeed, we had to adapt.

Aaron and I set out to put together a new one-page plan, which he called "Powering Ahead."

"Okay," we said, "we have to think about how to grow revenue here."

"But you can't grow revenue in the middle of a downturn!" everyone objected.

"Let's see if we can figure it out," we said.

Like all companies, Generac began to carefully look through all of its activities, examining every expense, and made some very difficult cost cuts. Yet through all these difficult decisions, Aaron and I agreed to keep roughly fifty engineers and a similar-size group of employees to be used as a field sales force.

We gave the engineers two projects. First, we needed to make a massive change in the cost structure of our standby products. The team worked to dramatically increase the power of its moderate-size units while at the same time reducing costs. As a result, the company completely reengineered its flagship product line around a smaller engine. A standby generator designed to power most of a good-size home plunged from more than $7,000 to less than $3,000 (Value Driver 1).

Second, we asked the engineers to develop a line of gasoline-fueled portable generators (Value Driver 2), the kind of power plants on wheels that you pull out of the garage or storage room. You often see them on construction job sites. At that point, Generac had previously exited the market and had no presence in portable generation. But in just two years, the new product line designed by the company's engineers moved Generac to the number two player in the country.

Aaron also invested in a new field sales force. Historically, Mother Nature played a big role in marketing for Generac. In a very difficult economic environment, when cutting sales and marketing expense seemed easy, Aaron went in the opposite direction. He built a team of field sales representatives tasked to find and recruit electricians, plumbers, and entrepreneurs to become dealers. Over time, Generac created the premier network of more than 5,000 dealers who would sell, install, and service their generators (Value Driver 3).

We've learned over the years that when things get tough, companies use price reduction as the primary marketing tool.

So we also launched a pricing study on our home standby generators. We found that we'd priced our generators 15 percent below the competition, despite our standing as the leading player in the market. We immediately did what many thought was impossible: we took a price increase in the worst financial downturn since the Great Depression. But the price increases stuck and volume remained steady, dramatically boosting earnings (Value Driver 4).

By identifying and then pulling four key value drivers, we came up with a way to grow the company, even in the middle of a national economic downturn. And we hadn't finished.

CCMP and other investors bought back a good chunk of Generac's debt at a substantial discount, then reinvested that money in the company by exchanging it for equity. In doing so, we bought time. Time for Generac to implement its Powering Ahead plan. In late 2009, when the rest of the world was adapting to its new economic environment, Generac was doing something different. It was growing. In February 2010, we took the company public and used the public offering to pay down some further debt while continuing to grow the business (Value Driver 5, see "Build a Fortress Balance Sheet," the topic of chapter four). Tim Walsh, my partner, adeptly led that process.

We then split the company into residential and commercial

divisions and began acquiring related companies (Value Driver 6, strategic mergers and acquisitions).

Generac succeeded, even in the worst of times, because we worked with Aaron to develop and execute a new one-page plan that covered all five steps. We bought the company at $13 per share and generated so much cash that we paid $11 in cash dividends to shareholders. Company revenue has more than doubled and profits have more than tripled. The stock has traded above $50 a share.

The housing market today is still less than half of its 2006 peak, and yet Generac has quickly grown. Instead of waiting for the next storm to drive sales, Generac used its own strategy to make its own storms.

Take a look at Generac's Powering Ahead plan below:

"Powering Ahead" Strategic Plan — GENERAC

Grow Residential Standby Generator Market
- Awareness
- Availability
- Affordability

Gain Industrial Market Share
- Upgrade distribution
- Build relations with specifying engineers
- Expand product offering
- Increade awareness in "optional" standby power market

Diversify End Markets with New Products and Services
- Leverage brand
- Leverage distribution
- Leverage supply chain

Enter New Geographies
- Ottomotores local manufacturing, higher-power products and distribution
- Build additional distribution
- Focus on natrual gas products
- Leverage Magnum distribution

Figure 1: *Generac's* Powering Ahead *Plan.*

Note all the strategic acquisitions it has completed (Figure 2). And then consider the company's financial results (Figures 3.1 through 3.3).

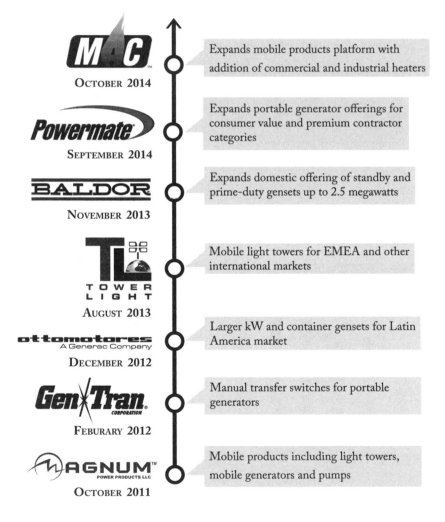

Figure 2: *Generac's strategic acquisitions 2011–2014.*

TOTAL NET SALES & GROSS MARGIN %
($ IN MILLIONS)

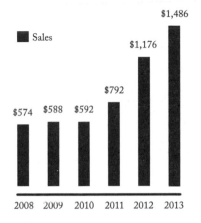

ADJUSTED EBITDA & MARGIN %
($ IN MILLIONS)

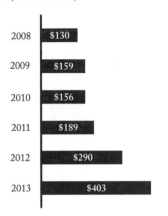

FREE CASH FLOW ($ IN MILLIONS)

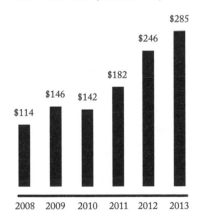

Figures 3.1, 3.2, 3.3: *Charts from Generac's 2013 Investor Presentation.*

In the pages that follow, we will identify the value drivers of each company that we discuss. Use those examples to help you identify the key value drivers in your own company, which in turn will enable you to write an effective one-page plan for your business. As you develop that plan, remember to test it with others in your organization, including young, high-potential coworkers. That's the road to success.

A Few Key Tools

To create a good one-page plan, you'll need a few tools to help identify the company's key value drivers. These are the ones I use whenever we are evaluating a business. If this is a relatively new process for you, it might help to hone your skills by very intentionally reviewing some of the following concepts. The key is to think through them conceptually but not get too hung up in the details.

1. Business Definition

I first ask myself, "What is the proper definition for this business?" Are our primary competitors local, regional, national, or global? You can figure this out by examining the three Cs: cost, competitors, and customers. Use them to clearly grasp the playing field of your business.

The boundaries of your competitive field in business correspond to the out-of-bounds lines on a sports playing field. If you pursue something out-of-bounds, you probably lose the game. Generac, for example, is a national business. Its primary customers, electricians and companies such as Home Depot or Lowe's, sell to consumers across the country. Since power needs and regulations differ greatly by country, playing around the globe becomes very difficult for a company like Generac. The success of any company's strategy depends on figuring out a precise business definition.

2. Competitive Dynamics

Once you have identified the geographic boundary of your business, you can begin to look at where your company stands. How attractive is the industry you compete in? Where does your company rate in comparison to its competitors? How well does it perform? Several interesting tools exist to help you answer this question.

Many people like to use SWOT analysis and study the strengths, weaknesses, opportunities, and threats of a company. I prefer Michael Porter's five forces analysis, which Porter developed because he believed that the SWOT analysis felt too ad hoc. The five forces analysis seeks to take a look at the microforces around a company to determine both how attractive an industry is and how a specific company can apply its core competencies, business model, and network to achieve a profit. The framework looks at competitive rivalry, threat of new entrants, threat of substitutes, buyer power, and supplier power.[4] By understanding these five forces, we discovered how Continental could prosper in the historically unprofitable airline industry. Continental had been destroying value for not only itself but also for the whole industry by doing things like flying excess capacity to places people didn't want to go and by leading industry-destroying fare sales. When we stopped doing dumb things, the whole industry got better. And Continental prospered.

Whatever methodology you choose, you must have a good grasp of the situation your company faces *before* determining your value drivers or writing your one-page plan.

PORTER'S FIVE FORCES ANALYSIS

NEW ENTRANTS

SUBSTITUTES   **EXISTING COMPETITORS**   **BUYER'S BARGANING POWER**

SELLER'S BARGANING POWER

3. Profit from the Core

Chris Zook, an outstanding Bain & Company partner, developed this concept. He did a lot of original research to show that nine out of ten companies that had sustained profitable growth for more than a decade had focused on their core business rather than on diversification. Companies profit far more when they either double down on areas of strength or make all their acquisitions in areas closely related to their core strengths. When companies leave their core, they normally generate terrible returns.

Perhaps you remember the high-end home design retail concept called EXPO, a division wholly owned by Home Depot. The problem was, the initiative took a lot of attention away from the "orange box," the core Home Depot stores. It never worked. Designers and home owners visited EXPO and viewed very high-end product in a showroom, then went back to their custom builders, who would source the product from their own network of mom-and-pop dealers. EXPO never returned its cost of capital, and ultimately we shut it down.

4. Customer Retention

Most businesses don't truly understand their relationship with their customers and what makes those customers tick. Are they gaining or losing share? While the link between employee satisfaction, customer satisfaction, and profitability is well researched, Fred Reichheld, another Bain & Company partner, along with Earl Sasser, one of my Harvard Business School professors, took this concept to the next level. They developed a consistent methodology to measure customer satisfaction and retention, tying it to profitability. This tool, called a Net Promoter Score (NPS), diagnoses the loyalty of your customers. NPS has become the gold standard for truly understanding the relationship between a business and its customer, critical for any company.

The great thing about tracking your NPS is that you can take action when your customers become disenchanted with your service. In the airline business, for example, a quick diagnostic would tell you that customers defect when your schedule doesn't match their needs, your prices are too high, or you have perpetually late flights.

Once you think through Business Definition, Competitive Dynamics, Profit from the Core, and Customer Retention, you can usually identify your key value drivers. And *then* it's time to write your one-page plan.

Writing Your Go Forward Plan

I call about 80 percent of the one-page plans I write the Go Forward plan. The other 20 percent get an appropriate name from a creative CEO (like "Powering Ahead" at Generac). The Go Forward plan originally got its name at Continental.

Gordon Bethune and I wrote a one-page plan for Continental that we thought of, very generically, as "the Turnaround Plan." Continental's owner, private equity icon David Bonderman, did not like the word "turnaround." I think he felt embarrassed to have his first deal called a turnaround, less than eighteen months after he bought the company (even though that is exactly what it was). He called me and suggested the alternate name, "Going Forward." Thus, the plan became known as the Go Forward plan, and the name stuck.

Every Go Forward plan has four cornerstones written across the top: Market, Financial, Product, and People. These four categories provide the backbone that holds everything together. I always try to come up with catchphrases for each cornerstone to make them all memorable. At Continental, for example:

⇨ Market became *Fly to Win*
⇨ Financial became *Fund the Future*
⇨ Product became *Make Reliability a Reality*
⇨ People became *Working Together*

Each of these phrases meant something specific to our employees. *Fly to Win* meant that we would no longer fly to places that lost money. It meant that we would turn from nearly two decades of losing money and now would start making some. *Fund the Future* meant that we would reinvest in the airline: new carpet in the airports, new paint and interiors on the planes, a new fleet, and better uniforms for employees. *Make Reliability a Reality* meant that we would no longer be the last-place airline, the laughingstock of the flying world. We would get you to your destination on time, with your bags, serve you meals at mealtimes, and show you movies when you got bored. Finally, *Working Together* meant that we would end the days of fighting between management and line workers. We would all win together and get rewarded when we did so.

A simple, clear, sharply targeted Go Forward plan helps everyone in the company to remember where you're going and how you intend to get there. By the way, let me remind you that you don't have to be a CEO to develop a Go Forward plan. Doing so can be equally valuable for your division, function, or department.

While I could offer a lot more detail about how to develop your own one-page plan, I think a good story works much better and makes those details easier to remember. One of the most interesting turnarounds this country has ever seen, the Continental story, also illustrates the enduring power of the five-step approach developed in this book. While times have certainly changed since then, the essential strategy we used to turn around Continental works just as well today. I recommend you read the *Harvard Business Review* article, which you'll find in the appendix.

Once you read the Continental story, pull out a sheet of paper and write the one-page plan for your business. Remember, you have to take that first step.

MY MENTORS

Mitt Romney: A Risk-Taking Turnaround Leader

I doubt many people need an introduction to Mitt Romney, as most of us know his résumé by now. He's the son of George Romney, the former president of American Motors and governor of Michigan. He attended Harvard Business School and Harvard Law School, worked at Bain, and then began Bain Capital. Eventually he served as governor of Massachusetts and became the 2012 Republican nominee for US president.

I joined Bain in 1988, a difficult time for the company. For the first time ever, Bain had to lay off employees. During that trying period, Bain's name took a hit on all the business school campuses... but it's also when I first saw truly great turnaround leadership. When Bain itself needed a turnaround, it turned to Mitt Romney. And without knowing it, Mitt played a huge role in my career, with some advice and two simple moves.

Mitt told me that one big secret to success is realizing that in every personal interaction, you either gain or lose share. There is no neutral interaction. "Greg," he told me, "Just make sure you're always gaining share." Most of us tend to overlook the importance of individual personal interactions. But if you are always aware that in every interaction you can gain or lose share, it significantly changes your approach.

As part of the Bain turnaround, Mitt changed the firm's compensation and promotion structure from a heavily tenure-driven model to an entrepreneurial model where compensation was largely based on the profitability of your local office.

He then allowed three of us "young guns" to open a Dallas office in 1990, during the middle of a big economic downturn. So Mark Gottfredson, Ted Beneski, and I took off for Dallas. Stan Pace soon joined us. We knew we were taking a huge risk, because Bain itself wasn't doing well. After we lost our only client (a story I'll tell later), we looked at each other and said, "We're either going to have to figure out how to sell consulting services or we need to start looking for other jobs. This isn't going to last much longer." Fortunately, we did learn how to sell. In three years we grew the Dallas office to a staff of 120. The growth of the Dallas office helped me to make partner in four years, about half of the normal time, and to be elected to the policy committee (Bain's board) shortly thereafter.

Without question, I owe much of my early success to Mitt Romney.

Orit Gadiesh: Bain's Culture Carrier

Orit Gadiesh is the longtime chairman of Bain & Company. Orit joined Bain in 1977 after graduating from Harvard Business School with high distinction; she was also a Baker scholar. This alone is remarkable, given that Orit came to the

United States from Israel, after serving in the Israeli army, without speaking any English. She had to do her HBS cases with a Hebrew-to-English dictionary in hand.

Orit is an extraordinary consultant but an even better leader and culture carrier. She was one of about a dozen partners who focused intensely on Bain's clients while Mitt Romney was negotiating with the banks during Bain's turnaround.

I'll never forget a speech that Orit gave at a firm-wide meeting in the early 1990s. Orit noted that while Bain had been turned around financially and operationally, the effort would all be for naught if the company did not stick to its core values of integrity, diversity, and transparency as it helped clients get results. She called this Bain's True North.

Orit's focus on culture was every bit as important as Mitt's focus on financial and operational transformation. The turnaround at Bain required both.

Stay Focused with Some Simple Life Rules

> *By failing to prepare, you are preparing to fail.*
> BENJAMIN FRANKLIN

LET'S SET BUSINESS ASIDE for a moment and talk about something much more important: your life.

Do you ever feel as if your life is flying by so fast that it's all you can do to keep up with your daily activities, leaving little time for anything else? Do working, eating, sleeping, doing chores, and taking care of family take up all your time?

Do you wish you had more time to focus on your faith, family, friends, fitness, and hobbies?

Does the concept of work/life balance seem like the world's greatest contradiction, an almost impossible gerbil wheel of guilt?

Congratulations! If you feel any of these things, you are just like the rest of us.

If you want to change, to live a highly significant life, however, then you must stay on course to fulfill your life mission—although first, of course, you have to know what your life mission might be.

What do you think you're called to do on this earth?

I floundered badly in this area until I finally developed a Go Forward plan for my life, stopped trying to achieve the impossibility of work/life balance, and focused instead on work/life integration.

Let me walk you through the process I used to make my life more meaningful and fulfilling. This process has helped many of my friends find fulfillment in their lives, and I hope it will in yours too.

What Are Your Blue Chips?

My wife, Ronda, and I periodically host young couples or business executives in Colorado for various retreats, ranging from mentoring weekends to relationship building within management teams. As part of these retreats, I always steal a concept I learned from a terrific organizational consulting firm, Senn Delany. I put a bunch of poker chips on our dining room table: white chips on one end, then red chips, then blue chips toward the center. I place our guests into two teams, ask them to pick someone from their team, and then tell that person to put one hand behind his or her back. "In one minute," I say, "pick up all the chips you can, one by one. No scooping! Let's see who can pick up the most chips."

Almost always, people will start at the end and pick up as many white chips as they can. They snag most of them, if not all of them. Sometimes they grab a few red chips. But only rarely does anybody ever get around to picking up any blue chips.

I then sit everyone down and ask, "What if I told you the blue chips were worth twenty-five points, the red chips were worth ten points, and the white chips were worth a single point? Would you do the exercise any differently?"

Of course they would. So would you.

Then I tell them, "The same principle holds true in business and in life. When we build our to-do lists, we have a tendency to tackle all the easy items first. We grab the white chips, the things that come flying at us every day. We can go for long periods—days, weeks, months, years—without ever making it to the blue chips, the things that *really* matter to us and to others."

The whole reason for putting together a one-page plan for your life is to help you clearly identify your blue chips, and then to develop a workable strategy to ensure that you focus on them. These blue chips are the value drivers in your life, the things you treasure above all else. Your one-page plan helps you to prioritize your blue chips, so that you don't lose them in the avalanche of white and red chips or ignore them in the wave of technology coming at you. Your plan reminds you, "These are the most important things in my life. These are the blue chips I need to pick up first. White chips may be easier, closer, and more numerous—but if I focus on them, I will end up with a life of 'achievements' that in retrospect will have mattered hardly at all."

Everywhere I go, I carry around my own personal Go Forward plan. I look at it four or five times a week and ask myself, "How am I doing with my time allocation, with my efforts, with my daily actions as measured against my personal Go Forward plan?" When I fail to do that, I find that the white chips inevitably creep into my life. The day-to-day demands on my time naturally tug me away from my blue chips, the things that matter most to me.

Do You Integrate Your Work and Your Life?

I'm probably as busy as I've ever been. I run a large private equity firm that owns fourteen companies and sit on the board of four of them. I also serve on five outside profit and non-profit boards. I am on the road an average of four days a week and am gone most weekends on family or mentoring activities.

We live in an ADD world. With every new device that promises to connect us in some amazing new way, our attention spans continue to shrink. Already our smartphones and tablets give us immediate access to social media and the Internet, which constantly bombard us with a million stimuli at once, all clamoring for our attention. E-mail. Instant messaging. Addictive games. RSS feeds. Snapchat. Video chats. My kids, all in their twenties, seem to come up with a new way to communicate with each other every week.

And, oh yes, for guys like me, even old-fashioned phone chats.

A lot of pull and tension exists in my life, as it does in all of our lives. If I don't intentionally counteract that pull and tension by doing what I must to make sure that I fill my life with significance, then day-to-day events can easily highjack my schedule. And I'll find that days, weeks, months, even years go by without me ever really focusing on my blue chips.

You too must avoid wasting too much time on social media and the stimulus overload it can create.

Long ago, I learned that striving for a work/life balance is a really poor way to think about life. If you really want to have a significant and fulfilling life, then you really need to focus on work/life *integration*. You need to integrate the things that are truly important to you into your life, every day. You need to find a way to merge your life so that you can truly accomplish the things you consider most important.

If you haven't already done so, begin to do some hard thinking about what matters most to you as a person. What are *your* blue chips? What would you like others to say about you at your funeral? What are your own "eulogy virtues"? If everything got stripped away except for the things you consider most important, what would remain?

How Do You Make Decisions?

Do you want to have some fun? Need an interesting conversation starter for a lunch or dinner? Ask your friends or coworkers how they make life decisions. They will almost certainly give you a blank stare. But don't let them off the hook.

"It's not that hard," tell them. "You make thousands of decisions a day, from routine decisions like when to get up and what to eat for lunch, to big ones like what faith to follow, who to marry, what job to take, and what house to buy. How do you make them?"

They'll still be staring at you, but you will have their rapt attention.

It's amazing how we make hundreds, if not thousands, of decisions a day and yet can't fully describe how we make them. Shouldn't we each have a process for making them—at least for making the really important ones?

If you don't have a process for making decisions, let me propose one. I have refined this process with my good friend Britt Harris. Britt is one of the top investors in the world and is the CIO/CEO of the Teachers Retirement System of Texas, managing over $130 billion in assets. He serves as an advisor to the Federal Reserve and as a guest lecturer at Texas A&M, Harvard, Yale and Princeton. I'll mention him again later. Britt and I make our own decisions using the Five Fs: Faith, Family, Friends, Fitness, and Finance. As you make decisions, ask yourself:

⇨ *Faith:* **Will this decision bring me closer to my Maker or push me further away?**
You've seen the bracelets that say WWJD. Some people use them as a reminder to always take faith into account as they're making life decisions.

⇨ *Family:* **Will it benefit my family or destroy the relationships I value most?**
We all have a tendency to overcommit our time. But we need to ask ourselves: Are we just pulling time away from those who really matter to us?

⇨ *Friends:* **Will this decision bring me closer to my good friends or push them away?**
How many good friends have you lost track of over the years? Imagine how things could improve if we prioritized time with our friends ahead of less important activities.

> ⇨ *Fitness:* **Will it require so much time or stress it will**
> **hurt my health?**
> Most of us perform better in life if we take time to
> exercise daily, get a full night's sleep, and eat properly.
> ⇨ *Finance:* **Will this decision put me in a poor**
> **financial position? Will it allow me to be a good**
> **steward of the resources entrusted to me?**
> Managing your money properly allows you the free-
> dom to make good decisions without constraint.

As you prepare your own one-page Go Forward plan, use all Five Fs to make the proper trade-offs. Trade-offs are necessary because you only get one page!

It might help you to create your own Go Forward plan by showing you what mine looks like. But before I get to that, let me set it up by telling you how it came to be.

My Story

Almost as soon as I left Burger King in 2006, I hit a crossroads in my life. Although I had achieved a lot of success and amassed a lot of wealth by age forty-five, my life felt fairly unsatisfying, unfulfilled, and uncomfortably devoid of the kind of real significance I craved. I realized with a shock that I deeply wanted, but didn't have, the kind of spiritual grounding that I had enjoyed earlier in my life. I also wanted the family and friends

I cared about most to know that I truly valued them. That's when I decided to apply the five steps to my personal life. I hoped the process would add meaning and revitalize my life in much the same way it had improved the bottom line for many businesses.

At the beginning of this process, my mind naturally traveled back to my childhood and strong spiritual heritage. I grew up in Hesston, Kansas, a sleepy farming town of about 3,000 residents. About 95 percent of those residents are Mennonite. The town has seven Mennonite churches and just one Methodist church. We used to jokingly say that all the heathens congregated in one place.

I felt very fortunate to grow up in an exceptional family with a deep Christian heritage. My grandparents on both sides were both very dedicated, humble servant leaders. My maternal grandfather served as a Mennonite bishop and preacher; the chapel in Aspen, Colorado, is dedicated to him. My paternal grandfather ran a farm. I had great parents. Dad worked his way up from accounting clerk to CEO of the Hesston Corporation, a Fortune 500 agricultural company. He ran the companyand traveled the world during my childhood, exposing me broadly to business (I profile him later in this book). Mom dedicated herself to taking care of my younger brothers and me. My terrific brothers have fine families and have gone on to great success in their own lives and careers.

Hesston is a unique place because, despite its small size,

it has a huge manufacturing base. In my boyhood years, it boasted one very large company called Hesston Corporation, founded by my great-uncle, Lyle Yost. The company soon attracted a lot of related manufacturing jobs and businesses. Those of us who grew up in that small community learned to work very, very, *very* hard.

I got my first job in third grade, working for my great-uncle. Every day I would ride my bike to his farm, about five miles from my house. I'd get out the hose, sit down, and start reading books and watering trees. The tiny little pine trees I watered lined a driving range my uncle had put in, saplings that he didn't want to die in the brutal Kansas summer heat.

Before I started that job, I negotiated my wages. "Greg," my boss/great-uncle said, "what do you think it would take you to water these trees?"

"How about seventy-five cents an hour?" I asked, naming a figure on the high side for a nine-year-old at the time.

"Fine," he said. "That sounds fair." We shook hands on the deal and I rode my bike home.

When I told my mom that Uncle Lyle had agreed to pay me seventy-five cents an hour to water his trees for four or five hours a day, she got very frustrated with me. She immediately ordered me into the car, drove me back to my uncle's farm, rang the doorbell, and told him, "He'll do it for fifty cents an hour." I believe Mom was just trying to teach me the important lesson that every young boy from a rural home learns: "Pigs get fat and hogs get slaughtered."

My uncle looked at me and said, "Okay, fifty cents an hour."

But I did learn a second important lesson that day: never let Mom negotiate. She cost me a third of my paycheck and I hadn't even started working yet!

As I got older and moved through high school, my tree-watering job gave way to others. I used to get up in the morning, mow and trim the local golf course, and then in the afternoon, deliver office furniture. In the evenings, sometimes I'd even bale hay. In Hesston, you worked very hard from the time you could hold a simple job until you graduated from high school. But you also learned a great set of core values about how hard work paid off and especially about how to treat people with dignity and respect. All of us heard the Golden Rule quoted again and again: "Do unto others as you'd want them to do unto you." Anyone who grew up in Hesston had that solid perspective ingrained into them right from the crib.

Perhaps you come from a different faith tradition, or from no faith at all, but still you had a similar value-based experience drilled into you by your parents. I appreciate that kind of heritage. I love studying the world's religions and truly appreciate their similarities in morality. For me, however, faith in Christ has changed my life. From my perspective, Christianity is the only religion I've seen in which one can enjoy a relationship with God without having to earn it, but enjoy it purely through faith in Christ—a gift known as grace. "Good works" follow from a desire to be more like Him.

Very early in life, I got introduced to the importance of faith, family, and friends. I "accepted Christ" into my life as a small boy. Thereafter, I had some terrific mentors. Two of the most important were my great-uncle, Lyle Yost, and a pastor and artist, Paul Friesen (also profiled later in the book).

After I left Hesston to attend college at Washburn University in Topeka, Kansas, I did my MBA at Harvard, then went to work at Bain and subsequently led several turnarounds. My career took off; but through my twenties, thirties, and early forties, a false sense of pride set in. I justified my actions by "being good" and "doing good" instead of seeking to nurture whatever produced that "good" in the first place. Externally I acted like a deeply moral person. I was faithful to my wife. I sat with my family in church almost every Sunday morning and helped out in AWANA (a Sunday night program for kids). Most of the time, I upheld my value standards in my interactions with my coworkers and employees. We donated a lot of time, talent, and treasure to several charities and even helped to start and grow a private Christian school on forty acres of land I sourced in The Woodlands, Texas.

But in fact, especially with my time, I really only paid lip service to my faith, to my family, and to my friends. In Christian circles, I had become what might be termed "a tickled tither." I would give my tithes—a sizable portion of my money, a bit of my talent, and less of my time—and that seemed good enough to me. My contributions made me feel really good about myself and tickled my ego... a classic tickled tither.

But I was only lukewarm spiritually.

Eight years ago, when I was forty-five, I found myself tired from the "success" of turnarounds. I felt restless and unfulfilled.

"How could you possibly be unfulfilled?" a close friend asked me. "You have all these positive things going on in your life. You have a loving family, an interesting life, and great kids. You have wealth. You travel all over the world." All of that was true. But I still felt deeply unfulfilled. I said to myself, "There *has* to be more than this."

While I seemed to be doing well enough in the spiritual realm, one Bible passage in particular troubled me. In a passage from the Book of Revelation, Jesus Himself delivers a blistering critique to a wealthy congregation in Asia Minor. "I know your deeds," He tells the church of Laodicea, "that you are neither cold nor hot. I wish you were either one or the other! So, because you are lukewarm—neither hot nor cold—I am about to spit you out of my mouth. You say, 'I am rich; I have acquired wealth and do not need a thing.' But you do not realize that you are wretched, pitiful, poor, blind and naked" (Revelation 3:15–17).

That passage seemed written just to me. *I* was a card-carrying member of the church of Laodicea. And suddenly it hit me.

Satisfactorily underperforming. That was me in my personal life. And I knew I wasn't alone. When I spend time with CEOs, senior executives, and politicians—apparently the wealthiest and most successful people on earth—many of them say they feel the very same way. I've learned that depression knows no boundaries. It pays no attention to money, to fame, to fortune. Even wildly popular celebrities struggle, although on the surface they may look very happy.

I hadn't hit any form of rock bottom. I didn't struggle with sex, drugs, and rock and roll. Few observers would have looked at me and said, "Man, that guy has *issues*. He needs to get his life turned around." But I knew something was deeply wrong and that I had to change my life. That's when I put together a personal Go Forward plan.

A Walk through My Go Forward Plan

I'd like to briefly walk you through my personal Go Forward plan to show you its four main components. Yours will look different from mine. The key thing is that it has to be yours.

As you review my Go Forward plan for life, perhaps it will get you thinking about your own life and what you believe will make you truly, deeply happy. Any successful plan depends on

GREG BRENNEMAN'S GO FORWARD LIFE PLAN

Deep Walk with God…
Become One of His Intimates

⇨ Daily Quiet Time (prayer and meditation during daily runs).
⇨ Bible Reading.
⇨ Scripture memory.
⇨ Purposed Reading.

2

Lasting Christian Legacy to
My Family

⇨ Invest in Ronda by doing ministry together.
⇨ Time alone with my parents every year.
⇨ Time alone with each child every year.
⇨ Integrate our new daughter-in-law into the family.
⇨ Pray, Play, Fellowship together:
  o *Woodlands*
  o *Beaver Creek*
  o *Baylor*
  o *Asbury*
  o *Mission Trips*
⇨ College Contracts.
⇨ Attend NCS together with sons.

3

Fully Utilize Platform…
Mentor Others

⇨ 400+ books to CEOs at Christmas… deliberate follow-up.
⇨ Host Houston CEO dinners with meaningful topics… 55 CEOs every fall.
⇨ Couples mentoring with Ronda. Weekend retreat every year. 5–7 couples total.
⇨ 40+ purposed speeches in the new year… Faith, Family, Friends, Fitness, Finance.
⇨ Be available for 3-5 mentoring sessions a week.

Lasting Stewardship Legacy…
Think Money Out, Not Money In

⇨ Drive outsized returns at CCMP by providing "values-based" leadership in firm and across portfolio companies.
⇨ Dilligent service on my Boards.
⇨ Have a fortress balance sheet. No debt.
⇨ Give away money in our lifetime.
⇨ Make giving a family priority… Christmas giving.
⇨ Purposed Kingdom Giving— local, global, affiliate:
  o *Focus, Focus, Focus*
  o *Time, Talent, Treasure*
  o *High Return on Capital Given*

identifying your blue chips, your personal value drivers. What things in your life do you consider most important?

Deep Walk With God: Become One of His Intimates

The famous theologian A.W. Tozer once said, "God does not have favorites, but he does have intimates." I wanted to become an intimate of God. I still do.

But how do you become an intimate of God? You make sure that you spend time with Him every day. It's an investment, like investing in your business. To get the return you want, you have to invest the time. For me, that meant reading the Bible, praying, memorizing Scripture verses, and building genuine community. Those are my value drivers, my blue chips.

Probably most importantly for me, and maybe for you too, is the accountability that comes from great friends. I have three other guys to whom I'm very close: Hal Chappelle, Bill Nath and Kyle Vann. I meet with them for two hours Sunday morning before church, from 6:30 a.m. until 8:30 a.m. If any of us is traveling, we call in. We meet like this about forty weeks a year, excluding a couple of holidays and some weeks in the summer. We often talk at other times during the week too.

And what do we do in our times together? We share our lives and we give each other counsel. Every week we listen to a sermon and memorize Scripture verses. But most importantly, we just spend time with one another, sharing the ups and downs of life, praying for one another. We're there to support each other.

All of these are guys are CEOs of their own businesses. I picked men with similar life experience to my own so we could relate easily to one another. These guys have become a very important part of my life and a key part of keeping me grounded.

I did not have close friends like this until 2006. I didn't think it was worth it and so I didn't allocate the time. I also had a hard time finding guys who faced pressures similar to the ones facing me. It took a while for our little group to form. When I first started developing my Go Forward plan, I got invited to join a much larger men's group. Over time, a natural affinity developed among the CEOs in that group. Our core group continued to narrow down until, a few years ago, it became just our group of four.

I've noticed that very few high-achieving men have anything like this. They just don't have a group of trustworthy guys they can be with, talk to, share their lives with. I didn't have it until I reached my late forties.

We all have a tendency to say, "Well, that isn't important. I don't have time for that! And anyway, I already have my family." I said the same thing. But for me, the grounding that these guys provide is priceless.

Do you know who feels happiest that I have this group of

guys in my life? It's my wife of thirty-one years, Ronda. She can see the enormous difference in me when I have these guys challenging and supporting me.

It isn't easy to do, but trust me: it is well worth your trouble to build a close circle of friends who will be honest with you.

Lasting Christian Legacy to My Family

What does it mean to impart a lasting legacy to my family? Let me offer a couple of examples.

A pastor friend and I used to mentor small groups of younger men. Twice a year we'd take them to the mountains of Colorado and teach them using a curriculum we'd developed. One day, Ronda looked at me and said, "Greg, why are you going on these two boondoggles a year? You're traveling all the time for business. Instead of leaving the family again to do these mentoring trips, what if we found a way to do them together?"

She was right. So about seven years ago, she and I instead started to mentor groups of handpicked young couples. Every Memorial Day, we host seven couples in Colorado and, along with Britt and Julia Harris, take them through a terrific curriculum that basically answers the question, "What do we wish we knew when we were your age so we could have had an even better marriage, done a better job parenting, and been better stewards of the resources granted us?" We are fortunate to do this from a position of humility, strength, and experience.

The Harrises have been married thirty-four years to our thirty-one.

While these young couples tell us they love the experience, for me the most valuable part of the whole encounter is getting to spend concentrated time with my wife. We grow closer together as a couple. It's one key way of imparting a lasting legacy to my family.

And what about our kids? For as long as I can remember, every year I've taken each of our children on some special outing, just dad and son or dad and daughter. On that weekend or special event, we play hard and I pour myself into them. They are now in their twenties but we still enjoy these times.

I try to do something similar with my parents. I spend some special time with Mom and Dad every year, or at least close to every year. Last year, for example, a friend invited me to play golf at Augusta National, the home of the Masters tournament. "My dad is turning seventy-four and he's an avid golfer," I told my friend. "I know it's presumptuous to ask, but could I bring him with me?"

"Of course," he said. "Bring your dad."

Dad and I got to play two rounds at Augusta, plus the par three. We stayed in a cabin right on the course, had a drink in the champions' locker room, and visited the Crow's Nest, where the amateurs stay. We ate in the dining room where a lot of players had begun to congregate after their own practice rounds. Augusta National may not mean much to you if you're not a golfer, but to golfers, it's the holy land. It's like visiting Mecca or the Temple Mount in Jerusalem. It's a very special, beloved place. What a great way to spend time with my dad! A couple of months later, I took him and my sons to Pebble Beach as part of spending some more intentional time with them.

Fully Utilize My Platform... Mentor Others

God has given all of us, including me, a platform in the world. The real question for each of us is "How will I use it?" Will we use it for good or for bad? My platform happens to be that I know a lot of CEOs and men and women who lead organizations. I felt the calling to see if I could spend some time with a few of them and maybe make a meaningful difference in their lives.

Britt Harris and I pulled together an annual CEO dinner in Houston, to which we invite fifty-five CEOs and high-potential young men. We always have a speaker who has applied value-based principles to his business—sometimes big public businesses, sometimes small businesses, sometimes entrepreneurs, but always folks who have done some very interesting things. In this way, we hope to encourage each other in our own companies.

Although I'm lousy at reaching out to people, I discovered that I can use my love of reading to start interesting conversations about faith and life. Every year at Christmastime, Ronda and I pick out a favorite book and send it to my mailing list of CEOs and other leaders. By now, we send out about five hundred books a year. About two hundred and fifty of those books probably get thrown on a shelf somewhere, because these are very busy people. But I estimate that about half of them actually get read. I get a call from about 50 percent, who say, "Hey, could we have lunch or breakfast or dinner and talk about the book? I'd really like to chat for a while." If you do the math, that adds up to about 125 great conversations a year.

As I travel on business, I set up breakfasts or lunches or dinners or coffees to have these in-depth conversations with my friends, many of whom I've known for a very long time. These interactions add a lot of significance to my life, and they don't usually center on business. In fact, they usually focus on faith, family, friends, fitness, and then maybe after that, finance/business. We tend to have the deep conversations that many of us simply don't take the time (or make the time) to have. This is what I meant when I said you need to focus not on work/life balance but on work/life *integration*. I consider these interactions a blue chip on my Go Forward plan, one of my key value drivers.

Lasting Stewardship Legacy... Money Out, Not Money In

In chapter six, "Think Money In, Not Money Out," I'll talk

about the importance of a business generating revenue and not focusing solely on cutting costs. But on the personal side of the ledger, it's exactly the opposite. You need to think about Money Out, Not Money In (see chapter seven).

What are you giving back to society and to the world? How are you using your platform to help and encourage others? We spend most of our careers asking ourselves, "How do I get to the next level in expanding my portfolio? How do I generate the next dollar? How do I grow my business?" But we all know that in the long term, our true value doesn't lie there. Instead, our real value lies in asking, "How can I very thoughtfully give back the time, talent, and treasure that's been given to me?"

As we proceed, I'll give a few examples of how we've done this as a family. For now, I encourage you to ponder the question for yourself. What kind of financial legacy do you want to leave that blesses others? What are you doing now? What might your own version of "Money Out, Not Money In" look like?

Give It a Try

Your plan will look different from my plan. This is just *my* plan. It reflects my interests, my values, my blue chips. You have to build your own Go Forward plan around your own blue chips.

As you've seen, some of my blue chips revolve around my Christian faith. You may have a different faith, whether Jewish,

Muslim, Hindu, Buddhist, or something else. You may have no faith base at all. But that doesn't mean that you don't have key value drivers in your life. You too have specific blue chips. Certain things are vitally important to you, things that you want to make sure you get done before you leave this planet. And those things are too important to leave to chance or to postpone until next year or next decade.

When I finally realized that I needed to make my life more meaningful and significant, I applied the five steps to my life... and it worked. We all can all get a lot better, but in order to do so, we need to get focused. I hope that you will take this tool, apply the five steps to your life, and discover how to make your days more rewarding, more effective, and more significant.

I feel fulfilled today in a way that I didn't a decade ago. Most of that happened because I learned to focus on work/life integration, not work/life balance. That choice has made my life simpler and much more enjoyable. My decision-making process is clearly defined—I use the Five Fs. And when I intentionally integrate my business Go Forward plan with my personal Go Forward plan, the difference between Monday and Sunday almost disappears. It becomes just my life, not my business life and my personal life—and this has brought me more joy and fulfillment than I ever thought possible.

It can do the same for you. I suggest you give it a try.

MY MENTORS

Lyle Yost: The Most Extraordinary Man I've Ever Met

Lyle Yost, my great-uncle, became a millionaire in a time and place when most people would have thought such a feat impossible. He pulled it off largely because he had an unwavering bead on his mission in life. Whenever I'd ask him, "Uncle Lyle, what were you put on the earth to do?" he would always answer, "Greg, I was put on the earth to mechanize farming to make it easier for farmers." Period. Stop. End of statement.

Most people remember Lyle as an extraordinary inventor. In the old days, after you reaped a wheat field and you wanted to get the wheat into a truck, you had to jump in the back of the combine and hand shovel the grain into the truck. My great-uncle called that crazy, so he invented the wheat auger. Today, augers move all sorts of grains from the combine to the truck, and then into grain silos.

He didn't stop there. Formerly when farmers combined their hay, it didn't automatically get baled. Instead, you had to take a pitchfork and throw it, loose, on the back of a wagon. Uncle Lyle hated inefficiency, so he invented the machines that make those large round and square bales, enabling an individual farmer to bale and transport his own hay. In the autumn, when you see hay bales on the side of the road, think of my great-uncle Lyle.

Uncle Lyle turned those innovative ideas into a Fortune 500 company called Hesston Corporation. At one time, Hesston Corporation employed about 5,000 workers in a town of 3,000. That should give you a sense of the huge impact he had on our region.

Uncle Lyle also was a remarkably humble Christian philanthropist. He had a huge desire to give away all his money before he died, and he tried several interesting approaches to reach his goal. Since Boeing and Cessna and Lear all had operations in Wichita, Kansas, just thirty miles up the road, Uncle Lyle took an interest in aviation. He traveled the world, and in the late sixties and early seventies, he visited Central America—in his opinion, the perfect place for a dairy, creating both jobs and food for the people.

He approached some church officials with his idea, but when the men didn't act quickly enough, Uncle Lyle took matters into his own hands. On his own, he decided to buy up all the used dairy equipment in our area and ship it all down to Central America. He founded the largest dairy in Latin America, which still exists today.

In time, the church hierarchy came to embrace his operation. The Mennonite Economic Development Association (MEDA) was formed, took what my great-uncle Lyle had started, and built on it. These days, MEDA does economic development work in needy countries all around the world. My great-uncle

Lyle didn't let conventional thinking stop him from doing what he thought could be done better.

He also had a profound commitment to take care of his own. Lyle's younger sister, my grandmother, Zella, passed away at age ninety-five, around 5:00 a.m. Two hours after her death, Lyle's daughter walked into her father's room to tell him the news. Before she could say anything, my great-uncle said, "Susan, I have something that I need to tell you."

"What, Dad?"

"Zella passed away."

"Dad!" replied his astonished daughter. "How did you know?"

"Well," he replied, "about five o'clock, she came and sat by my bed. We had a nice chat. She said she was ready to go be with Jesus, and I watched her go."

Just a couple of months after my grandmother died, my great-uncle Lyle also passed away. I really believe he was waiting to die until Zella went, still protecting his little sister.

Every year, the Kansas Business Hall of Fame inducts one new member. Individuals such as the Cessna brothers, Frank Carney (the founder of Pizza Hut), Charles Koch and his dad, Fred (founder of Koch Industries, the second-largest privately held company in the United States), have been inducted. They're all genuine icons of business.

In 2006, the Kansas Business Hall of Fame inducted Lyle Yost into its ranks. It meant a great deal to him. In 2012, shortly after he died, I got a note from the Kansas governor informing me that I'd also been inducted into the Kansas Business Hall of Fame. At first I thought it was a fraternity brother prank. But once I realized they meant it, I wrote a short speech for the induction ceremony in which I told the story of my great-uncle Lyle and what he meant to me. What an honor to come after him! I can hardly think of a better capstone to the extraordinary life of Lyle Yost.

Build a Fortress Balance Sheet

> *The time to repair the roof is when the sun is shining.*
> JOHN F. KENNEDY

D URING THE FINANCIAL CRISIS of 2008, when banks were melting down and the nation's whole monetary system seemed on the verge of collapse, I spent a bit of time one fall morning with my friend Jamie Dimon, chairman and CEO of JPMorgan Chase. I walked into his office about 9:00 a.m. and found him with his sleeves rolled up and his tie undone—far from the norm for the usually dapper Jamie. Clearly, he had gotten no sleep.

Jamie and I first got to know each other during a week-long trip to Israel in the late 1990s, after Jamie left his job at

Citigroup and before he took over as chairman and CEO of Bank One in Chicago. I was president of Continental Airlines. Since then, our paths have crossed frequently.

Jamie called me a year or two after I left Continental to help him work through the United Airlines bankruptcy. Bank One was the dip lender to United and had a huge income stream coming from the United Airlines credit card. Jamie also introduced me to Home Depot founder Ken Langone, which led to my joining the board of Home Depot in 2000. Jamie also was instrumental in recruiting me to my current position as chairman and CEO of CCMP. At the time, JPMC was a large limited partner in CCMP, but due to the Volcker rule, it no longer invests with us.

So Jamie and I have known each other for a long time. Still, I had stopped by to see him at a most difficult time in his life.

"It was nice of you to see me," I said. "I know you're incredibly busy, facing crisis after crisis. You must have a ton of meetings today."

"Greg," he replied, "it is great to see you. I don't really know my schedule for today. I've canceled all my normal meetings. We have detailed updates every day on our balance sheet and on rapidly changing current events. These days, I need to be available to quickly react to whatever crisis comes up next."

It was Jamie who introduced me to the term "fortress balance sheet," and I've never seen anyone understand the concept better or build a stronger one. Jamie is responsible for a very complex balance sheet at JPMC, and yet he always manages to simplify it and zero in on the relevant risk. He did a miraculous job during the toughest economic period to hit this country since the Great Depression. He not only saved JPMC but also led the bank to an incredible gain in market share and quickly assumed the leadership mantle in all of its financial services.

What Is a Fortress Balance Sheet?

It takes four key steps to build a fortress balance sheet, and you don't have to be a CEO to find this information helpful. Let me list each step quickly, and then we'll dive into each one in more detail.

1. Don't run out of cash. Maintain plenty of liquidity.

Make sure you have plenty of cash, including cash on your balance sheet *and* cash readily available via credit lines. This is a principle we need to underline: <u>Never, ever, *ever* run out of cash</u>. Failure to do so is like cutting off your oxygen. You will die quickly.

The Continental pilots told me that they were taught in the military to think about fuel the way we think about liquidity. "The only time a navy fighter pilot can have too much fuel," they said, "is when he's on fire."

2. Know how much leverage your company can handle.

Train yourself to think like an operator. If the worst thing that could happen to you actually happened—the country had another financial crisis, your sales dropped 30 percent, some competitor entered your market and started taking market share from you—how would your business perform? How would your balance sheet be stressed? Would you still have plenty of cash?

While most of us understand the perils of too much debt, you can also have too little debt. Think like Goldilocks and the three bears: Not too much debt, not too little debt, but just the right amount of debt.

3. Keep your debt maturity stack well into the future.

You absolutely must match your debt maturities with your business needs. As a general rule, make sure you have little to no debt coming due in the short term. We have a saying at CCMP: "Private equity is a long-dated option; you just need to make sure that no one can shorten the date." The only way your date can get shortened is if you run out of cash, your debt comes due, or if a banker can call in your loan early for some other reason.

4. Drill down on your one-page plan and develop a detailed set of measurements.

For each item on your one-page plan, it is incredibly important that you develop a goal and a stretch goal. You must know how to measure your performance and your progress. If you can measure your performance and your progress on the value drivers you identified on your one-page plan, then you're almost certain to end up with increasing sales, improved margins, more profit, and better cash flow. And that will lead you naturally to a fortress balance sheet.

How did Jamie drive JPMC to a leadership role in financial services? He demanded that the bank maintain a fortress balance sheet at all times. While other banks added loads of debt to juice their returns (some banks, like Lehman Brothers, had about 97 percent debt and only 3 percent equity, so they could not withstand even a reasonable downturn), Jamie made sure JPMC had modest leverage, properly matched to the maturity of its assets. When other banks sent a huge percentage of their assets into high return classes with huge fees, like syndicated mortgages that blew up when the housing bubble burst, Jamie made sure he had diversified his exposure. He made a heavy dose of safer investments, such as bank loans to solid midmarket companies.

Most of all, while other banks lacked available cash when their customers asked for it, Jamie made sure he had plenty of liquidity to meet all the needs of his firm and all the demands of his customers. Jamie's relentless focus on maintaining a fortress balance sheet, in good times and bad, put him in a position to come out a clear winner when the market collapsed.

Hank Paulson, US Treasury Secretary from 2006 to 2009, asked Jamie and JPMC to bail out Bear Stearns and Washington Mutual, and then to take equity that the company did not need, as a signal to others that they could safely do the same. In each case, Jamie thoughtfully and prudently did the right thing to benefit both JPMC shareholders and the United States. He could make these moves only because he insisted on maintaining a fortress balance sheet. Without a doubt, his actions saved the global banking system and prevented its complete collapse.

Quite frankly, Jamie did one of the more remarkable management jobs I've ever seen. This country hasn't given him nearly the credit he deserves. The revisionist history of that period and the regulatory and compliance regime that has taken over since has been hard to watch. In my view, it is destroying our banking system. Yes, some good ideas have come from the effort. More capital on bank balance sheets and long-dated compensation with claw backs—required management givebacks if financial results are restated—for Wall Street executives are both good ideas. But the levels of conflicting oversight from Washington make it abundantly clear that politicians struggle to understand how the financial system works.

Several true American heroes emerged during that difficult time, but I put Jamie at the top of that list. He did an amazing job. His efforts saved our financial system—and he did it primarily by building and maintaining a fortress balance sheet.

Don't Run Out of Cash

Why do most businesses fail? The answer is very simple: they run out of cash.

The same is true with governments, something we see with Greece right now. The same is true of individuals; they declare bankruptcy when they no longer have cash in the bank. Charities and churches fall into the same hole when, for example, they carry too much debt by building too many facilities.

Cash is king.

Leading a turnaround requires a maniacal focus on cash, not just on net income or revenue. Unfortunately, most dying businesses fail to recognize (or at least remember) that fact. And yes, it really is possible to have a profitable business but still fail because you run out of cash.

Always make sure you have plenty of liquidity to give yourself the time to turn around a struggling business. If the key to buying attractive real estate is location, location, location, then the key to building a fortress balance sheet is cash, cash, cash. That can be cash you have in the bank or a line of credit from a bank that allows you to quickly secure funds. But the key is always having enough cash.

I first learned to restructure balance sheets and preserve

cash during my days as a consultant at Bain. So let me take you back to our first client in our Dallas office: a real estate powerhouse named after its founder, Trammell Crow.

The Tale of Trammell Crow

Mark Gottfredson, Ted Beneski, and I moved from Boston to Dallas in 1990 to start Bain's Dallas office. We had just one client at the time, a Monterrey-based Mexican titan called Grupo Industrial Alfa.

We had been commuting for a year from Boston to Monterrey to consult with Alfa as it dealt with the impact of the anticipated North American Free Trade Agreement (NAFTA). At the same time, a big privatization movement was sweeping Mexico, and many national government–owned companies, including the steel business and the telecommunications business (TELMEX), were being sold. My assignment was to work with a junior member of the controlling family, Armando Garza Sada, and the head of strategy at Alfa, Ricardo Saldívar, to determine which government assets Alfa should bid on. Alfa could buy the steel business or TELMEX but not both. (Interestingly, all these years later, Armando is now the chairman of Alfa and Ricardo is the president of Home Depot Mexico.)

Armando, Ricardo, and I saw the choice of assets as a no-brainer. At Bain, I had helped to write the Free Trade Agreement for Telecommunications and Transportation, so we knew that TELMEX had a concession agreement from the government that would guarantee its profitability for a long time. Besides, we had lined up Southwestern Bell as a partner. The steel business, on the other hand, had 30 percent tariffs protecting the business, tariffs scheduled to go away over three years. That guaranteed a very rough and bumpy ride for Mexican steel. So Alfa bought TELMEX, right?

Guess again.

I'll never forget what the patriarch, Bernardo Garza Sada, told us when we went in to pitch the TELMEX deal to the Alfa board: "We've been in steel for fifty years; we're going to be in steel for another fifty years. We're not going to buy TELMEX. We're going to buy the government's steel company." And then he asked us to leave.

He doubled down on steel, and shortly afterward, Bain's engagement at Alfa ended.

Southwestern Bell partnered instead with a very smart Mexican banker named Carlos Slim Helú to buy TELMEX. The market played out as expected. Alfa suffered and Helú went on to become one of the richest men in the world.

We felt gratified at eventually being proven right—but how did being right help us? We'd lost our only client, just days after opening the Dallas office. We went forty days and forty nights without a single client.

Finally, we managed to land a consulting assignment with

the Trammell Crow Company (TCC), at the time one of the largest real estate firms in the world. Trammell Crow himself, a famous real estate magnate and philanthropist, founded the company. We walked into TCC right on top of the national real estate crash of the late 1980s and early 1990s. The company had partners in almost every major city in the United States and even had loads of partners developing buildings in cities not considered major.

TCC had a unique business strategy. It took bright young people right out of the leading MBA programs, such as Harvard or Stanford. The company made them partners and gave them very small salaries, about $20,000 a year. These young guns then would go out to source and build commercial office, industrial, and retail properties. TCC would finance these properties with as much debt as possible, using equity from large institutions such as insurance companies, some equity from the Crow family, and sweat equity from the young partners.

A large number of these loans were cross collateralized, so that the equity behind a loan on one building in Austin, for example, might also serve as loan collateral for another building in Houston or in New York. The Crow family and the young partners also frequently gave the banks guarantees against their own personal assets.

Buildings can be levered quite high; you can often put less than 10 percent down and be in debt to insurance companies or banks for the remaining 90 percent. And that's what the company did to build a highly levered empire.

This system worked so long as prices went up, which they did for some time due to economic growth and high inflation. When this happened, the Crow family became billionaires and the young partners became millionaires—at least on paper. As a result, these young real estate tycoons often spent like millionaires, buying fancy cars, expensive homes, and other luxury items. Because they had such low salaries, almost all of their spending came from money borrowed against the equity they had in "their" buildings.

But what happens when prices go down? Equity in the buildings evaporates, and since the borrowing that the partners did to support their lavish lifestyles was backed by bank loans that promptly got called, the partners found themselves in a tight squeeze. They had no cash to meet either the capital calls on the buildings or even to pay their personal loans.

And now you know why they say "Cash is king." When you don't have it, you are a peasant.

That's when TCC called us. We needed a client after getting kicked out of Alfa, and TCC needed some help. They knew they were in trouble, since it was pretty clear that their "equity" was worthless and that the banks and insurance companies who held the debt effectively owned the buildings.

(By the way, this scenario repeats itself in a slightly different fashion every decade or so. It played out again when the 2007 housing crisis hit and the mortgages of many homes eclipsed the homes' values.)

I walked into TCC as a young Bain consultant and immediately got asked, "What's your plan, Greg?"

Before you can solve a problem, you have to understand it, so I replied, "I'd like to get a simple balance sheet, income statement, and statement of cash flow so I can understand your business."

I could tell by the way they looked at me that I had asked for something they didn't have. No wonder they didn't know for sure how well or poorly they were performing! It's hard to have a *fortress* balance sheet if you don't even have a balance sheet.

They quickly led me to a large conference room, filled with hundreds of boxes overflowing with thousands of documents. "These are all of our real estate projects," they said. "You'll find all the information on our partnerships in this room. Perhaps you can construct the statements for us."

For the next six weeks, we went through all that data and sorted out the complex and confusing situation. My original training as a CPA helped me dig through all of those boxes, despite the tremendous amount of work involved. When the music finally stopped and we figured everything out, we discovered that these guys had $4 billion of recourse debt. In addition, nearly *all* the buildings were cross collateralized and almost all of the debt had personal guarantees attached to it. Individual partners of TCC, including members of the Crow family, had guaranteed those loans, which were all basically underwater. In fact, many of the projects required cash infusions just to keep going. Capital calls needed to go out and did go out for the cash needed to finish the projects. But the partners were out of cash and the oxygen in the room was running out fast.

So what could TCC do? How could the young partners get out from under this mess without declaring personal bankruptcy?

It just so happened that at that time Section 182 of the IRS tax code allowed partners to exchange equity in a project for forgiveness of debt on that project, without declaring income. The young partners really had only once choice: to turn in all their equity in exchange for freedom from the debt. They would have to figure out on their own how to handle the personal debt they had accumulated for their fancy cars and homes.

The Crow family, at the center of the storm, had a different decision to make. Yes, they had a massive cross collateralization problem, $4 billion of debt outstanding, and personal guarantees; but they also had equity in some of those buildings and cash to help make capital calls. They alone could dig out of this mess.

I watched as the amazing Don Williams, the CEO of TCC,

and his team sat down with the lenders. Don took a bunch of keys with him into the boardroom and placed them on the table. "We can't figure out what you own," he said, "because there's so much cross collateralization from building to building. If we can't figure out what you own, it is unlikely you can; but here are all the keys. You can take what you want and fight it out amongst yourselves—or we can work out a situation where we can all win together."

Not surprisingly, the banks and insurance companies took the second option. They worked out a deal in which the lenders took a bit of a hit on the debt owed to them. The cross collateralization across the buildings was broken up so everyone knew exactly which buildings they owned. The Trammell Crow family put some money back into the buildings and the agreement worked out great for everyone. As the markets came back and the properties appreciated, the lenders were paid and the family did very well.

This process proved to be very helpful to me. A few years later, we faced nearly the same situation at Continental. The full story of the situation we faced at the airline, and how we dealt with it, is in the appendix.

But what about the young TCC partners? We worked with them to change the strategy of TCC. "Never again can you have a company operating like this," we said, "where you are spending like mad and running out of cash without anyone knowing it." Together, we broke the firm into two pieces. While the Crow family became the development arm of the business, deciding what to build and how to finance it, the young guys who actually built the properties became the owners of a property management and leasing company, a fee-based business requiring very little capital. They went on to create one of the great fee-based businesses in the world, ultimately selling it at a big profit years later.

The young TCC partners were very lucky, even though not all of them (or even any of them) felt that way at the time. Most of them moved on without declaring personal bankruptcy and then went on to have successful, even extraordinary, careers. There is a saying: "If you owe a little, the banks own you; but if you owe a lot, you own the banks." TCC clearly benefited from this truism, but most stories in which someone runs out of cash don't end nearly as well.

The moral of the story: never, ever, *ever* run out of cash.

Know How Much Leverage You Can Handle

Debt in business is neither good nor bad. Debt is a neutral tool. I've referred earlier to my friend Britt Harris. He has a wonderful saying about money that can be applied to business debt: "Debt is a wonderful servant but a ruthless master."

Used properly, debt can give you a proper capital structure and effectively leverage your business, allowing you to grow much faster and increase your shareholder returns. Used in excess, it can destroy your equity value and cause you to run out of cash. If you have too much debt, you won't be able to turn around a business or take a satisfactorily underperforming organization to full performance. If you have too little debt, you will deliver suboptimal return on capital and will become a target for activist investors.

So how much debt should you put on your business? It depends. You need to understand your business really well to answer that question meaningfully. Let me give you a couple of examples.

CCMP owns a couple of players in the cyclical exploration and production (E&P) sector of oil and gas. E&P companies consume a lot of capital for drilling, which they fund from the cash flow of their oil and gas production, plus occasionally from additional debt. Oil and gas is a commodity business. In the last two to three years, we've seen prices as high as $140 a barrel and we've seen prices as low as $40 a barrel. That swing in price creates dramatically different cash flow and has a massive impact on the business. In fact, it is pretty easy to destroy value in E&P of oil and gas without realizing it. Many an E&P CEO has followed the flawed logic of borrowing to drill wells, thinking all is well so long as EBITDA[5] is growing.

Oil wells deplete over time, some quite quickly, so if the returns on your drilling activity are poor, although your EBITDA can be increasing, eventually your debt will grow so high that you can't pay it back—and no one will lend you more. You will be out of business. Congratulations, you just ran out of cash.

The key is always calculating the return on the next dollar of capital, the incremental dollar, that you spend drilling wells. If you don't, you could go broke at the same time you think you're doing well.

We are fortunate at CCMP to have an outstanding partner, Chris Behrens, an E&P expert who makes sure our companies focus on projects with high incremental returns. We always ask, "What actions are we taking *now* to best position ourselves if oil prices drop?"

You can prepare for such volatility in a number of ways. First, you may decide to invest in only the highest return projects, refuse to invest more than your cash flow, and keep your debt balance very low. Or second, you might hedge your oil and gas prices so that you lock in a future sales price that permits you to feel comfortable about how you're handling your debt. Prudence would suggest that you do both to protect your equity value. Energy companies get into trouble when they don't. In fact, right now we're seeing a number of energy companies going under for this very failure.

It's pretty easy to understand where and why businesses get into difficulty when they opt for too much leverage. We read about it in the papers almost every day. But what happens when a company has too little leverage? Let's take a look at the story of one business that made that mistake.

A Tale of Woe, in Reverse

What happened to us at The Home Depot a few years ago demonstrates that you can have a balance sheet with too little debt and too much cash. Just such a cash-rich balance sheet made Home Depot a potential target for activists.

In the mid-2000s, Home Depot had a goal to become the biggest company possible. The CEO launched a strategy in which, in an ideal world, Home Depot would double its sales and approach the size of GE. He executed the strategy using the $5 billion-plus that Home Depot generated in cash flow a year to buy industrial businesses far removed from Home Depot's core. The company also built new stores as fast as possible, even though these stores generated lousy returns in a fully saturated market. Predictably, Home Depot's return on invested capital (ROIC) declined. But it was easy to keep going, because the company had plenty of cash and almost no debt.

The firm's debt-free balance sheet and low ROIC eventually caused investors to get frustrated and the stock price to drop. Our board, led by Chairman and CEO Frank Blake and CFO Carol Tome, settled on a very logical plan for capital allocation: stop building stores with low returns, increase the dividend, and add a little debt to the company to buy back shares. We also told our shareholders that we would become world-class at driving returns by investing in store merchandising, interconnected retail, and our orange-aproned associates.

We pressure tested our business model for the worst crisis possible and determined that we could easily maintain a reasonable amount of leverage, which for Home Depot was two times debt to EBITDA. We used our excess cash to increase our dividends to shareholders and buy back stock. The result? Over eight years, Home Depot's stock rose more than 500 percent.

To get your own leverage just right, build a financial model and pressure test it for the worst of times. Never take all the leverage the banks will offer to give you in the good times— they are not very good at stress testing businesses. Never put your company at risk for debt that can't survive a serious downturn. If your business is sensitive to commodities, then protect yourself in the short run with hedges. Think like an operator and always err by taking a little less debt and holding a little more cash. You don't want too much leverage or too little leverage. It needs to be just right.

Keep Your Debt Maturity Stack Well into the Future

To make sure your debt doesn't come due at a bad time, you need to take three critical steps.

First, always match your debt to the life of your asset. There is a reason that your personal credit card bills come due every month, your car loan must be paid off over five years, and your home mortgage lasts thirty years. Those loans have been set up to match the life of the underlying asset. Groceries last a month, cars about five years, and homes much longer.

The same is true in business. Make sure that your business loans are long enough to not come due before you have the chance to earn the funds to repay them. It is okay to have short-term working capital lines, but never use them to finance long-term assets, like retail stores or manufacturing plants. Make sure your business has plenty of time to generate the profits you need to repay the loans.

Second, remember that the financial markets are not always open for borrowing money. During the financial crisis, many firms went under because the short-term cash they had grown accustomed to receiving dried up. These firms went bankrupt because they ran out of cash. Always use the open windows to refinance your company and push the debt maturity out as far as is practical, and make sure your debt does not all expire in any one year. We do this type of refinancing at CCMP all the time. We did it at Generac, Edwards, Milacron, Chaparral, and many more. In fact, we do it at almost every company we own. Why? It goes back to the underlined principle of this chapter: never, ever, *ever* run out of cash.

Third, seek out advice from an expert, someone who is truly

on your side and does credit agreements for a living. Don't underestimate how complicated this issue can get, and if you're not an expert, don't negotiate against someone who does this every day! Credit agreements can be very difficult to read. Some of them have covenants that allow the bank to reclaim your company if you don't reach your targets, while some agreements are "covenant light." Covenant light financings are almost always best, because the banks or bondholders cannot call the loan. This has saved us in many investments. Whatever the case, the terms and covenants *do* matter, and you need to pay careful attention to them.

We have a partner at CCMP, Kevin O'Brien, who I consider the world's greatest negotiator of credit agreements. He understands credit better than anyone I've ever known. He is the center of excellence in this area of risk management for us. It's critically important for you to have that kind of expert around to ask, "What if this happened? What if that happened? What do our banking covenants say? How do they work?"

Develop Proper Metrics

Let's end with the obvious. The better your business performs, the less likely you are to run into a balance sheet issue. In business, I like to say that sales and profits cure all woes. At the core of every fortress balance sheet you find a well-run business.

As we all know by now, a well-run business requires a very good one-page Go Forward plan, focused on the key value drivers of that business. Each item on the Go Forward plan needs a target so you know when you have succeeded. These targets should be measured, managed, and tied to your compensation system. We'll dive into compensation in chapter ten, but suffice it to say, a fortress balance sheet begins and ends with a great business plan.

The best balance sheet in the world will extend the life of a business only for so long. In the end, the only way to ensure success is to execute a great operating plan for an extended period of time. So if you're keen on building a strong fortress, understand that strong operations are the only way to become impregnable.

MY MENTORS

Ken Langone and Bonnie Hill:
How to Be a Great Director

Ken Langone: Drive and Integrity

Everybody on Wall Street knows Ken Langone. Ken grew up in Roslyn Heights, New York, to Italian-American working-class parents. He put himself through both Bucknell University and NYU. He formed a relationship with Ross Perot and served as the banker that took Electronic Data Systems public. Along with Bernie Marcus and Arthur Blank, he founded Home Depot in 1978. Jamie Dimon introduced me to Ken in 1999, and shortly thereafter, Ken asked me to go on the Home Depot board. Ken has been a mentor to me ever since.

Ken is an enthusiastic big bear of a man who has a huge hug for friends every time he sees them. He'd give you the shirt off his back if you needed it. Ken has incredible drive, impeccable integrity, and a strong Catholic faith. This has led Ken to champion the Home Depot associates ever since the company began. Thousands of associates over the years have used Ken's personal number to report a problem they've seen at Home Depot—and Ken always responds. You want Ken in your foxhole.

Ken fiercely protected Home Depot and its fortress balance sheet until he retired from the board a few years ago. We went through some difficult times at Home Depot during the time I served with Ken. He always worked passionately hard on behalf of the company. Ken always led the board to do the right thing "right away and all at once."

Bonnie Hill: Rebuilding Credibility

Bonnie Hill had an amazing career that spanned academia, politics, and business. She earned her PhD in Education from the University of California at Berkeley and served as the dean of the McIntire School of Commerce at the University of Virginia. Bonnie also served as a cabinet member for California Governor Pete Wilson and as director of the US Office of Consumer Affairs in the George H.W. Bush administration. In business, Bonnie was a vice president at Times Mirror Company and on numerous corporate boards, including Albertsons, Hershey, Yum!, and of course, Home Depot.

Bonnie joined the Home Depot board in 1999 and took over as lead director when Ken Langone retired in 2008. I was fortunate to join the Home Depot board in 2000 and took over as lead director from Bonnie when she retired in 2014. As you can see, I had some big shoes to fill.

Bonnie took over as lead director shortly after Frank Blake became CEO. The board badly needed to rebuild credibility with its shareholders, and Bonnie was the perfect person to do it. She relentlessly worked with management and met with shareholders to explain the company's strategy and our focus on proper corporate governance. Bonnie also became a featured speaker at almost every major corporate governance and director training forum. Her calm and thoughtful leadership during this time reflected positively on the Home Depot board and earned Bonnie the well-deserved honor of being named one of the top directors in the United States. Both Bonnie and Ken taught me how to be a great director.

Choose Freedom

> *A man in debt is so far a slave.*
> RALPH WALDO EMERSON

H OW WOULD IT FEEL to know that your decisions about what you want to accomplish in life and where you need to spend your time to reach those goals are not limited by your financial condition? How would it feel to know that you are not constrained by too much debt and too little cash?

Just imagine a world where you can pursue what you have been put on this earth to do. You can fulfill your life mission. You have complete freedom to execute your one-page personal Go Forward plan, without concern for your finances. You never have to waste any energy on whether you have the needed financial resources. You never have to take a job you hate just to fund your lifestyle. Would that feel good?

Financial freedom is a wonderful thing. On the other hand, financial issues are the number one cause of divorce and at the root of a host of stress-related diseases.

So let me give you a tool and some suggestions on how to develop financial freedom. Managing your finances is pretty binary. It will either work out well for you or it won't. There is not too much middle ground. Let me show you how to master money instead of it mastering you.

Determine Your Financial Finish Line

Let's start by beginning with the end in mind: How much money do you need to achieve financial freedom? Your financial finish line is a hard number. It is simply the amount that gives you enough in the bank to enable you to live the lifestyle you have chosen, without needing any more money. Period. Stop. End of day. It also helps you cap your lifestyle so that you don't allow your expenditures to increase with your income.

Before I walk you through a simple example to help you calculate your financial finish line, let me say that this is not an exercise for the faint of heart. The math is pretty simple, but how you determine "How much is enough?" says a lot about you, your priorities in life, and your personal Go Forward plan. In the end, your financial finish line is much more than a number.

If you are married, you should definitely do this exercise with your spouse. Don't try to "lone wolf" this one. The interesting discussions you will have are certain to align you together in your marriage. And isn't that a lot better than the default of arguing about which one of you is spending too much? If you are single, your priorities might look a little different, but the process remains exactly the same. In either case, put your personal Go Forward plan in front of you as you start the process. It will keep your financial finish line consistent with your life plan.

You can make the calculation of your financial finish line as complicated as you want. Genius financiers will notice that I've made a few assumptions to keep the process simple, but let's not focus too much on that, since it won't matter much anyway, and I'd like to keep our discussion uncomplicated.

Get started by pulling together an annual estimate of what you need to live on in your peak spending years. Very likely, these are the years when your kids are in high school or college. Don't write down what you hope to spend, but what you actually *need* to take care of your family and pay for life's expenses. If you are married, share your dreams with your spouse and have all those great debates to determine what kind of house you plan to live in, what kind of cars you will drive, what kind of schools your kids will attend, how you plan to take care of your parents or other relatives. Wrestle them all to the ground.

Always set aside at least 10 percent to give to those less fortunate, plus another 10 percent for savings. If you are single, you just have to negotiate with yourself.

Once you finish your spending plan for the peak years, check it again. How does it compare to your spending today? Do you plan to ramp up your lifestyle or tone it down? Does it feel good? Does it feel responsible? Once you have a hard maximum annual number, you can move on.

Let's work through an example.

How much is enough for an average American family? A 2014 *USA Today* article calculated the cost of living for the average American who determined he or she was living well: about $130,000 a year. If you add 10 percent savings to that figure, that's another $13,000. And if you add 10 percent giving, the number rises another $13,000. So in effect, the average American says he or she will feel satisfied with about $160,000 a year. Your number may be higher or lower than $160,000; it doesn't matter. Following the *USA Today* example, let's assume your number to live well is $160,000 a year. It is not lost on me that the average household income in the United States is less than $160,000 per year; we all tend to want more than we have. Happiness always seems to be just around the corner.

It's now quite simple to calculate your financial finish line. Divide the $160,000 per year you need to live by the 5 percent you expect to earn annually. (I am assuming the money you save will appreciate 5 percent every year. If you save and invest in stocks and bonds through an index fund, history would tell us that you should be able to make that much over time. You may be a wizard of an investor who can earn more, but be careful. This is your retirement money. Be safe.)

This means you need $3.2 million to hit your personal financial finish line. You can say, "Once I have $3.2 million in the bank, I will generate $160,000 in income per year and can live at the lifestyle I identified as the right lifestyle for me. I will have complete financial freedom."

I need to make two important comments at this point. First, if you're an entrepreneur or you own a business, you might need some capital for that business. In that case, you must add whatever capital you require to get to your financial finish line. Second, as you get closer to retirement, your number may go down both because you can live on less, but also because you have pension funds or social security benefits that *might* offset your costs.

But congratulations—you've just determined your financial finish line!

Now, go back and take a detailed look at your current budget. How much are you making? How much are you spending? What are you saving? Don't guess at the number; sit down and figure it out.

Once you know your annual savings level, you can determine

how many years it will take to reach your financial finish line. Don't forget to count the 5 percent in appreciation you get every year on the money you save! Let's say you have a great job and can save $100,000 per year. At that level, if your financial finish line is $3.2 million, it will take you a little over twenty years. You can and should track your progress along the way.

What Is Your Financial Finish Line?

Now do your own calculation—how long will it take you? What year will you get there? Will you arrive in ten years? Twenty years? Never?

Does your calculation scare you? Will you end up depending on someone else when you retire? Will you need to work until you are eighty? Do you need to reduce your expenditures and reevaluate what you really *need*, as opposed to what you *want* so you can save more?

If you're not saving any money (or very little), you'll never have financial freedom. I'd be willing to bet that at least half of my readers are in this category. If you're in that half, you're probably saying, "I did the calculation and I'm never going to be able to retire. I'm always going to be in debt to someone." Then to you I say, *now* is the time to change. *Now* is the time to reduce your expenses, start saving, and begin moving toward financial freedom.

If you're in the other half, you're probably feeling pretty

smug right now, saying to yourself, "I've won the prize! I've hit my financial finish line! I have a personal fortress balance sheet!" Congratulations to you... but perhaps, just perhaps, those in that position should focus now on sharing with the less fortunate. I wrote chapter seven for everyone, but aimed it especially at those who have financial freedom.

Five Simple Rules

Building a personal fortress balance sheet gives you enormous flexibility to execute your personal Go Forward plan. It gives you choices on how to best follow through on your value levers, your blue chips. It's unbelievably rewarding and fulfilling to have that kind of freedom—so long as you use it well.

We have taught our children a few very simple rules so they won't make bad choices along the way to adulthood, poor decisions that can put them in a serious hole. Perhaps these rules may help you too. These five straightforward rules may seem simpler than what you've seen elsewhere, but I wanted my kids to have a good handle on these issues by the time they became young adults.

1. Keep a budget and make sure you have enough cash.

If you've never kept a household budget, start one. You don't necessarily have to reconcile your expenditures down to every coffee you buy, but create and track a budget that you develop yourself. Remember that the dictum "what gets measured gets managed" goes for your personal life too. And keep a cash cushion so you'll be okay when emergencies come up.

Reconcile your budget to your actual expenses monthly. Don't just guess how you are doing; *know*. Make sure as part of that budget that you allow for the things that will keep you physically healthy. Take care of yourself, because medical bills are expensive! Medical costs are increasing over time, not shrinking. Taking care of your physical health brings a lot of benefits, not the least of which is improving your financial health.

2. No auto or credit card debt.

Credit cards feel very tempting. They allow you to spend beyond your means. They also have very high interest rates.

My personal rule is to use debit cards only (where you spend only the money you already have in the bank) or to pay off all credit cards in full each month, as soon as the bill arrives. Stay away from accumulating credit card debt on items that depreciate quickly, things that lose a lot of their value the moment you pay for them. Many people accumulate credit debt by buying groceries, furniture, and other perishable items, but that just doesn't make good financial sense.

The same is true for car loans. We all know that cars depreciate sharply as soon as you drive them off the lot. So why borrow to buy a car? Just pay cash for whatever you can afford to own.

I drove inexpensive used cars (an old Ford Pinto and a Dodge Colt) long into my career, when I could have afforded something much nicer. Why? My wife and I had focused on getting to our financial finish line and giving to others along the way, and we knew we could save a lot by driving older-model cars.

So just say no to any auto or credit card debt. Accumulating debt to buy rapidly depreciating assets at high interest rates is a very bad idea if you want to have financial freedom.

3. Limit your education debt and always run a payback on your educational expenses.

When my own kids were high school sophomores and juniors, I asked them to think about what they wanted to do for a living once they graduated from college. Where did they want to work? What kind of job did they want? We spent a lot of time together dreaming about their future. We began with the end in mind.

I then asked them to begin to identify colleges that would equip them to secure that ideal job. Did these colleges offer the right majors? How did they rank nationally? Did their graduates have a good record of securing the kinds of jobs my kids really wanted?

Next, I had them figure out what kind of starting annual pay they could expect to get out of their chosen occupation.

What was the average salary range? What did the potential for advancement look like?

Finally, we went back and said, "If you had to borrow the money to go to school, what would be the payback on your education?" While the payback for something like nursing or accounting or engineering is pretty good, the payback for a history major, a philosophy major or an English major is much less certain. That doesn't mean no one should major in those things, of course; but perhaps—if you have to borrow to go to school—you should double major in an area where you can get a job that will allow you to pay back your education debt.

College students often change their minds during school about their majors, which is fine. But if they have to think about an end game, a career, far ahead of time, then they are more likely to make wise financial decisions about their education. And even if they do change their minds, parents can always come back later and say, "Okay, *now* go do the research for me. Initially you picked XYZ job; we know how much income that job would generate. Are there good jobs for graduates in the new major you want to pursue? How much are you likely to earn? What is the payback on the new major? Can you pay back the student loans you took out, if any?"

As I write, student loan debt in the United States has risen to more than a *trillion* dollars. Much of it will go into default, mainly because those who incurred the debt did not have a plan to pay it back. In addition, the government willingly provided a guarantee for the loans, and universities often didn't deliver good value for the education they provided. Defaulting student loans could easily be the next financial tsunami to hit the country.

If you or your kids need to borrow to go to school, consider ways in which you can keep down the cost. Malcolm Gladwell, in his book *David and Goliath*, claims that if you attend a university where you can be in the top third of your class, you are much more likely to stick to your chosen field and have a prosperous, fulfilling life than if you attend a prestigious institution where you are an average student. Read Gladwell's book before you insist on sending your kids to the "best university they can get into." Set yourself up for success. We have a wonderful community college system in this country that equips students with the basics for a fraction of the cost of a traditional four-year school. Keep your student loan debt as low as possible.

4. Don't allow your total housing costs to exceed 20 percent of your gross income.

This 20 percent guideline includes not only your mortgage or rent, but also utilities, taxes, insurance, upkeep, the whole package. If you do this calculation on your current situation and find that your housing costs exceed 20 percent of your gross income, then probably you ought to change where you live. You're likely living above your means.

I recognize that if you live in a large city on the coast, like New York, Los Angeles, or San Francisco, and you're early in your career, you may have housing costs over 20 percent of your income. Just recognize that as your income goes up, you should not necessarily increase your lifestyle.

5. Always include a minimum of 10 percent savings and 10 percent giving.

The 10 percent savings rule is pretty much nonnegotiable, because you need a cushion for when things go wrong. Later I'll talk more about the 10 percent giving guideline, but I think it's pretty important to give back to the less fortunate. And let's face it—if you're reading this book, odds are there are a whole bunch of people less fortunate than you. I know that's certainly true of me.

Talking to Kids about Money

I was fortunate to grow up with parents and in a community with a very strong sense of stewardship and a very conservative posture toward debt. This is not true for most people I know. For them, financial matters were considered very private, very personal. Generationally, that's how it's been in our country for a long time.

But how are we serving our kids well if we aren't willing to talk to them about how to handle money? We need to give them life skills, including instruction about family finance.

As our own kids grew up, we very deliberately discussed money matters with them. We didn't want money to be a forbidden topic. While they didn't need to know everything about how much we made and all of our financial decisions, they did need to know how to manage money.

Jeff Smisek, a good friend and colleague at Continental and the former chairman and CEO of United Airlines, gave us a good idea. Jeff is a really smart businessman and was a terrific partner during the Continental years, but his advice here had an outsize impact on our family. When each of our children reached the age of about four years old, we gave them an old-fashioned ledger in which they could keep track of debits and credits, plusses and minuses. They used those ledgers until they were sixteen. Ronda and I functioned as their bank.

Whatever income they had—birthday money, or maybe we'd pay them for good grades or doing a special chore—they would record the amount as a plus in their ledger. Every time they spent money (or maybe they got fined for getting in trouble or mouthing off), they'd get a minus in their ledger. So from a very early age, they learned how to put debits and credits in their ledgers. They weren't handling actual money yet, but they were learning about it. They learned how the banking system works and about basic accounting. And they were learning it from their parents.

Our kids are now all in their mid-twenties and they love reading back through the old childhood ledgers. Those precious books tell a host of amazing, funny stories about their lives—maybe that toy they just "had" to buy, or some punishment they received. "Fifty-five *dollars* for being mouthy and talking back? Mom must have been *really* angry that day!" We just sit and laugh together. It amazes us how much they learned about life through this simple exercise.

Once they turned sixteen, we opened real bank accounts in their names (we were cosigners) and deposited in the bank all the money recorded in their ledgers. They also started using debit cards, as most teenagers do, to spend money out of their own accounts. And as they got jobs, they put the money they earned into their own accounts.

Many teenagers today appear to believe that money grows on trees; they imagine it just pours out of a debit card some-how. But long before our kids had actual money, by using their ledgers, they knew how debits and credits worked. They knew where money came from. During those years, they always gave 10 percent of their income, immediately after they earned it, to the less fortunate. They still do.

As each of our children got ready to leave for college, I drew up a contract for them to sign, laying out our expectations of them in return for funding their education. The agreement with Andrew, our oldest son, began like this: "Whereas Andrew realizes his parents' moral financial obligations to him are over, and whereas he'd like his parents to fund his college to get off to a good start in life, and whereas his parents will be happy to do that to get him off to a good start, therefore...." We then listed four or five behavioral actions that we wanted to see. We wanted to see Andrew in church every Sunday, for example, and in a Bible study during the week. We wanted him to avoid illegal drugs or alcohol. We wanted him to earn reasonable grades.

When I handed the contract to Andrew in the spring of his senior year of high school, he balked. "Dad," he said, "this contract isn't fair!"

"Andrew," I replied, "why do you say that?"

"Well, we didn't negotiate it," he answered. "We didn't even have a discussion about it."

"Andrew," I replied, "when you were out with your buddies, I went up to your room and looked around. I didn't see a single thing that I wanted. Not one thing. So as near as I can tell, your mom and I have a fair amount of money that you'd like us to give you for college, and all you have that we want are a few very simple behavioral items."

I let that sink in and then said, "I'm going to teach you the first lesson in negotiation, Andrew. It's called leverage. You don't have any." I told Andrew he could either sign the contract and we'd be happy to pay for his college, so long as he lived up to the contract, or he could choose not to sign it, and he could pay for college himself. He went up to his room to think it over.

Of course, an hour or two later, he came down with the contract signed.

To our surprise, our kids put up their contracts on a wall in their dorm rooms, and when their friends asked them to do something really stupid, they'd point to the contract and say, "I'd lose my college funding if I did that." So the contract served several purposes. We are not naive; we also felt very happy we did not know everything that went on during their college years!

Each semester, we distributed the college money we had agreed to provide. Our children were responsible for budgeting and managing these funds during the semester. They'd also sit down with me at the end of each semester, at least during the first few years of college, to review what funds they had left, what they'd spent, and how they were doing against their budget.

When Bethany, our second child, was getting ready for her junior year, she said to me one day, "Dad, you haven't given me my college contract yet for this year."

"Bethany," I said, "why don't *you* write your college contract?"

She looked at me in a quizzical way and asked, "Dad, why would *I* write it?"

"Well," I replied, "you're now twenty-one. You're responsible— so why don't you go write your own contract?"

She went upstairs and wrote out the contract she wanted to live by during her junior year. When she brought it down to me, I read it, tore it up, and threw it away.

"Dad," she said, "why did you do that? Aren't you going to sign the contract?"

I looked at her and said, "Bethany, you don't need a contract anymore."

She had been trained appropriately, had managed her money well, and our training had come to an end. She was completely capable of handling her college money without a contract.

What If You're Under Water?

"Greg," you might be saying, "these guidelines and your counsel sound great for a young person just starting out in life. But what if someone has taken a few wrong turns and finds himself in a financial bind? What then? What can he do?"

This isn't rocket science. In fact, a person in trouble financially does the same thing someone new to the game must do. All it means is that the person starts in debt rather than at ground zero. Any financial counselor worth the name will say, "Let's sit down and put a budget together to determine where you are. Then, let's look at your debts and figure out how to pay them back." That's how programs like Financial Peace University work.

I've done this with individuals who have gotten themselves into serious debt. When I ask them to put together a budget, in their first attempt, their expenses usually exceed their income. If they don't, I have a pretty good idea they've fibbed. "This is what we're spending," they say; but if that were *really* the case, then they would not have a financial problem. So I ask them to try again. "How many times a week are you eating out?" I'll ask. "How many times do you go to Starbucks a day? What does your cable plan cost?" Yada, yada, yada. Once you get to the *real* budget, the tough choices become apparent. Everyone realizes that, at least for a time, they have to live on a whole lot less than they want to.

In fact, living on what they make is not enough. To get out from under the debt, a significant percent of earnings should go to paying down that debt. This means they will have to accept a true austerity plan.

At the end of the day, it's really just math. To get out of debt and build a fortress balance sheet, you must hold your expenses to a minimum, figure out a way to generate more income, and fight your way out. The basic process is exactly the same for companies, organizations, and individuals.

I have helped about a half dozen churches get out of debt too. One situation stands out. A large community church built a campus right about the time of the financial crisis. The church didn't make wise decisions and had large cost overruns, donations fell below expectations, and their debt ballooned. In fact, based on the database of at least one group that measures these things, it became the most indebted church per attendee in the country.

When the leadership asked for my advice, we started talking about the necessary moves to reduce and eliminate the debt. Of course, that required some hard choices. At first, the pastor objected. "No, this is God's church," he declared. "We're going to do this, we're going to do that."

"Can I stop you for just a second?" I asked. "This is *not* God's church, at least not at the moment." The pastor looked at me, confused and a little hurt. I continued, "This church is owned by the *bank*. It can truly be God's church only when you get it out of debt. God does not need your money, but he does need your adherence to good financial stewardship."

The leadership team soon saw my point and agreed to move ahead. I represented the church at a negotiation with the bank and said, in essence, "We have three choices here. We can buy back the debt at fifty cents on the dollar and we'll solve the problem that way. Or you take back the keys to the church building. Or you give us real low-interest payments for the next five years or so, and we'll fight to get the debt paid off." Not surprisingly, the bank chose the third option.

The church had to write its version of a Go Forward plan, lay off a third of its staff, and really prioritize. Expenses were capped and wages were frozen for several years. The church adopted an austerity program to pay back its enormous debt.

Five and a half years later, thanks to hard work and a generous congregation, the church completely freed itself of debt. It went from being the most indebted church in the nation to absolutely no debt. Even better, half of the money that comes in now goes to help people in need, as opposed to getting poured into more projectors, more musicians, more buildings, more church programs and functions. It's an incredible story, really... but it required absolute austerity for five and a half years.

Funny thing, though. Nobody really missed the things that got cut. A great lesson for us all!

The *really* cool thing, however, is that now that the debt has been redeemed, I'm told you could not find a happier bunch of people anywhere. It's not the bank's church anymore, and the people know it. They actually *are* God's church. It's really fantastic.

Make no bones about it, whether the debt is saddling a church, a business, or a person, it's a tough road to creating a fortress balance sheet.

Since we're focusing here on the personal side, let me ask a few simple questions about your debt. Do you have one parent working or two? Do you drive old clunker cars or do you get a new car with a big loan? Do you eat out once or more a week or stay in and cook for yourself? I hate to say it, but the road to getting debt-free is really pretty simple, even if it's hard. Simple and easy aren't the same.

Honestly, it doesn't matter how many zeros there are in the debt. It doesn't matter if the debt belongs to a huge company with a hundred billion in sales or to an individual who makes $40,000 a year. Getting rid of it is hard work.

I've seen a lot of individuals rally around this effort to create a personal fortress balance sheet, and it changes their lives. Believe me: you will feel an incredible sense of freedom if you don't owe anybody anything!

My Mentors

Paul Friesen: The North Star

I got to know Paul Friesen, now in his mid-nineties, when he served as our pastor. As a missionary's kid who grew up in India, Paul escaped with his life at the age of twelve from a terrible car wreck. Every time I've ever seen him, he's taken the opportunity to tell me that God's provision on that fateful day prepared him for the rest of his life.

Paul was an outstanding preacher, but he's best known for his work as a potter and sculptor. I remember Paul delivering sermons while sitting at his potter's wheel. On my desk at work sits one of his sculptures, a beautiful piece called South Wind, made out of cherry wood and inscribed with a few carefully chosen Bible verses. I look at that stunning piece of artwork every day. It's so very full of meaning to me.

Despite Paul's packed schedule, he took the time to teach our seventh grade Sunday school class. On one occasion in the dead of winter, he and my uncle took a group of us to Colorado, where we stayed in a cabin that no one had ever bothered to winterize. Our only heat came from a fire we had to build in the fireplace, and when nature called, your only choice was the frozen great outdoors. In many ways the outing was a disaster—but Paul willingly took the time to invest in us as kids, and I never forgot it.

Over the decades, Paul and I have forged a very special relationship. He still lives in Hesston, although now in a vibrant retirement community. He often sends me letters that sound like something out of *Tuesdays with Morrie*. A couple of years ago he wrote, "Greg, I want to tell you what it's like to get old. It's not fun at all and I wouldn't write this letter to you unless you were a very dear friend." And then he proceeded to describe what it felt like to watch the years drift on by.

I last went to see Paul a few months ago. When I arrived at his room, I found him at his computer. He gave me a huge hug and we had a great conversation about a new Bible study he's doing on the Minor Prophets (the last twelve books in the Hebrew Scriptures). After more than nine decades on this planet, Paul is still learning and exploring! We ended our visit with an amazing time together in prayer.

Every time the Brenneman family suffers a death—my grandfather, my grandmother, my great-uncle, all of whom I've been very close to—the first guy who approaches me at the funeral is Paul. He's always there and always has been. Paul and I can go for two years without having an extended conversation, and then pick it up again as though we'd never been apart. He's been a constant influence.

It was Paul who taught me that what really matters in the end is your faith, your family, and your friends. His example constantly reminds me to spend my time where it counts the most. Even now, I can hear him gently say it: "Don't let your life mission drift!"

Paul Friesen always has been my True North. Whenever I need to recenter myself, I think about Paul, look to Paul, or talk to Paul. If you were to identify somebody who has lived his life humbly, giving it to others and then giving it back to the Kingdom, that someone would be Paul Friesen.

Paul Friesen taught me how to choose freedom.

STEP 3

Think Money In, Not Money Out

> *Without continual growth and progress, such words as improvement, achievement and success have no meaning.*
> BENJAMIN FRANKLIN

D
URING THE FINANCIAL CRISIS of 2008, JPMorgan Chase bought Bear Stearns, the troubled investment bank and brokerage firm. As part of that transaction, the bank inherited a small private equity operation that it asked CCMP to manage. The best thing about the request was that, as part of the agreement, we convinced Joe Scharfenberger to join us at CCMP as a managing director in our consumer/retail group. Joe was a great cultural fit from the beginning. Among other qualities, he has an extraordinary eye for growing retail concepts.

While at Bear Stearns, Joe had made a very small minority investment in a Houston-based discount specialty boutique named Francesca's Collections. After the sale of Bear Stearns, we took over responsibility for managing Francesca's. Around the same time, I happened to be talking one day with a CEO friend in Houston who asked if I'd ever heard of the company. He wondered if I could spend a little time with Francesca's young CEO.

Since the company was based in Houston and we now had a responsibility to manage it, I replied, "Of course. I'd be glad to visit." When I arrived for my first meeting, I found the company's corporate headquarters in a ratty warehouse. The offices up front literally had ceiling tiles falling in, and the hot distribution center in the back looked even worse. Not the best first impression! But then I heard the Francesca's story from its terrific young CEO, John De Meritt.

John had founded the company with three wonderful siblings, a sister in her early fifties and a brother and sister in their late forties, all of them very strategic and very hardworking. Their parents had emigrated from Korea and had never learned to speak English. The father had operated a convenience store in a Korean section of Houston, and even though he got shot twice there in the decades he ran the family business, he and his wife somehow managed to send their three kids to the University of Houston. The middle daughter had worked in the finance department at Continental Airlines, where I got to know her a bit. For some time, she juggled three jobs: working at Continental, starting Francesca's, and serving as chief merchant. All four of the founders had boundless energy.

After my office appointment, I visited a Francesca's store, where it took me all of fifteen minutes to tell that they had created a very special business, despite running the operation out of a shoebox. Somehow, they had turned specialty retail on its head.

They shipped merchandise to their stores every day to keep product fresh (versus the normal quarterly plan-o-grams of other retailers). They collapsed the supply chain so that they could open a purchase order in a single day (versus a thirty-day-plus process for others). They sourced new merchandise in five to six weeks (versus twelve-plus months for others). And they designed their own clothes, jewelry, gifts, and other items, branding it all with their own private label, allowing for about 70 percent profit margins (versus about 40 percent when distributing someone else's brand).

"These guys have a really unique business model," I told my partners.

I'd served on the board at J. Crew, so I knew how retail clothing concepts normally work. You pick blue sweaters for Christmas, eighteen months in advance, and then you just hope that blue sweaters are "in" during the holidays. J Crew had about a twelve- to eighteen-month lead time on product. When J. Crew bought those sweaters, it'd sell them for an entire season, essentially three months. The product might come in five different sizes and eighteen different colors. Not so at Francesca's; the product was sourced in about six weeks and sold out in about two weeks and came in just three basic sizes: small, medium, and large.

But what really got my attention that day was the margin on the products generated by this fast-turning retail operation: *70 percent!* It just stunned me. Yes, the small company had only about fifty stores, but the founders very plainly had a good thing going.

John and I began to get to know one another just as the financial crisis of 2008 hit. One day he asked me, "Greg, how many stores do you think we should build in 2009? Our stores are doing really well."

Indeed they were. They had a cash-on-cash payback of about six months, when normal for retail stores runs about three *years.* (Cash-on-cash payback refers to the cash you use to start a store, and how long it takes for that cash to come back to you.) I had never seen payback that fast.

"I'm thinking of opening eight or nine stores in 2009," John told me.

"John," I said, "I think you ought to build forty stores next year."

My new friend's jaw nearly dropped. "Greg," he said, "what

do you mean, *forty?* That would dramatically increase the size of the company!"

"It's true that it's the world's worst time in the economy," I replied, "but you're still doing amazingly well. The best real estate in the world is becoming available because most retailers are shutting down great sites. Many jewelry stores are vacating 'main and main' in the corners of the malls. And you are the best person I have ever seen at selecting real estate."

John pondered my advice and eventually took it. Instead of adding nine stores in 2009, he opened forty stores. And the company continued to do well, despite the sick economy.

Toward the end of that year, John called my secretary, his voice full of intensity. "I need to see Greg," he told her. She immediately came to me and said, "Hey, I think something's wrong with John or his family. He *badly* needs to see you. I told him you were going to Seattle, and he asked if he could get on the plane with you."

"Absolutely," I said. "Put John on the plane with me."

After we took off, John wasted little time getting to the point. "The siblings are ready to sell," he told me. "But they want to sell the business only to you. They've already figured out what they believe you can pay."

We continued our discussion in the air, and by the time we landed in Seattle, we had a deal. CCMP would buy 84 percent of the business from John and the other founders, while they would keep 16 percent. We took over Francesca's in March 2010, and from that point forward, we grew the business like mad. We added sixty stores in 2010 and added about eighty-five stores per year while we owned it. In November of 2010, we took half of our money back, and in July of 2011, a little over a year later, we took the company public. Very quickly, we had no debt on the business and made over four times our initial investment. John became a rock star CEO with a terrific reputation.

I'll never forget the day Francesca's went public on the NASDAQ. I had breakfast that morning with one of the sisters and her parents, who had come to the United States from Korea all those years ago. They felt so proud of their three children! And they had every right. I can't imagine where our country would be today if we didn't open our arms wide to industrious immigrants.

That's the power of growing a company. We got such an outsize return, so quickly, because we focused on growing a small business that we thought had world-class potential. And we did it even in the middle of an economic downturn. Growth is the key. You have to think money in rather than money out.

Cost Cutting Is No Panacea

Reducing cost can actually cost more than it's worth. We've already seen how Home Depot degraded customer service by replacing many full-time skilled plumbers and electricians, experts beloved by customers, with unskilled part-timers. And in the appendix you'll read how the no-frills division of Continental called CALite simply bombed.

After Continental's brutal experience, several other carriers also tried this "lite" strategy, including Delta, Air France, and British Airways. It never worked. We would just laugh whenever we saw other carriers experiment with it. Eventually, they all abandoned it too. The whole experience led my partner at Continental, CEO Gordon Bethune, to remark, "You can make a pizza so cheap that no one will want to eat it." Continental had cost cut its way to an airline so cheap that nobody wanted to fly it.

Don't miss the lesson: *a maniacal focus on trimming cost can lose you more revenue than you gain.*

"But if that's true," someone asks, "then why do so many turnaround attempts go straight to cutting cost?" They do so because some costs almost always need to come out, like the surplus of partners and nonvalue-added advertising we saw earlier at PwCC. You also need to trim costs that customers don't value. More often than not, however, executives go straight to cost cutting because it's far easier to reduce cost than it is to grow revenue.

Think back to the analogy of blue chips, red chips, and white chips. Cost reduction is almost always a white chip, or at best a red chip. Revenue growth, however, is always a blue chip. Growing revenue always produces better results than focusing solely on cutting costs. So yes, managing your costs is important; but if you want to increase profitability in a big way, you *must* focus on generating revenue.

Why Obsess on Growth?

Why the obsession with growth? For one thing, it's a lot of fun to create jobs and new opportunities for so many people. Creating good jobs is really our primary mission as businesspeople. It is what we were put on earth to do. It is why I often say, "revenue growth is next to godliness." It is *that* important.

The founders of Home Depot—Bernie Marcus, Arthur Blank, and Ken Langone—started in 1978 with an idea. Today, about 350,000 associates work at Home Depot. That's what I call doing a lot of good!

I like what Dorothy Sayers had to say on the subject. Born in Victorian England in the late nineteenth century, she was one of the first women to graduate from Oxford. She earned a reputation as a respected theologian and playwright. She once wrote, "A human being must have occupation, if he or she is not to become a nuisance to the world." She also wrote,

> *Work is not primarily the thing one does to live, but the thing one lives to do. It is, or should be, the full expression of a worker's facilities, the thing in which one finds spiritual,*

mental and bodily satisfaction, and the medium in which one offers himself to God.

I love Sayers's words; but really, we are not that altruistic. Creating jobs is not the core reason why we so strongly emphasize growth. We focus on profitable growth primarily because *that's how we get paid.*

Our limited partners at CCMP are all good people, and while they love it when we create jobs, they expect us to make hefty returns for them. They want to give us a dollar and receive two or three in return. They want a payback on their money higher than the public equity market can deliver. If they didn't think we could accomplish that, they wouldn't let us lock up their money for ten years. They'd just put their dollars in a mattress or invest it in public stocks and bonds and have access to their funds anytime they wanted it.

Investors give us their money for one reason: they believe we can deliver extraordinary returns. And in fact, our focus on growth has allowed us to grow our companies organically at a rate much faster than the growth of the US economy, which creates a lot of value.

The only way to create returns that consistently outperform the stock market is to grow companies at a rate much faster than the economy's growth. Research shows that by focusing on growth, you can create a mighty flywheel effect that quickly sparks a positive spiral. Profitable companies offer better promotion opportunities and attract better employees. Happy employees offer better customer service, which makes customers want to return. Those customers tell their friends to come. You don't have to spend as much money trying to acquire new customers, which increases your profits and makes for happy investors. And the flywheel just keeps gaining more momentum.

Consider Some Evidence

Growing companies was a big part of the reason I came to CCMP in 2008. Let me tell you a little bit about my thinking.

To start, just a little background on private equity that led to my decision. Throughout most of the '80s and '90s, nascent private equity was operationally intensive; you had to roll up your sleeves and figure out how to make a company work. The Continental turnaround, for example, was a private equity deal. But toward the end of the '90s and the beginning of the 2000s, the public equity markets took off, and so did private equity. During this era, PE became so easy that I like to joke that any educated chimpanzee could do it; and by the mid-2000s, you didn't even have to be an educated chimpanzee. You could be just a regular chimpanzee and still excel in private equity. Why?

The banks made it easy. They took perfectly good companies and put loads of debt on them with what's called "stapled financing." The banks said, "We're going to sell this company to the highest bidder. Here is a financing package that goes along with the company, so you don't need to worry about the debt. Just put in a little sliver of equity." So investors would put in their little sliver of equity, the public equity market would go up, and soon the PE firm would sell that little sliver of equity for plus or minus three times whatever the investor put in. Easy. How could you miss?

But with the coming of the financial crisis of 2008, that whole game of stapled financing and PE firms just processing deals ended. I like to tell people that 2008 reminds me of the biblical story of Joseph in Egypt. We had just finished seven years of feast and were about to enter seven years of famine. Great operating skill would be required. Not coincidentally, I joined CCMP that year. It interested me because we had returned to the times when you had to operate and grow a company. That signaled to me that I should move to what some call the "dark side," from being a CEO of companies to investing in companies as a private equity owner.

While a lot of private equity firms looked for ways to use operating talent, CCMP went about it differently. The partners had succeeded in business for a long time, but they recognized the industry was changing. They believed, as I did, that the future of private equity would belong not exclusively to those who traditionally created value through buying and selling, but also to those who could have a decisive impact on the companies while they owned them. In the capital markets, this is called "delivering Alpha." Rather than riding up and down with the markets, it's about having a positive operating impact on the business.

I wanted to enter a private equity firm where I could be a full partner in running the firm and growing companies, not junior to the financial partners, as is the case in most firms. I wanted to operate in a "two heads are better than one" model where there was a traditional PE partner with a financial background on every company, along with an equal partner with operating background, like myself, who had been a CEO on every deal. At CCMP, that is exactly the model we adopted. Since that time, Rich Zannino (former CEO of Dow Jones) and Doug Cahill (a very talented CEO we had worked with for many years) have joined too.

Revenue growth in our business is the difference between just getting your money back or making a three-times-plus return on your investment. In consumer retail, for example, two factors drive the multiple you get when you sell your company: revenue growth and profit margin. High-growth retail companies command huge sales multiples, more than double that of slow-growing retail companies. Our coheads of consumer/retail, Rich Zannino in the United States and Tom Walker in London, scan the market to find founders of growth retail companies interested in partnering with us, particularly ones that have a value orientation to consumers. This has led to investments like Francesca's and Ollie's in the United States, and Pure Gym in London.

We also target industrial companies, where we believe we can grow revenue at a rate at least three times the growth rate of the economy (5 percent or greater revenue growth when the economy is growing at only 1 to 2 percent), 20 percent or better EBITDA margins, and 70 percent or better free cash flow conversion. If you do that, then you have great odds of selling your business at really attractive values. Companies like Edwards, Generac or Milacron fit this profile.

By contrast, if your revenue grows only 1 or 2 percent, your EBITDA as a percent of revenue remains in the teens and you have to invest a lot of cash back into your business. In that case, you will top out on your multiples at about eight times EBITDA—meaning you'd be just as well off sticking your money in a stock index fund at Fidelity or Vanguard, with a lot less work.

How to Generate Profitable Revenue Growth

The three basic steps to driving profitable revenue growth are unbelievably simple to describe but extraordinarily difficult to do. Nevertheless, they must find a place in your own Go Forward plan.

1. Stop doing things that lose money.

The fastest way to make money is to stop doing things that lose it. Money-losing operations always consume a ton of your time and that of your management team. It may feel tempting to ignore money-losing businesses or to think you can eventually fix them, but be hard on yourself. Ask the tough questions:

"Have I ever made money doing that?"

"Will I ever make money on it?"

"Will it ever be worth my efforts?"

If you answer "no," then just bite the bullet and shut it down.

Consider one quick example. When I first arrived at Continental as a consultant, 18 percent of the flights were cash negative. I knew the fastest way to make money was to stop doing things that lose it. I sat the scheduling team down and started asking questions.

"Why are we going from Greensboro to Greenville six times a day when both customers who want to fly that route are on the first flight?"

"It's strategic," someone told me.

"When did it last make money?"

"It never did," came the reply.

"How strategic can that be?"

Silence filled the room. "Does someone's boyfriend or girlfriend live there?" I asked. "Why don't we just charter you a Lear jet? It would be cheaper."

We soon eliminated that route, along with other cash-draining flights, and let go about 7,000 employees. Profits followed almost immediately.

Be ruthless! Don't tolerate businesses or divisions that consistently lose money (or even those that make only a small profit).

2. Focus on your core.

Remember the concept of Profit from the Core discussed in chapter two?

I have come to appreciate the simple exercise of asking customers what they want and what they will pay for. When asked what they want, customers will write you an epistle a foot thick. When asked what they want *and* will pay for, you get a single-page, double-spaced list. That list represents your core. Work on those things! My CCMP partner Jon Lynch heads our investor relations group. Jon relentlessly represents our investors for us every time we discuss an important issue. I love that Jon never lets us stray from our core.

It is always easier to drive profits from the core areas of your business than by working at ventures with little connection to the areas where you have expertise and a competitive advantage. Many investors like to buy interesting businesses that have little connection to what they do best. They almost always think, *I'll transform my company into something very different.*

It rarely works.

My current partner at CCMP Rich Zannino oversaw a terrific turnaround at the *Wall Street Journal*. Rich served as the CEO of the parent company, Dow Jones, in the mid-2000s. Rich recognized that the venerable paper had begun to totter, mostly because it had continued to do things that customers didn't value. Traditional advertisers were dropping out at an alarming rate because, while they saw that consumers now wanted to view content online, they didn't see how advertising in the paper would help them to reach those online customers.

The business needed a fairly radical turnaround, and Rich led it through one, starting by cutting out long articles that few readers found interesting, and then adding new initiatives based on current customer desires. He took the newspaper from five days a week to six, added an online edition, dramatically shortened articles, and added several interesting sections, such as Off Duty, the Review section, and the Personal Journal section. Rupert Murdock saw the results of Rich's efforts and paid a huge premium for Dow Jones.

At Continental Airlines, focusing on the core meant flying in and out of our main hubs: Houston, Cleveland, and Newark. Every route we could fly in and out of those hubs made us far more profit than any flying we did elsewhere.

Once we cut the money-losing routes and found our profitable core inside our three hubs, we could grow—and grow we did. We added about 10 percent capacity per year and lots of destinations. When we arrived, the airline flew from Newark to only three destinations in Europe. By the time we left, it flew to seventeen. Continental flew to no destinations in Latin America or Asia; by the time we finished, it flew to six destinations in Latin America and five in Asia. When we built our airline around our profitable hubs, ignoring everything else, our core got stronger and stronger and more and more profitable.

Home Depot made a similar decision. After some false starts, it chose not to focus on international growth beyond Canada and Mexico. It decided not to focus on EXPO or on a separate tile center or on any number of other experiments, such as Home Depot Supply, a set of businesses intended to serve the industrial sector. Instead, it chose to focus on its core, its retail stores, the more than 2,000 orange boxes that produced all its profits. Home Depot also doubled down on interconnected retail, building a website with billions in sales. This allowed the customer to buy exactly in the manner he or she wanted. They could buy online and ship to their home, or buy online and ship to the store, or buy online and have it delivered from the store. Not only was this great for the customer, but it also dramatically increased the inventory turns for the company. In addition, Home Depot added creative new services to the core. For example, the company partnered with Hertz Penske to provide rental trucks at the stores. Not only did Home Depot get a commission on the truck rental, but it also received all the incremental sales that came from moving supplies (boxes, tape, blankets, etc.).

Or consider what happened at Burger King. When we toured our company-owned restaurants for the first time, we found dirty, unfriendly places that sold mediocre food. Recall that the former owner of Burger King, a British spirits company called Diageo, had acquired Burger King as an ancillary part of a larger acquisition. The franchisees felt angry, frustrated, and confused. I always joked, "The worst possible owner of an American fast food company is a British booze company. The British can't cook, and Diageo makes about 80 percent profit margin on its liquor, so it had very little interest in running Burger King." Since the restaurant chain was not part of Diageo's core, it got treated like an afterthought.

Three very talented private equity firms bought Burger King: TPG, Goldman Sachs, and Bain Capital. We named a former franchisee, Jim Hyatt, as COO. (Jim has since become a very good friend and now serves as the CEO of Church's Chicken, where he's doing a tremendous job. A couple of years ago, Jim and I even climbed Kilimanjaro, along with our wives.) Jim instituted a system-wide operating platform to clean up the restaurants and to get the core business back to profitability. He wanted to create a place where paying customers actually wanted to go.

We quickly adopted three primary operating initiatives and

rolled them out to the entire chain: Clean and Safe, Hot and Fresh, and Fast and Friendly. We also created metrics to measure each initiative and hired a third party, EcoSure, to verify compliance.

Clean and Safe set strict operating standards for the stores. It focused on a total store freshen up and a strong emphasis on cleanliness and food quality.

Hot and Fresh, among other things, outlined specific targets for food temperatures. We started doing made-to-order Whoppers, because we found that for every minute a Whopper spent in the heat chute, it lost ten degrees of heat. So if the sandwich went into that chute at 170 degrees, five minutes later it was down to 120 degrees—and a Whopper at 120 degrees tastes very different than a Whopper at 170 degrees.

The Fast and Friendly initiative trained employees how to greet customers, but just as importantly, it targeted the speed of each store's drive-through. About 70-75 percent of sales came through the drive-through, which meant that if just three cars were in line, others would join them. But if drivers saw a fourth and a fifth car, they wouldn't get in line, figuring it would take too long. So to increase sales, we needed customers to move quickly through the drive-through.

All three of these initiatives helped us to get back to our profitable core. Jim Hyatt gets a ton of credit for what we accomplished.

In your own business, don't get distracted from the things you do really well. Where do you make the majority of your money? Make that area as strong as you can, and then make it even stronger.

3. Consider synergistic product additions or acquisitions adjacent to your core.

Where do you have cross-selling revenue opportunities that can enhance your business?

At Continental, we asked, "What adjacent acquisitions could we do?" Since Panama was geographically central to our operations out of Houston and Latin America, we acquired 49 percent of a Panamanian airline named Copa, the maximum allowed by law. We then helped Copa acquire the same 737s we had in the Continental fleet, enabling it to transition to all brand-new Boeing airplanes. Very quickly, on a percent of revenue basis (and thanks to the hard work of Stanley Motta and Pedro Heilbron), Copa became the most profitable airline in the world. At one time, 49 percent of Copa was worth more than all of Continental Airlines.

At Burger King, after we solidified our core operations, we began addressing the issue of our loss in customer traffic. Unless you get more customers in the stores, you have to keep raising your prices to make up the revenue loss caused by your declining numbers of customers. I used to joke, "Guys, if traffic continues to decline, we're going to have to price the one Whopper we sell at a million dollars."

So we looked hard at our menu, comparing it especially with McDonald's and Wendy's. "What do they have that we don't?" we asked. We discovered that Burger King hadn't changed its menu in a very long time. We had no whole muscle chicken sandwich, for example, even though Wendy's was making a ton of money on its spicy chicken sandwich. We had no handheld chicken, like chicken strips or nuggets. We had no salads. Big chunks of our menu had never been developed, prompting customers to go elsewhere. For a short period of time, this neglect allowed Wendy's to overtake Burger King as the number two player, after McDonalds.

So what did we do? Since our company always had a "have it your way" ethos, we didn't want to just copy what others had done. We wanted to update our menu with our own twist, but we needed to have something *special* in those newer product offerings. You might remember items like Chicken Fries, the Angus Burger and, of course, specialty Whoppers. We hired a very talented advertising agency named Crispin Porter, which helped us revive both "Have it Your Way" and the "Creepy Burger King" seen in many commercials. Burger King had used twenty-nine slogans over the years, but "Have It Your Way" was the only one anyone could remember. Who could ever forget "Hold the pickles, hold the lettuce, special orders don't upset us"? We aimed our advertising directly at our Super Fans, males aged eighteen to twenty-nine. Many years before, the chain had a Burger King head that sat atop helium tanks, used to blow up balloons for children in stores. Crispin Porter found that head on eBay and bought it. Do you remember the commercial where the Burger King got inserted into famous NFL plays? Or when the Burger King would show up on *The Tonight Show with Jay Leno*?

We also expanded our operation by making the construction of new restaurants more affordable. The US Burger King system hadn't grown in many years, in part because the company had decreed that restaurants needed to sit on one acre of land and have from fifty-five to sixty seats in the dining room. That requirement made no sense to me, given that 70–75 percent of our business came via the drive-through. So I said, "What if we built stores on half an acre and arranged our dining room seating more like they do at Starbucks? We won't have big booths where one person can take up room for six, but will have loose tables that customers can arrange themselves, based on who they want to eat with."

I heard repeatedly that we could never get by with just thirty seats in a restaurant; my critics insisted they needed a much bigger dining room. So we set up cameras in our busiest restaurants and asked, "How many customers, at any one time, are actually sitting in the dining room?" At the peak of the peak times—Easter Sunday for churchgoers—we never counted more than twenty-eight customers at a time in our busiest restaurant. So it simply wasn't true that we needed sixty seats in each dining room.

We then developed what we called the ROC (Return on Capital) facility. We designed each building to sit on half of the former footprint, with half the number of seats, and with a very fast drive-through. The ROC facility took the cost of building a restaurant from about $1.7 million to under $1 million, thus making many new locations economical.

At Home Depot, a few synergistic acquisitions also spurred growth. We bought a four-store business in Mexico called Total Home and rebranded it Home Depot de Mexico. CEO Ricardo Saldívar and his team have grown the company into more than one hundred stores. We further bought a company called Black Locust, which allowed us to become experts at dynamically pricing our store product to make sure we always remained more than price competitive. We bought yet another company called Blinds.com, which sells made-to-order blinds online. All of these synergistic acquisitions helped us to grow while staying true to our core.

What Are You Waiting for?

Growth is fun when you're creating jobs and promoting co-workers. It's also highly profitable. Growing a business really does come down to executing three key items:

⇨ Stop doing things that lose money

⇨ Build a profitable core

⇨ Do very synergistic adjacent acquisitions

Have you done this in your business? If not, what are you waiting for?

MY MENTORS

Bernie Marcus: Always Think Money In

Bernie Marcus was born to Russian Jewish immigrant parents in Newark, New Jersey. He grew up in a tenement, worked his way through college at Rutgers University, and became a pharmacist. He had a natural knack for retail, however, and ended up as an executive for a hardware store called Handy Dan. When Bernie and Arthur Blank found themselves fired from Handy Dan, they teamed with Ken Langone to start the home improvement store Bernie had dreamed about in the first Big Box format. They called it The Home Depot, and the rest, as they say, is history. The Home Depot built more than 2,000 stores and made all three of them billionaires. Bernie ran Home Depot as CEO for its first nineteen years.

Bernie is an exceptionally astute merchant. He has forgotten more about how to maximize sales and grow a company than most of us will ever know. Bernie and Sam Walton were very good friends, walked stores together, and started the process of moving away from constant discounts to everyday low prices in their stores. Bernie fought relentlessly to make sure Home Depot customers got the best product at the best price with the best service.

I'll never forget a story that Home Depot's retired CEO

Frank Blake told me about walking some Home Depot and Walmart stores with Bernie and Mike Duke, Walmart's CEO after Sam. Bernie was relentless in his constructive criticism of both the Walmart and Home Depot stores. Mike called Frank after and said, "I felt like I just walked stores with Sam Walton. That was brutal."

"You did just walk stores with Sam Walton," Frank replied. "Those guys came from the same mold. They were incredible merchants."

Bernie is also enormously generous with his time, talent, and treasure. I'll never forget stopping by to see Bernie in his office during the design of the Atlanta aquarium, his gift to the city. He stayed involved in every part of the project, including selecting the animals and specifying the process for melting glass to create the tanks.

I learned a lot about how to think about "Money In" from Bernie in my two years we spent together on the Home Depot board. Bernie is a legend, one of a kind. But I learned even more about the importance of "Money Out" through Bernie's generosity and mentorship.

Think Money Out, Not Money In

> *You have not lived today until you have done something for someone who can never repay you.*
> JOHN BUNYAN

T HERE ARE TWO KINDS of people in the world, those who are privileged and those who aren't. Unless I'm badly mistaken, I'm guessing that everyone reading this book lands in the first category.

Our basic needs are taken care of. We live in surplus. We don't worry much about food, clothing, or shelter. We land on the high end of Maslow's Hierarchy of Needs (Figure 4), which means we have the wonderful luxury of focusing on "self-actualization."

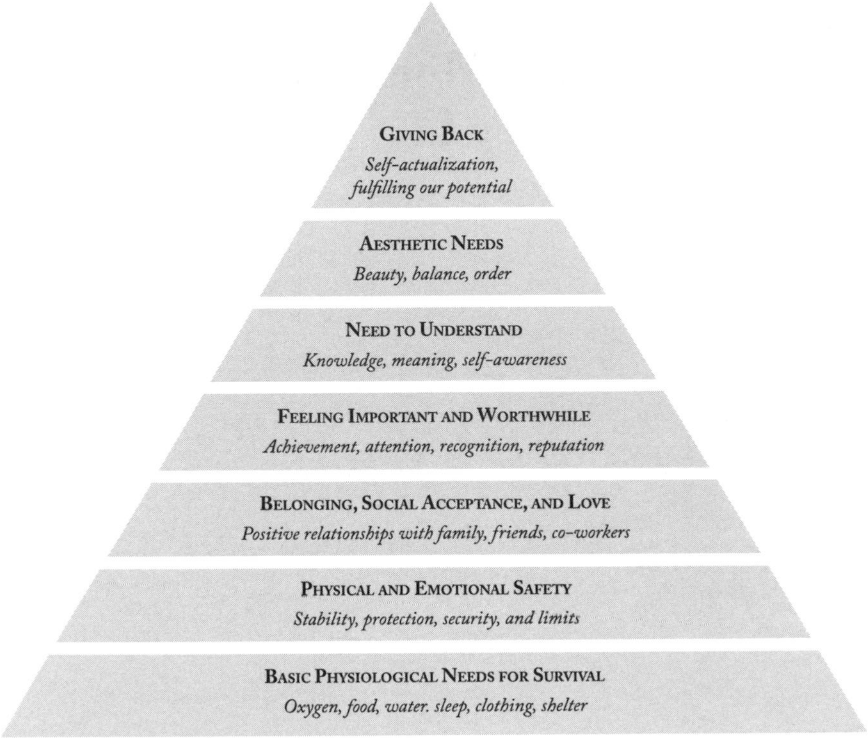

Figure 4: *Maslow's Hierarchy of Needs.*

I'm all for that! But I believe we find a big part of our self-actualization and of our self-worth when we freely choose to help the less fortunate.

Did you know that more than 80 percent of the world lives on less than ten dollars a day? Or that more than half live on less than $2.50 a day? The World Bank calculates that the poorest 20 percent of earth's population accounts for 1.5 percent of the planet's total private consumption, while the richest 20 percent accounts for around 75 percent of global private consumption.

You get the point. You're either privileged and can step into your privilege, or you're someone who needs a little help. Most of us are privileged, often because we've done well in business.

Step Three for businesspeople means that they have to think about money in and not money out, about investing money to create profitable revenue growth and thus make lots of money themselves. But what about on the personal side?

In your personal life, I believe that you need to think money out and not money in, the exact *opposite* of business. But like business, it is not just about giving your treasure, but about giving your time and talent as well. We experience the most joy, gain the most fulfillment, and live a significant life by developing a lifestyle of generosity. Only when we choose to be generous, to step into the privilege granted to us, do we begin to experience what real life is all about. Giving is the only antidote to materialism.

We privileged people are also dangerous people. What is a dangerous person? A dangerous person is someone who has the time, talent, and treasure to help change the world, either for the better or for the worse. The question for all of us is, will we use the surplus granted to us to help others? Are we willing to be dangerous for a good purpose? Or will we consume all our resources or store them up for ourselves? I'd like to make the question more complicated than that, but those are the two basic choices we have.

So as you make your way toward your financial finish line, what obligation do you have to others? What will you do with the resources you accumulate? And what happens *after* you reach your financial finish line?

A few years ago, I went searching for best practices in generosity. I interviewed a dozen men who were at least ten years older than I was, had enjoyed more financial success, and yet who were unusually generous. I respect all of these men. I wanted to learn what worked for them and what didn't work, so that our family could manage well the resources God had given to us. I found it a very helpful exercise and, as we go along, I'll share some of their advice.

A Rare Point of Agreement

With all the rancor and strife that too often unsettles our world, it always encourages me to find some genuine points of agreement. One of those points of agreement centers on generosity. It's one of the rare things—maybe the only thing?—that every major religious and secular philosophy or worldview agrees on. It's worth a quick review.

Let's start with atheism. Richard Dawkins, the best-selling author and atheist, says, "Let us try to teach generosity and altruism, because we're born selfish."

Immanuel Kant, the famed Enlightenment philosopher, believed that by giving to the poor, the rich merely returned money to its rightful owner.

Buddhism instructs its adherents, "Teach this triple truth to all: a generous heart, a kind speech, and a life of service and compassion to renew humanity."

Confucianism offers the counsel, "He who wishes to secure the good of others has already secured his own."

Hinduism declares, "May those who give have all things; may those who withhold have nothing."

Islam states in its holy book, the Quran, "You will never be truly righteous until you have given alms of what you dearly cherish."

Judaism states, "Good will come to him who is generous and lends freely, who conducts his affairs with justice" (Psalm 112:5). It also says, "A generous man will prosper; he who refreshes others will himself be refreshed" (Proverbs 11:25).

Warren Buffet and Bill Gates, two of the richest men on the planet, have asked fellow billionaires around the world (there are more than 1,800 of them) to make a pledge to give away at least half of all they own during their lifetimes or after they die. Buffet has stipulated that all his fortune be given away within ten years of his death.

From this brief review, you can see that both religious individuals and those who claim to follow no religion at all speak with one voice about generosity. They all urge their fellow human beings to reach out to the less fortunate and provide whatever help they can. It's one of the very few universals you'll find on our fractured world.

A Closer Look at the Judeo-Christian Ethic

I've already told you that I grew up within the Judeo-Christian worldview, specifically as a Mennonite youngster in a town full of Mennonites. Our culture was all about working hard and treating others with respect—a society dominated by Jesus's Golden Rule. We were taught to give back our time, our talent, and our treasure. Our elders taught us to give at least 10 percent of our income to help those in need. We had a very broad sense of community in Hesston. If you think of the Amish and their barn raisings, where the whole community shows up to build a new barn for newlyweds or to rebuild an old barn that had burned down, you've got the idea.

I got exposed to many other worldviews during my college years and at the start of my business career. Over time, I let a little of my upbringing slip away. I still focused on being good and doing good, but I did so more out of habit than conviction, more to quiet my conscience than to live by my faith. I donated a significant percent of my income to my church and to support other causes, but the idea of true generosity hadn't really gripped me yet. I was still busy accumulating.

Sometimes I would grow frustrated with charities that constantly asked for money but seldom used it well. At other times, I grew cynical of the teaching about giving I heard from the pulpit, especially when the pastor clearly had not studied the entire body of Scripture on giving and generosity. And so I alternated between being a "tickled tither" (proud of myself that I still gave more than the 10 percent tithe) and a frustrated giver.

That all changed at around age forty-five.

Shortly after I applied the five steps to my life, generosity became a much bigger part of my routine. I started focusing on it and quickly learned about the massive joy that comes from giving cheerfully rather than out of stone-cold duty. I started to deeply ponder the words of a few generous business leaders and religious teachers who had a strong grip on biblical giving. I did a lot of my own research and soul-searching.

I relearned that (1) debt is bad, (2) savings is good, (3) giving is fun, and (4) stuff is meaningless.

Interestingly, the Bible has more to say about money than about any other single topic. Let me give you just a few of the highlights from my study.

I'll begin with Psalm 50:7–12, which declares that God is very well financed, thank you very much, without a penny from us. Everything we have comes from God and we're merely stewards of his abundance:

I do not rebuke you for your sacrifices or your burnt offerings, which are ever before me. I have no need of a bull from your stall or goats from your pens, for every animal in the forest is mine, and the cattle on a thousand hills. I know every bird in the mountains, and the creatures of the fields are mine. If I were hungry I would not tell you, for the world is mine, and all that is in it. Do I eat the flesh of bulls or drink the blood of goats? Sacrifice thank offerings to God, fulfill your vows to the Most High, and call upon me in the day of trouble; I will deliver you, and you will honor me.

The Bible speaks a lot about money, not because God needs to say it, but because we need to hear it. Like debt, money is a neutral commodity. It is a wonderful servant but a ruthless master. Either we will control our money or it will control us. How we manage our money will make it either a cancer in our lives or a blessing to others, and therefore draw us nearer to God's heart or push us further away. Jesus made that pretty clear:

No one can serve two masters, for either he will hate the one and love the other, or he will be devoted to one and despise the other. You cannot serve God and money. (Matthew 6:24)

Contrary to the populist banter widely spoken in some political and religious circles today, God does not despise wealth. In fact, many godly men in the Hebrew Scriptures were wealthy: Abraham, Moses, Boaz, Job, David, Joseph, Daniel. All of them controlled very large estates and material assets.

When you get to the New Testament, you discover that money is neither emphasized nor deemphasized. The New Testament focuses strongly on our relationship to God through Jesus Christ, but also makes it clear that God calls us to be good stewards of whatever he gives us. Jesus told a story in Matthew 25:14–30 that we often call the parable of the talents. It concerns money that a landowner gave to his servants with a clear expectation of how they were to manage that money. He called them, and God calls us, to be good stewards of the money we control.

As part of this stewardship, we are instructed to budget properly. Proverbs 24:3 states that an enterprise is built by wise planning, becomes strong through common sense, and profits wonderfully when the steward keeps abreast of the facts.

And what about giving? The Bible calls us to give joyfully and sacrificially. Again, God doesn't need our money; we give it away so that money doesn't become our god. I like what author John Piper wrote about this subject: "God increases our yield, so that by giving we can prove that yield is not our god." Giving regularly is simply fasting from money so we don't become dependent on it. God blesses us materially so that, first of all, we can take care of our families:

But if one does not provide for his relatives, and especially for members of his household, he has denied the faith and is worse than an unbeliever. (1 Timothy 5:8)

He also blesses us materially so we can take care of others in need:

But if anyone has the world's goods and sees his brother in need, yet closes his heart against him, how does God's love abide in Him? (1 John 3:17)

For Christians, generosity comes from recognizing what Jesus sacrificed for us on the cross and then wanting to give back to Him. Generosity comes from the heart. Theologian Martin Luther said it best: "There are three conversions a person needs to experience. Conversion of the head, conversion of the heart, and conversion of the wallet. Our choices about money are indicators of our spiritual condition."

What's the Right Amount to Give?

What's the right level of generosity? Many pastors insist on a 10 percent tithe. They get that figure primarily from a text in the Hebrew Scriptures (Malachi 3:8–10). But in fact, the 10 percent tithe was not really the standard, even in ancient Israel. If you add up all the special offerings listed in various biblical passages, the giving requirement for ancient Israelites came much closer to 23 percent of income. I have heard a few pastors, but not many, describe that higher ancient standard. Why isn't this presented more thoroughly? Perhaps there is a concern that folks would head for the exits!

In addition, the "storehouse" spoken of in Malachi was closer to the entitlement system we have today (Social Security, Medicare, food stamps, etc.).

Neither Jesus nor anyone else in the New Testament provides a hard and fast rule for giving, either in how much to give or what causes to support. The two examples of generous giving featured in the New Testament focus on giving it all. In the first, the story of the widow's mite in Luke 21:1–4, a desperately poor woman gave all she had without anyone asking her to do so. And in the second, the account of the rich young ruler in Matthew 19:16–20, the wealthy man gave away nothing and went away sad after Jesus challenged him to divest himself of all his money and so free himself from money's iron grip on his soul.

The apostle Paul writes the longest passage on giving found anywhere in the Bible, but the closest he gets to a "rule" is his appeal to his Christian friends to "excel in this grace of giving" (2 Corinthians 8:7). He also repeatedly compliments generous individuals and churches.

So what is the "right" answer? You'll have to answer that one for yourself. For some pastors, it's 10 percent of one's pretax income to the local church. For those with super surplus, who already have hit their financial finish line, it may be well over 10 percent of assets, to be given more broadly.

As to the right causes, Christians tend to give to Christian causes. Mormons tend to give to Mormon causes. Jewish people tend to give to Jewish causes. Others give it elsewhere, according to their interests. Almost everyone agrees some of our giving should go to the poor.

One of the mentors I admire most is David Weekley. David is the founder and owner of Weekley Homes, one of the largest home builders in the United States. David decided a long time ago to give half of his income, half of his time, and most of his significant talent to charity. He now applies his extraordinary instincts as an entrepreneur to help worthwhile charities scale their operations. David doesn't just write checks; he sits on the charity boards and often provides them with helpful consultants. If you're just looking for a check, you might find an easier guy to ask than David. But if you really want to become a better person and grow, David is your man. If he invests in a charity, its probability of success goes up about 500 percent. Our family often invests in causes that involve David.

No matter which philosophy we follow, whether atheism, agnosticism, Buddhism, Confucianism, Islam, Judaism, Christianity, or something else, Americans en masse give away way less than 2 percent of their annual income. Studies show that even people with incomes above $100,000 and religious leaders don't do much better. Really—is that the best we can do?

For my own giving rule, I prefer 2 Corinthians 9:7, where Christians are instructed, "Each one should give what he has decided in his heart to give, not reluctantly or under compulsion, for God loves a cheerful giver." I also believe a portion of our giving needs to go to our local church.

For all of us, the question really comes back to this: Do we want to be dangerous by living a life of significance? Do we truly want to make a difference?

If we say yes, then we must be willing to give to the less fortunate. How can we neglect to do so, when every major religion or philosophy, whether faith-based or not, requires it?

Keys to Thoughtful Philanthropy

So what best practices can help us to thoughtfully give away our money to worthy causes? Let me return to the interviews mentioned earlier, with the dozen men ten years or more older than myself. I've learned a lot about giving from these men. I've been inspired by their stories, encouraged by their example, and energized by their commitment. All of them have stepped into their privilege and use it to bless others. They're also remarkably humble, to a man.

I've learned that if you really want to become a more generous giver, it helps to have people around you who set a good example and who want to walk with you in the journey. From my own mentors, I've learned the following.

1. Give quietly, regularly, and cheerfully.

Fasting from money basically means being willing to give a portion of it away to the less fortunate, and doing so regularly. When we hang on to money in a tight-fisted manner, struggling to keep every last bit of it for ourselves, it has a way of owning us rather than us owning it. It becomes the dictator and we become its slaves. Do you know of anyone who worked like a dog for years to buy some dream boat and then the dream became a controlling nightmare? I wonder if something like that was in the mind of the man who wrote millennia ago, "Whoever loves money never has money enough; whoever loves wealth is never satisfied with his income. This too is meaningless." (Ecclesiastes 5:10).

Meaningless, indeed. But nothing that some good fasting can't fix.

I like what C.S. Lewis wrote about this guideline in one of his most popular books, *Mere Christianity*:

> *I do not believe one can settle how much we ought to give. I am afraid the only safe rule is to give more than we can spare. In other words, if our expenditure on comforts, luxuries, amusements, etc., is up to the standard common among those with the same income as our own, we are*

probably giving away too little. If our charities do not at all pinch or hamper us, I should say they are too small. There ought to be things we should like to do and cannot because our charitable expenditure excludes them. I am speaking now of "charities" in the common way. Particular cases of distress among your own relatives, friends, neighbors or employees, which God, as it were, forces upon your notice, may demand much more: even to the crippling and endangering of your own position. For many of us the great obstacle to charity lies not in our luxurious living or desire for more money, but in our fear—fear of insecurity. This must often be recognized as a temptation.[6]

And if you're going to make the smart choice to be a giver, you might as well give cheerfully. Don't be like the stingy man described in Proverbs 23:6–7, an old grump who gives but not happily: "Do not eat the food of a stingy man, do not crave his delicacies, for he is the kind of man who is always thinking about the cost. 'Eat and drink,' he says to you, but his heart is not with you." Who needs that? Rather, think of someone you know who embodies the far better sentiment described in Proverbs 15:15, which tells us, "the cheerful heart has a continual feast." Choose the feast.

Giving ought to be like physical exercise: regular and heart-pumping. Regular giving does something good for the psyche that irregular giving can never do, just like working out on the treadmill every morning will always benefit you more than two hours on the treadmill once every other month.

2. Integrate your giving into your life.

I've observed that the individuals who seem most effective and satisfied with their giving appear to have fully integrated generosity into their lives and to their interests. They feel called to certain charities.

Entrepreneurs such as my uncle Lyle Yost, or David Weekley of Weekley Homes, or Bernie Marcus of Home Depot, for example, seem to excel either at starting up new charities or at intercepting charities at an early stage to help them grow. David Weekley calls this getting to charities before they "pro up."

On the other hand, professional managers (like me) tend to be most effective when they assist charities that can use their time, talent, and treasure—and perhaps the application of the five steps—to take them from "good to great." A few great examples quickly come to mind, such as Home Depot founder Ken Langone and all his efforts at the NYU Langone Medical Center in New York City, or Lee Cooperman of Omega Partners and his efforts at Columbia Medical School and St. Barnabas Medical Center.

Some of my friends have made generosity the center of the second half of their careers. Examples here include Kyle Vann, one of the four members of my small group of men. Kyle volunteers as chairman of Generous Giving, an organization founded "to spread the biblical message of generosity in order to grow generous givers among those entrusted with much." I think also of Waters Davis, my best friend from Harvard Business School, who serves as president of the Houston chapter of the National Christian Foundation, a group that works with individuals and families to wisely give money away.

What are you good at? What do you enjoy? Where can your unique skill set best be used? The answers differ for each of us, since we all have different skills and unique passions. Look for those charities that help the poor and where you can best apply your talents.

3. Involve your family and friends.

Another way to integrate your giving with your life is to partner in giving with your family and friends. Such collaboration can make giving more meaningful and enjoyable and has the added benefit of training your children to be generous.

How you handle money will have a huge impact on your marriage and on your kids. You may have heard the old saying, "Rags to rags in three generations." It's an old saying because it's true. It reflects the all-too-common story of one generation working hard to go from rags to riches, the next generation living on the fortune, and the third generation losing it or squander ing it because the heirs lost touch with the hard work necessary to create the money, thus winding up in rags once more.

About seven or eight years ago, when our kids were still teenagers, we decided to "reverse Christmas." For a long time, our Christmas Day had followed the pattern common in most American homes: we gave out a lot of presents and we spent a lot of time together. But these days, every Christmas morning, we read the Christmas story, open a very few gifts, and then spend the rest of the day as a family determining where to allocate our giving for the coming year.

We assign each of our kids certain charities, things that interest them, and they also come up with their own ideas. They then track the charities' performance, give us an update, and make a proposal to the family about what to fund. We have found it a terrific way to spend Christmas Day.

We started doing this with a very small amount of money and now have grown it to a substantial sum. By this point, we do nearly all our giving as a family. That makes the process far more rewarding, both to our children and to us.

We also enjoy giving alongside our friends, such as Bill and Jennifer Nath. Bill is another member of the small group of men with whom I meet every Sunday. Bill and Jennifer also enjoy giving with their family and have some of the same charitable interests we do. We often travel together on "vision trips" to the charities we support. We have found that joining with others in our giving leverages our efforts and makes the process a lot more fun.

4. Give wisely.

Learn to give away your money using the same care and precision you employ in your business life. Consider a few best practices I learned from the men I interviewed.

Don't create reliance.

Almost every one of the generous men I interviewed told me about a time when he thought he'd really screwed up an organization with his gifts, mainly by allowing the organization to become too dependent on them. Some of these stories ended very badly, while other groups recovered after a period of pain. To a man, however, these mentors told me they wished they had done it differently. We have experienced the same issue in our own giving. After making a couple of painful mistakes, we decided to limit our giving to no more than 10 percent of any organization's annual budget.

Hold nonprofits accountable for delivering results.

Set up annual metrics for the nonprofits you support, just as you would in business. Most of the men I interviewed either avoided making multiyear gifts or tied them to annual deliverables. Do what you can to ensure that the money you give away actually achieves the purpose for which you gave it.

That takes some research. How much of your donation goes to overhead? To fund-raising? To salaries? Does the charitable organization have a good reputation? Can any of your own associates or colleagues vouch for it? Will the money you give away make the world a better place? Do some digging before you write the check.

Limit the amount of your estate that goes to your children.

Everyone I know wants to make sure that their children learn the joy that comes from work. Most of the men I interviewed have focused on leaving just enough behind to ensure that their children could enjoy an upper-middle-class lifestyle as adults (even though these men could have given them much more). They also worked to make sure, as their children grew up, that they didn't drive the nicest cars, have the nicest clothes, or buy the latest technology. They wanted their children to be humble and considerate of others.

Give away your money in your lifetime or shortly thereafter.

I already mentioned that my uncle Lyle Yost gave away his money during his lifetime, and that Warren Buffet set up his estate so that all his money will be given away within ten years of his death. Among the men I interviewed, this was a common theme. I've heard too many stories of "charity drift" and family feuds to believe that large estates usually get properly stewarded well into the future. Wouldn't you rather have the fun of seeing the money used well by others *during* your lifetime? Remember that during breakfast, the chicken is involved but the pig is committed. Be the pig, not the chicken, when it comes to generosity. Give during your lifetime.

Charities We Support

People often say to us, "You seem to do a lot of research on charities. Where do *you* give?" We have found a number of charities that leverage our family mission statement, "Faith at Work." While this list is not all-inclusive (we give to about twenty charities) and it may not encompass your area of interest, I'd like to highlight a few charities that we think do a good job.

1. World Vision

World Vision is the world's largest Christian humanitarian organization. It operates in more than 100 countries and focuses on providing the poor with water, food, health care, education, microenterprise, and child trafficking protection, as well as services in several other areas. World Vision's impressive ground operations in each country, all staffed by citizens of that country, can't easily be replicated. World Vision has the size and scale to make a huge difference around the globe. We focus specifically on education projects in Honduras designed to lead to jobs for that nation's young people.

2. WorkFaith Connection

WorkFaith Connection is a Houston-based charity headed by the energetic Sandy Schultz. The charity takes individuals who have fallen on hard times, including those right out of prison or rehab, gives them job skills, and lines up Houston-area businesses to interview and hire them. The organization assigns each program graduate a mentor who stays with that individual for at least two years. This huge community effort has produced terrific results, turning wards of the state into productive citizens.

3. City to City

Redeemer City to City, a dynamic church-planting ministry founded by Pastor Tim Keller, has planted hundreds of churches of various denominations in New York City and thousands around the country. Tim is a preacher and author who has dedicated his life to NYC. Many call him the C.S. Lewis of our time.

4. Baylor Global Mission Leadership Initiative

The work that Baylor President Ken Starr and Athletic Director Ian McCaw did in applying the five steps to turn around Baylor's athletic program is worth studying in its own right, but we have enjoyed partnering with World Vision and the Baylor School of Social Work to educate selected World Vision employees. The goal is to provide gifted foreign nationals with master's degrees to make them more effective in their jobs when they return to their own countries.

5. Pine Cove

About 40,000 youth attend camp each summer at Pine Cove, the second-largest youth camp in the country. It also has a program to take mobile camps to the inner city. The great thing about Pine Cove is that your donation to build more facilities can become self-funding, because it allows the organization to grow the number of paid campers, which provides the funds to serve more poor children for free.

6. New Canaan Society

About twenty years ago, my friends Jim Lane and Eric Metaxas started what is perhaps my favorite charity. Jim was a partner at Goldman Sachs and Eric is now a popular author who has keynoted the National Prayer Breakfast. NCS has chapters all over the country where Christian businessmen can gather to share war stories, hear great speakers, laugh, and smoke cigars. Many men have found the same community there that I enjoy with my Sunday morning men's group. I encourage you to check it out.

I've highlighted six of my favorite charities—and all of the proceeds of this book will be split among these six—but many more organizations do great and worthwhile work, both in this country and around the world. Find a few that match your skills and desires and develop a plan to wisely invest in them.

Give Cheerfully

As I wrote this section on generosity, I began reflecting on all the joy and other blessings we have received from giving in this past year. No doubt you have experienced something similar. I'll leave you with two mental pictures.

A few years ago I met a young Honduran boy named Luther. Our children, Andrew and Nina Brenneman, support Luther through World Vision. On a visit to Honduras, I got to see Luther's mountain home, which at the time had no electricity or clean water. Thanks to an impressive World Vision project, Luther and his neighbors finally got a reliable source of clean water for the very first time.

A second meeting involved a smiling and impressive World Vision employee, Millicent Kamara, who met with my wife, Ronda, and daughter, Bethany. Millicent graduated this past May from the Masters in Social Work program at Baylor I just described. Millicent will return to Ebola-stricken Sierra Leone to run World Vision's program for poor women and children.

Two meetings, two lives. How much hope? That all depends, I suppose, on how dangerous we privileged people decide to be.

MY MENTORS

Tim Keller: Heart for Intellectual New Yorkers

Dr. Tim Keller is an American pastor, theologian, and author based in New York City. He graduated from Bucknell University, Gordon-Conwell Theological Seminary, and Westminster Theological Seminary. Tim has written several bestselling books, including *The Reason for God* (based on objections to faith he heard in New York), *The Meaning of Marriage* (which he wrote with his wife, Kathy) and *Every Good Endeavor* (aimed at faith at work). Many think of Tim as the C.S. Lewis of our time, since both have an amazing ability to attract and reach a skeptical intellectual audience. His real heart is for the people of New York.

Tim started a church, Redeemer Presbyterian, which meets in several locations around Manhattan and has grown from under ten members in 1989 to over five thousand today. Tim also has planted nearly two hundred churches of various denominations in Manhattan and thousands more around the country through an organization he started called City to City. Church attendance has gone up dramatically during Tim's time in New York City, thanks to his efforts.

Tim's ability to blend insightful preaching and writing, strategy, and financial acumen is rare in the pastoral world.

It is this gift that has allowed Tim to have an outsize impact on our culture and on me.

Tim executes the five steps, especially "Money Out," in a manner that touches souls and enriches lives.

Build a Team (Clean House If Necessary)

> *The first responsibility of a leader is to define reality.*
> *The last is to say thank you. In between, the leader is*
> *a servant.*
>
> Max De Pree

I GOT TO SPEND SOME time with Senator Lloyd Bentsen when he joined the Continental Airlines board, shortly after he left politics. Most people remember the late senator for a trio of impressive things.

First, he was a great senator from the state of Texas, a friendly rival to George H.W. Bush (although they really weren't far apart politically. Senator Bentsen was a very conservative Democrat while President Bush is a very moderate Republican). I'm grateful that I got to know them both.

Second, he served as secretary of the treasury under President Bill Clinton, where he did an amazing job. Had the political forces of the day let him implement all his plans, he could have fixed Social Security for good. He wanted to slowly increase the retirement age (from sixty-five) for young people, to match the increased longevity of the population (we live almost twenty years longer now than when Social Security began). He also wanted to match the annual inflationary increases of benefits to the costs of goods seniors actually consume rather than the more rapidly rising consumer price index. The senator also wanted to add incentives to work inside of our social safety net programs. Can you imagine how much better off our country would be today if the administration had been willing to champion such changes?

Third, and perhaps most memorably, in the 1988 vice presidential debate, a young Dan Quayle unwisely tried to compare himself to John Kennedy. "Senator, I served with Jack Kennedy," Senator Bentsen retorted in his deep, sonorous voice. "I knew Jack Kennedy. Jack Kennedy was a friend of mine. Senator, you're no Jack Kennedy." Most of us will remember that classic political smackdown for the rest of our lives.

After he attended a few Continental board meetings, Senator Bentsen unexpectedly called me. "Greg," he said, "I would like to set up some time to meet with you, maybe a couple of times a month. I'd also like to travel internationally with you."

His offer both thrilled and honored me. *Man,* I thought, *this is amazing! A former senator, recently retired secretary of the treasury, part of the Greatest Generation, iconic—why would he want to spend time with me?* But I saved my question for later.

At one point, we took a trip together to South America to do some spadework in additional markets where Continental might fly. We stopped in Argentina to see Carlos Menem, the president. When we drove up to the presidential palace, we found a motorcade and a band waiting for us. Ceremonially attired soldiers with uplifted swords lined the way into the palace. The senator looked at me and said, "Greg, I want you to get out of the car and walk in front of me into the palace. This is your meeting."

"Senator," I said, "I can't do that. There would be no band here for me. There would be no soldiers here for me. This has nothing to do with me. This is all about you. This is all about your decades of service and record of successful international diplomacy. Would you do me the service of walking in first? And then I'll come behind you."

He shook his head. "Let's walk in together," he said. "Let's go."

At breakfast a few weeks later, I told Senator Bentsen what an incredible honor it was to have him as a mentor. And then I asked the question I'd wanted to ask from the beginning. "Senator," I said, "what prompted you to call me up and offer to mentor me? And why have you chosen to spend so much time with me?"

With the same dry sense of humor he used in the vice presidential debate years earlier, he said, "Greg, you need it."

He was right. With Senator Bentsen in my camp—on our team, as my mentor—we had the very best possible, an A+ board member who helped our Continental team succeed.

You need A+ players on your team too. You can't succeed without them. So let's investigate what it takes to build a team of winners.

It All Starts with Your Board

You simply can't win on your own; organizations are too big. You need to combine the strengths of everyone around you through positive teamwork. That is the only way to achieve the goals you have set. In order to succeed, you *have* to build a great team. Business success is all about soliciting others to help as you develop your Go Forward plan and then empowering them to deliver on that plan.

Building a great team is critical, regardless of your level in the organization or job. You can be a chairman, CEO, senior officer, department head, supervisor, or store manager. No matter your job, you will only be as good as your team.

In today's environment, it really is not possible to reach your full potential without having a great board. You need a group of individuals who understand the environment in which you compete, can pressure test your Go Forward plan, and can help to identify the blind spots, whether in you or in your company.

Over the past twenty years, I have been fortunate to serve on some really terrific boards. I have worked with a long list of outstanding directors, including several chairmen or lead directors, such as Ken Langone and Bonnie Hill at Home Depot, Les Brun at ADP, and Larry Nichols at Baker Hughes. More recently, I have occupied the lead director chair myself at two public companies, Home Depot and Francesca's Collections. I have faced almost every conceivable difficulty that a board must confront, including the removal of several CEOs, selling two public companies facing hostile bids, addressing multiple class action lawsuits, working through a large computer security breach, dealing with drug and alcohol problems, handling the first social media breach by a CFO, removing underperforming directors, and a few more. Most of these stories will go with me to the grave. In short, as Malcolm Gladwell would say, I have my 10,000 hours in board work.

At CCMP, we also work hard to build world-class boards. Many PE firms load their boards with junior finance professionals; we don't. We go out and get the best industrialists we can and match them with our senior management professionals. Having a great board is that important.

So what are the primary responsibilities of boards?

Your first responsibility as a board member is to make sure the company has a great strategy. You are responsible to ensure that the company understands its marketplace and customers extremely well and then has a plan in place that will take the company to its full potential over the next five to ten years. The five- to ten-year timeframe is key, because busy managers find it very hard to think that far into the future. You must help them articulate a view, a plan, and have the resources to execute the plan. You need to make sure they go through the five steps. And you need to do this at least annually. As already noted, it is an evergreen process.

Second, it's your job to choose the CEO, the single most important decision you will ever make. You also need an evergreen succession planning process to make sure you're always developing at least two or three great internal candidates for the CEO position. Sometimes an external CEO is required, but you have a much higher probability of success if you groom someone you know internally. The succession planning process takes a lot of time. At Home Depot, we rotate the senior management team (the top fifteen officers) through the board each quarter, so each board member can get to know each officer. Although they have unstructured time together, typically a board member spends half a day with an officer, touring some Home Depot stores, and then the two grab lunch. We highly value this time, because when we have succession planning discussions, each board member has built a personal relationship with each member of the senior team. All of us know each of the top officers very well.

Third, you have a very important risk management job. Most board members don't consider this a particularly exciting part of the role, but it's critically important. You must be able to stand back and assess financial and reputational risks to the company and make sure all necessary processes and controls are in place to protect the organization.

So what do you look for in great board members? You need three things to have a great board: diversity, honesty, and courage.

1. Make sure your board reflects a diverse set of backgrounds and experiences.

Once you have a Go Forward plan, look at all the items you need to accomplish. What are the most difficult tasks? What do you know the least about? What skills do you already have on your board? What skills do you lack? Going through this exercise will quickly enable you to identify the gaps on your board. Fill them.

It is important that you have diversity of race, gender, experience, and ideas. It's particularly important that you have thoughtful women represented on your board.

You also need a minimum of one experienced board member in each of the following three areas, at least. First, recruit a sitting or recently retired CEO; these executives can quickly become great advisors to your CEO. Second, include someone close to the financial markets who knows how investors think; these leaders will push you to take a hard look at your strategy and your business, essentially making sure the board considers the five steps annually. Think of this as insurance against activist investors. Third, find someone who can be a great audit committee chair and who will take the lead role in risk management.

Beyond these three roles, you can add directors to meet your specific company needs.

2. Seek board members who will be very honest with each other and with management.

The culture of your board is very important. Everyone on the board needs to have a voice and the opportunity to get heard easily. You also want board members who know their role and who don't try either to manage the company or dominate every conversation. As a board member, I try to pick the one or two things I see as most critical at every meeting and have us focus on those. You will drive management crazy and do the company a grave disservice if you try to micromanage every issue.

You also want a board that, after all the debate has ended, can move forward from a unified position. Your members must have the utmost respect for the board process and for each other. Good board members seek first to understand and then to be understood. Make it your goal to mirror servant leadership for the CEO and senior management team. A servant leader is someone who puts the company and their coworkers needs before their own. This does not imply that they are wimps, merely that they are motivated by what is good for the whole and that they bask in the glory and achievement that comes from the success of the team.

3. Board members must have courage.

Serving on a board is easy until it isn't. If you serve long enough, you will certainly face the kinds of crises outlined previously. You need board members committed to protecting the company by courageously making very tough decisions thoughtfully, rationally, and without emotion. Board members must have the courage to make the right call, even if it isn't the easiest call.

How does your board stack up against these criteria? Do you need to add a member or two? Do you need to ask some members to leave? If you get A+ board members with the skill and diplomacy of Senator Bentsen, you will be well on your way to winning.

Four Key Questions

Let's focus now on your senior management team. If you don't put the right senior management team in place, you can't deliver results. It's impossible. So let's examine four critical questions to help you build a great team that can fully execute your Go Forward plan:

⇨ How do I build a proper organization chart and structure?

⇨ How do I select the members of my executive team?

⇨ How do I empower that team?

⇨ How do I compensate members of that team?

Build the Proper Organizational Structure

Before you take any CEO job, buy any business, or go on any board, use your Go Forward plan to sketch out an ideal organization chart. Don't look at the one that exists currently; start from scratch. Sketch it out according to what you're trying to accomplish, as described in your one-page plan. Ask yourself, "How *should* this company be organized? What roles do we need and what kind of players must fill those roles?"

Next, pull out the existing organizational chart and ask, "What players do I currently have? What does the chart look like today? Is it sufficient to enable me to execute my plan? What skills gaps do we have?"

Every time I've done this, I've found that either the company isn't organized properly to execute the plan, or more often, we don't have the right senior team in place. In a really good company, you will likely find you already have 75 percent of the team you need to take you from satisfactorily underperforming to your full potential, although you may need to reshuffle them a bit and add a few key executives. I have yet to go through this exercise, even in a *really* great company, and not find that I have some critical leadership gaps to fill.

A turnaround situation is quite different, however, and you normally will have only one in four senior leaders who can help you fix the company. With that in mind, consider one phrase I use a lot:

> *It is very hard for the sled dogs that drove the sled into the ditch to pull it out and head in the right direction.*

In turnarounds, you almost *always* need a new team.

When Gordon and I arrived at Continental Airlines, for example, we drew up what we thought of as the ideal organization chart. When we compared it with what existed, we saw a clear need for simplification. The company then had three separate divisions: Continental, Continental Lite, and Continental Express. We therefore had three of everything:

three human resources people, three CFOs, three controllers, three heads of operations, and so on. The airline had *sixty-one* officers.

Our Go Forward plan was all about consistency, not division. We wanted an airline that got people to their destinations on time, along with their baggage; served them good food when they got hungry; and showed them a movie when they felt bored. We wanted consistency in first class seats, consistency in our meals—and three divisions did not help us to accomplish our goal.

As we reorganized and asked which players could stay and which ones should go, we found that fifty of our sixty-one officers really had to leave. In many cases, we just eliminated duplication, but in some cases we made changes for other reasons. Some individuals didn't fit the culture we wanted to build. Some didn't get along with their coworkers. Some had trouble dealing with pilots, flight attendants, mechanics, and gate agents. We hired twenty new executives who fit the new organization chart, individuals who were terrific at their jobs, great team players, and tremendous culture carriers. In other words, they were great servant leaders. Getting that world-class team in place was every bit as important as getting the Go Forward plan right.

A very different situation confronted the board at ADP, where I served for many years as a director. ADP processes the paychecks for 16 percent of all employees in the United States, by far the nation's largest payroll processor. ADP touches millions of lives every day. Unlike Continental, ADP was a very well-run company. It had different issues.

Over the years, ADP grew, largely by acquisition. First it acquired payroll processors, and then it purchased benefits firms. It cobbled them all together into a huge, highly decentralized global organization. Because ADP tended to let its new acquisitions run independently, a lot of unnecessary overhead built up, including duplicate IT systems and inconsistent products.

The ADP board eventually directed the company's management team to ask, "If we were starting with a blank sheet of paper, what would our organization chart look like?" When they compared the old chart with the new one, they said, "Wow, these are *very* different."

The exercise led to the One ADP Initiative, in which the company consolidated and centralized its various functions, such as finance, IT development, HR, and legal. We also discovered that we needed to make a huge investment in developing IT products on modern, common platforms and then migrating our existing customers off the old products to the new ones.

As a result, we found that we did not need both a CEO and president/COO, a model ADP had used for many years to serve its sales force. For the first time, however, we did identify a desperate need for a chief information officer to execute the platform migration. We also knew the next CEO needed to have both sales and real product experience. We chose Carlos Rodriguez for that role, and he built an entirely new management team whose skills filled out the proper organization structure. The company saved about $100 million a year in duplication; developed new, modern products for every market segment; and dramatically improved customer service. As a result, ADP regained market share and its stock appreciated significantly.

Whether your company needs a turnaround or wants to go to the next level, align your organizational chart to match your Go Forward plan.

Select Servant Leaders for Your Executive Team

As we've seen, almost every business needs a team upgrade. Only very rarely, either in a turnaround or in a good-to-great situation, will your current team perfectly match your Go Forward plan. So keep in mind several things as you put together your new winning team.

1. Don't delay in letting some people go.

As managers, we always wait too long to make needed personnel changes. I've never said, nor have I ever heard any other manager say, "I wish I had waited longer to make a change."

On the contrary, everybody always exclaims, "Man, I wish I had done that sooner!"

A lot of research shows that a very small percentage of customers take up 80 percent of our time while adding very little value. Brokerage companies frequently look at this, in fact, and "fire" customers. The same is true inside our companies. A small number of very high-maintenance managers tend to drag down an organization. Think of Eeyore from the childhood Winnie the Pooh stories. Eeyore is always in the dumps, always raining on someone's parade, always consuming energy instead of creating energy. Eeyore works in a lot of our organizations. It's vitally important that you identify the Eeyores in your organization and then remove them.

Look for the folks who drain energy, who aren't on the bus with you, who won't follow the Go Forward plan. Another way to say this, which I often use:

> *If the value you add is less than your ability to be a pain in the butt, it is time for you to go.*

We all know these kinds of folks in our organizations. Remove them as quickly as you can.

Just a word of caution. As you let folks go, remember to treat them fairly and respectfully. Every time you show someone the door, follow the Golden Rule: treat him or her as you would want to be treated. Listen to them, to their arguments, to their problems. First, seek to understand them. Once you do, you can take the time to help them understand you. Try very hard to maintain a culture of caring, even when you have to say good-bye to Eeyore.

Sometimes, of course, they'd rather rebel. I did not experience such rebellion in the corporate world nearly so often as I do now on Wall Street. It must be something in the water. Even so, keep your cool and encourage them to move along so they can find the best place for their talents. Remind them that the change is actually good both for them and for you, since it allows them to find their highest use in their own business lives.

Remember too that others in your organization are watching. They will notice how you treat those who need to exit. Your actions will go a long way toward defining your culture. Your coworkers will take note.

Management changes are almost always necessary. So be honest with yourself and make sure you have the right people in the right slots.

2. Consistently apply the same tests.

I apply two simple tests whenever I want to hire an executive. I call the first one my IQ Dipstick Test. If I put the IQ dipstick in a candidate and it comes out two quarts empty when

I pull it out, there is no recovery. The person is just not smart enough to do the job. This sounds harsh, but it is very important.

I call my second test Fly Across the Atlantic. I ask myself, "Would I want this person sitting next to me on the plane for a ten-hour flight across the pond? Do I find this individual engaging and thoughtful, someone I like talking to, a team player who gives me energy? Or would I rather do anything to get away, even if that means sitting in coach between two NFL linemen across from the bathroom?" This test is equally important. You need to find folks that will look to create a win for the customer, a win for the company, and a win for co-workers. Servant leaders are uniquely win-win-win oriented.

3. Who do you know?

The best hires are usually the individuals you or your team already knows. When a senior executive job or board position comes open, the reaction of many companies and boards is to call a corporate recruiter. While you sometimes need to use headhunters—and they do provide a valuable service—my experience tells me that hiring through them gives you only a fifty-fifty chance of getting the right person. I strongly recommend that you start by trying to hire someone inside your network. Make a few calls and work hard to find the right person, using your own contacts and those of your board and senior team. Hiring people from within your network dramatically increases the probability of your success.

On every turnaround I've ever led, we've gathered our executives or board members in a room, laid out the Go Forward plan and the organization chart, and then made sure we had "A" players in each of the critical boxes. We put any remaining A players in the right slots, identified who needed to go, and then looked hard at the empty boxes, three and even four levels down. "Who do you know who would perform really well in this organization?" we would ask. "Who would you want to work with? Who would you want as a colleague?"

It's amazing how many managers and senior people reply with something like, "The number two person in finance at my former company would make a great CFO, but he'll never get the chance because they already have a CFO. But he's actually better than the guy in that job, so why don't we recruit him to be our CFO? It would give him a step up in his career and we'd get an A-plus player."

When I work with companies that could be performing better, I always find several B and C players in the most important roles. But B and C players rarely hire A players. If you want A players at all levels of the organization, you need A players at the top.

The same principle goes for board members. When we're looking for board members at big companies like Home Depot,

ADP, or Baker Hughes, we have corporate recruiters available to us, but the best candidates almost always turn out to be individuals known well by at least one, if not more, of the current board members. That's been true 99 percent of the time.

The key, of course, is having a large network of A players to talk to. We pride ourselves at CCMP in having a huge network; we maintain regular contact with hundreds of executives and managers. Where we have had an open management position, we've used our network to fill it most of the time.

Let's see how this all works in the real world.

Earlier I mentioned Milacron, a former American industrial icon with a 150-year history; astronaut Neil Armstrong once served as a company director. Beginning in the early 1980s, Milacron went into a long, slow period of decline, ultimately ending up in bankruptcy during the great recession. We saw the impact of this slow decline firsthand in our diligence. Milacron's principal manufacturing facility has a heritage room that chronicles its proud history from the early 1800s. The display ends in the 1980s, perhaps because that's when the tough times really began. When Milacron finally filed for bankruptcy, it didn't choose your garden-variety Chapter 11 reorganization, but a 363 process in which it literally had to choose between reorganization and calling Larry the liquidator to auction off the firm's equipment.

The core team and creditors worked together, and Milacron

survived the recession; that's when we purchased it. Milacron saw its future as a cyclical capital equipment supplier. We had a very different plan in mind. We believed we could help Milacron build itself into an industrial technology company.

While the period after the 1980s didn't treat Milacron well, barely one hundred miles away in Evansville, Indiana, Ira Boots set out to build his own company called Berry Plastics. By the time he retired in 2008, Ira had taken Berry from one facility and less than $50 million in revenue to a global leader in plastics and packaging with more than $4 billion in revenue. Berry wasn't a Milacron competitor, but rather a customer. Ira purchased equipment Milacron manufactured as well as equipment from other suppliers. We asked Ira to assist us with the diligence of the Milacron investment and made him chairman of the company after we bought it. He brought the unique perspective of the customer to our diligence and plan.

We thought Milacron had the potential to become a great company again, but to accomplish that, we would have to completely remake the business. Milacron had always viewed itself as an equipment company. "If you need a new machine every seven or eight years, call us; we're your guys." We believed, with Ira, that customers didn't want just new machines, they also wanted aftermarket service and support. Sometimes they didn't want a new machine, they wanted a rebuild; sometimes they wanted the very latest technology upgrade. And, oh yes, every once in a while, they wanted a new machine. We had in mind a dramatically different vision for the company and the industry, which we set about to build through organic investments and acquisitions.

CCMP bought Milacron in 2012 to serve as a starting block for building the world's best and biggest industrial technology company in plastics. After we bought Milacron, we bought a terrific Canadian company called Mold Masters and combined the two firms. We then moved manufacturing and the back office to low-cost countries, rebuilt the product line, and upgraded the sales force. In three years, we totally transformed the company, taking its EBITDA from $80 million to $200 million, with the potential to grow even further.

As we acquired these companies, however, we also acquired duplicate people and duplicate overhead. A culture of losing at Milacron needed to be replaced by a culture of winning. The salespeople at Milacron used the memorable phrase "loser sweats" to describe what often happened when they went out on sales calls. Their company's long history of financial distress made them so uncertain that they kept lowering the prices of their products, worried that they wouldn't land the deal. To create a new culture of winning, we needed to reinvigorate the place with a completely new management team.

When we drew a new organization chart to match our Go Forward plan, we found that we had almost no one who filled the key boxes. We needed a new CEO and new division managers who could create a positive culture that would unify the two companies.

We reached deep into our network to create a new management team. We brought in Tom Goeke, who had worked with us at a German company. Like Ira, Tom was a successful CEO and industry expert who brought the voice of the customer. He also brought a contagious enthusiasm and leadership style, which had been sorely missing. We brought in Ron Krisanda to run one-half of the new company's divisions; Ron was formerly the COO of Edwards, another of our former businesses. We brought in John Gallagher, whom we'd worked with many years before, to run the other half of the business. We brought in Bruce Chalmers, the controller from yet another of our businesses, to be CFO. Because all four of them are A players, they began to recruit great people underneath them. As a result, the new company quickly became successful, and today Milacron once again trades on the NYSE.

When you hire A players and senior executives you already know, your chance of success skyrockets.

4. Hire people who challenge you and complement your skills.

It's pretty easy for a CEO to put together a team of yes-men or women who will say whatever the boss wants to hear. But you really need people who are willing to thoughtfully state their minds, and then once the team chooses a direction, get behind that new direction. You also want folks who complement you and your skill set.

Knowing your own strengths and weaknesses is unbelievably important in selecting your colleagues. My best business partners always have had skill sets very different from my own.

When I came to CCMP, Steve Murray and I ran the business together for many years with great results. He was a key member of the team that created CCMP and had the foresight to recognize the need to change and adapt the private equity model. Steve came out of a finance background. He worked in finance his whole career, from the time he graduated from Boston College and then attended business school at Columbia. I had been an operator who worked for private equity owners. By combining our skills in a two-heads-are-better-than-one model, we managed to drive amazing results.

Today, Tim Walsh and I run CCMP. Tim came through the same lineage as Steve, on the finance side. Tim is an incredible investor, a great partner, and an even better person. We run CCMP together, and for the same reason: we believe two heads are better than one. We also work on a lot of deals together, including a couple (Generac and Milacron) profiled in this book. I firmly believe having someone with an operations background, who's also a full-time private equity executive, and someone with a financial background, who's a full-time private equity executive, working together with an incredible management team will easily yield the best results.

5. Go all the way down.

As you build out your organization chart, make sure you go all the way down. Don't put an A player in as CEO and A players across the top without asking them to go down in their own divisions to put in A players beneath them who can support the Go Forward plan.

I'll never forget visiting Continental's maintenance hangar in the middle of the night. I wanted to meet the workers. As I talked to the mechanics working the midnight shift, I realized that while 95 percent of our employees seemed really happy, this group didn't seem happy at all. They didn't understand the direction of the company or what we wanted to accomplish, which seemed very unusual, because everybody else in the company appeared to.

That disturbing experience taught me an important lesson: just changing out the lead sled dog doesn't alter the view for the dogs four or five spots back. They see only what's right ahead of them. The mechanics working third shift in maintenance did not see Continental through the perspective of Gordon Bethune or myself. They didn't see it even through the eyes of the airline's head of maintenance. They saw it through the supervisor who ran their shift. To them, the third shift maintenance supervisor *was* Continental. If that individual didn't adhere to our values of treating people with dignity and respect, or of informing everyone what was going on, then it didn't matter much to the mechanics what we did.

Walk into any retail establishment; you can usually tell right away how that store is doing. A great store manager will cultivate excited and enthusiastic employees who understand the business, the company, the culture, and what the leadership is trying to accomplish. But a top-down, condescending, and discouraging manager will make irrelevant whatever the CEO and his team are trying to do. At that particular store (or shift), the people will seem depressed, despondent, disappointed, and unmotivated.

At Edwards, a former sales guy served as the CEO. He wanted only to grow, grow, grow the company—but Edwards made vacuum pumps for the semiconductor industry, so whenever that industry went into a down cycle, he'd have to lay off a ton of full-time employees. We removed the CEO and put in place a guy named Jim Gentilcore, now an executive advisor at CCMP. Jim knew how to manage the business so that when it cycled up, he built the workforce, led by talented full-time managers. He used part-timers to provide the extra production needed. And when the cycle turned, as it inevitably does every three or four years, he'd let the part-time employees go while maintaining a motivated full-time workforce. Jim was a great servant leader who knew how to create a win for the customer, a win for his coworkers, and a win for investors. He is a win-win-win kind of guy, the kind of senior management individual you need in your own organization.

Empower Your Executive Management Team

Empower your senior people to do the things you've hired them to do. Your Go Forward plan and its metrics should make it really easy to assign specific tasks to particular individuals so that they understand the whole plan and then can focus just on what they're responsible for accomplishing. Ask them to come back with a detailed plan of their own for executing their responsibilities, and then meet with them frequently to see how they're doing. I call this process "trust but verify."

To do this well, you have to let your top managers run their own "shops." It's critical that you give them the power to build and manage their own teams. At the same time, it is imperative that this senior team operate with one voice and work together well.

In almost every company I've run, and in a few of our companies at CCMP, we've taken our senior teams off-site for a day or two of team building and training. As part of the experience, we have each member of the team take the Myers-Briggs personality inventory to help us figure out what motivates people and the best way to communicate with them. We then share their results with the whole group. The group learns how everyone in the group typically operates and discovers the best method to interact with each person—whether they're introverts or extroverts, for example, or feeling oriented versus more analytical. Everyone learns their respective acronyms and how they fit.

These tests don't take long to administer or understand but can help executives learn how to work together with coworkers who have very different styles.

Creating a Common Language

When dealing with your executive management team, it's also useful to develop a common language to ensure everyone is on the same page and all communications are clearly understood. I love to work with Senn Delaney and would highly recommend the firm. Larry Senn is an exceptional person who has developed a common "language"—phrases or trigger statements that I have found extremely useful in group training. I'll describe two of the most valuable, just to give you a flavor (I've previously mentioned blue chips, a third concept introduced to me by Sean Delaney). The first is Be Here Now.[7] All of us these days are distracted, multitasking, and multiprocessing. How many of us have sat on the computer, been on the phone, and answered e-mail on our iPhone—all at once? We take great pride in multitasking. But a raft of studies shows that the true definition of multitasking means not doing any one thing well.

A massive amount of research has been done around the concept of Be Here Now. If you can focus on one task at a time, one person at a time, be in one conversation at a time, then your productivity and the quality of your decision making skyrockets.

One key to Be Here Now is to start meetings on time. And yet, at most companies I've led, meetings always started late. So these days, at the first company meeting I hold, I usually lock the door and don't let anybody in after the meeting starts. After that, nobody comes late. We have a meeting at CCMP with our worldwide investment team that starts at 8:00 a.m. sharp every Monday morning. It *never* starts late!

Another big detriment to meetings is people bringing in their technology, whether iPhones or iPads or the like. When BlackBerries were all the rage, people lost their concentration entirely as soon as their device's red light started blinking. They wouldn't even know what triggered the light, whether junk e-mail or something important. Just the fact that it started flashing would drive them nuts.

At Quiznos, our CFO was addicted to his BlackBerry. I had trouble getting him and the rest of our senior team to concentrate. So I put a box at the front door and made them put all their gizmos in it. I needed them to focus if we were to have a highly productive meeting. I needed them to Be Here Now. After the meeting ended, I noticed that our CFO had left behind a doodle pad. During our discussion, he'd subconsciously sketched a complete, life-size copy of his BlackBerry. I signed it and gave it to him, along with a reminder written at the bottom: *Be Here Now.*

The distractive power of technology amazes me. Do you like it when you're talking to someone and you notice they're texting someone else? But I have a confession to make. I really struggle with Be Here Now.

I once took a church staff off-site to do some leadership training. The church had a couple of leaders, as in any organization, who habitually showed up late. I told them, "When you show up late for meetings, you're not being respectful of other people's time. You need to get focused. You need to Be Here Now."

After church one Sunday, the pastor's wife approached me, and with my wife and kids standing there, she gave me a big hug. "Greg," she said, "my husband came back from that retreat a completely different man. He's actually paying attention to me now, where before he was always distracted. He really listens to me. It's revolutionized our life together."

When we got to our car, Ronda turned to me and said, "What was *that* all about?"

I explained the story and the central concept of Be Here

Now. She just looked at me and said, "Well, the shoe cobbler's children have no shoes." Ronda would be the first to tell you I struggle with Be Here Now, all the time.

The second concept is called the Mood Elevator.[8] Again, a lot of research has shown that we make good decisions when we're in a good mood and bad decisions when we're in a bad mood. The highest state of mind on the Mood Elevator is gratitude. When you feel grateful, happy, and fulfilled, you make terrific decisions. When you feel upset, angry, frustrated, or disappointed, you make terrible decisions. The midpoint of the Mood Elevator is being curious. It's also the express button to the top. So when you find yourself saying about someone, "What an idiot," hit the express button. Ask yourself instead, "I wonder why he or she is thinking about things in that way?" And then enjoy the ride as the Mood Elevator takes you back to the top floor of gratitude.

As a management team, we talk about each of us making decisions while at the top of the Mood Elevator. If you find yourself at the bottom, take some time off. Go for a run, grab a coffee, walk around the block. Do whatever you need to do to get back to the top.

Using such common language enables you to remind others of these issues without insulting them. So if somebody's been through the training and you find them multitasking in a meeting, you can say to them, "I need you to Be Here Now."

Or when someone looks troubled, you can say, "I can tell you're on the bottom of the Mood Elevator. We both know you won't make good decisions there, so why don't you take a walk around the block? Grab a cup of coffee or do whatever it takes to get you back to curious."

Compensate Executive Team Members Appropriately

It's crucial to align senior leaders on the same objectives, tying their compensation to the Go Forward plan. Most of all, keep it simple. We do this in several ways.

1. Get good alignment.

I have served as the compensation committee chairman of many boards, both public and private. You learn quickly that you need to be careful what you ask for and what you reward senior executives for, because you are going to get it. The correlation between behavior and pay is *very* strong.

In our private equity model at CCMP, we seek to align the entire senior team with us as owners. If we win and our investors win, the senior team wins. Your end of the canoe can't be sinking and mine doing well, or vice versa.

We start with salaries pegged generally at the midpoint of the typical range for the job. On top of that, team members get an annual bonus determined by two factors. About 70 percent of the bonus is based on a common metric, like EBITDA, and 30 percent on individual performance, tied directly to the Go Forward plan. It's all very quantitative.

We also give senior leaders stock options struck at the price when we bought the company, so if we do well and sell the company at a big gain, executives make a lot of money. We also encourage senior team members to purchase shares; we expect them to put some of their own capital at risk for the gain. That creates terrific alignment and a great upside.

The public company model differs a bit. While the basic strategy for salary remains the same (usually the midpoint for comparable jobs) and the bonus is based on hard metrics, that bonus might be based on EPS or net income instead of EBITDA. Public company incentives tend to get broken out into two different securities. Performance-based restricted stock is one. If the company hits certain performance metrics over three years, the shares vest. Stock options is the other.

2. Minimize benefits given only to senior leaders.

Special health care, special life insurance, a car, tax gross ups—all of these benefits are things of the past. The reason is simple. None of them drive share price performance, nor do they drive retention of executives. It just becomes fixed cost, and you're much better off putting that money into incentives that pay out if the company does well.

3. Drive equity compensation down in the organization only so far as it is valued.

The further you go down in an organization, the less you find employees with an interest in equity. When we were doing our first pilot contract at Continental, for example, we offered stock options to pilots so that if the company did well, they would do well. When the negotiations locked up and they threatened to strike, they asked me to join the talks. One leader of the pilots' union met me at the door.

"Greg," he said, "we have a real problem."

"What's that?" I asked.

"We have all these issues and we may go on strike."

"Hey," I said, "I called Fidelity and checked my bank account before I came over here. I'm going to be okay if you strike—but are you going to be okay? It sounds like a really dumb idea. What's the real problem?"

"Well," he replied, "we don't want any of these stock options. That's just funny money. It's not real money."

"Okay," I said. "What if I gave you another buck an hour on your hourly rate to fly and we took away the stock options we offered?"

"That would be great," he said. So that's what we did. We gave them an additional buck an hour raise and no stock options.

When our stock shot from $6 to $120, the stock options we had as executives became worth a lot of money Gordon and I sold some stock that had to be publicly reported, and soon afterward the same representative of the pilot's union approached me.

"Greg," he said, "I can't *believe* you made all this money from selling your stock!" Yada, yada, yada.

I looked at him with a smile and said, "It's just funny money." We both had a good laugh.

As you go down the organization chart in any corporate entity, at some point you'll find that people would rather have hard cash to pay their bills than potential money from stock options. So even though the options you're trying to hand them might be worth $10,000, they'll think they're worth only $500. If they think they're worth $500, they'll be much happier with $1,000 in cash. Different levels of employees have different tolerances for risk. You need to understand what motivates them before you devise your compensation program.

So build a great team, one that fits your Go Forward plan. Train and compensate them well, and then let them run their own show. Trust but verify, and treat all of them with dignity and respect.

And then, after a lot of hard work, enjoy the benefits. (The funny money too.)

MY MENTORS

Armando Codina: A Great American

Armando Codina came to New Jersey as an eleven-year-old Cuban orphan in 1962 during Operation Pedro Pan. His mother made the trip more than three years later, took him out of the orphanage, and moved him to Miami. He would never live far from her again.

Armando had tremendous business success in not one but two industries. He first succeeded in creating an IT system for physicians. Later he became one of the most influential real estate professionals in the United States by focusing almost entirely on South Florida. Most would consider Armando the head of the unofficial Chamber of Commerce of Miami.

When I moved to Miami to become chairman and CEO of Burger King, Armando and his family adopted my family. Not because they had to, but because they wanted to. Armando is one of the kindest, most generous individuals I know. I also have watched the dignity, thoughtfulness, and decisiveness that Armando has displayed in some very difficult board situations, including American Airlines, Merrill Lynch, and General Motors. When Home Depot wanted to add another director, I recommended Armando and have had the pleasure of serving with him for the past eight years. He has incredible insight and tact and is an amazing servant leader.

Armando loves the United States and has taught me what it means to be a truly great American.

Build Your Life Team: Align and Prune

> *Give a lot, expect a lot, and if you don't get it, prune.*
> THOMAS J. PETERS

D O YOU ENJOY AN occasional glass of wine? Most of us do. But I wonder, might we enjoy it even more if we realized how much loving care goes into its production? I'm thinking especially of the time and attention it takes to grow the delicate grapes required to create most fine wines.

While I know nothing about running a vineyard, I read a recent blog describing how one individual chose to spend significant portions of her time helping tend the grapes of a little vineyard that a friend of hers planted behind his house in Sonoma County, California. "The problem is," wrote the author, "that vines need lots of attention if you want to manage them well."[9]

The author described how most of her friend's helpers come from San Francisco to enjoy a weekend in the country, although a few hail from as far away as Tennessee.

> *Work usually starts way too late when the sun is high and the heat is up, because no one can get their acts together at a sensible hour. But then everyone hits the vineyards and starts working.*
>
> *When we were there in early spring, we trimmed one-year-old vines down to knee height and lovingly wrapped cardboard protectors around them. We made sure the drip irrigation pipes were connected and cleared away the weeds.*
>
> *This time, we rip away the cardboard protectors and unravel each set of vines to find the strongest one. We cut off all the other stems growing from the base and leave four or five shoots on the main vine. Then we tie all the vines to the poles and clear up all the weeds, cuttings and cardboard protectors. All this in the afternoon heat, which has us sweating and puffing and feeling faint and wondering why we are doing this manual labor on a holiday weekend!*

Wow, did that remind me of the time I spent working on the farms where I grew up in Hesston, Kansas—except for the getting up late part! In the summer we would start very early and often end very late at night. I imagine the vineyard work described by the author is just the tip of the iceberg. I know growing grapes is a very intensive and intentional process. Growers have to align the type of wine they want with the specific variety of grape that produces that wine. They have to align their vines with the poles that help them to thrive and grow. And they have to weed around the delicate plants and carefully prune the vines to foster strong, healthy growth. In other words, good grapes don't just happen.

And neither do good relationships.

It Takes Work

Building good relationships, like growing healthy vines, requires intentionality and, very often, intensive effort. That's true of friendships, partnerships, and of practically any other kind of personal associations. If you want good relationships, you have to work at them, much like a vintner has to work at producing good grapes. You must align with those who have objectives in common with yours, and you must consistently, carefully, and thoughtfully prune the unaligned relationships you have, especially the ones that tend to sap your energy.

Think About Your Life

For a moment, try to identify the individuals from whom you

draw energy. Who makes you come alive? Who leaves you feeling better after a typical encounter than before it? Who mentors you (who is your Paul)? Who do you mentor (who is your Timothy)? Think about how much time you spend with these individuals and what real value you get out of your time together.

Now spend a few moments thinking of those who drain you. Who tends to sap your energy, drag you down, leave you feeling tired and exhausted? To execute your Go Forward plan in business, you have to remove the individuals who drag down your organization, while always treating them as you would want to be treated. In life, the same thing is true. To execute your personal Go Forward plan, you must diminish or even remove your contact with those who drain your time and energy, while always treating them with compassion and love.

In life and in business, we all struggle with those 5 or 10 percent of the men and women who, while perhaps well-intentioned, drain 80 percent of our time and energy. I don't have in mind here those who deplete us for a day or two, but those who consistently do so over a much longer period. We can't ignore members of our immediate family; we all have issues there, but we're called to invest in them regardless, to whatever degree we can manage it.

Rather, I'm thinking of friends, associates, and acquaintances who, in one way or another, wind up demanding significant amounts of time with us, but who tend to drain us. These folks have a habit of making their problems our problems.

How can you take your personal Go Forward plan, draw an organization chart to execute the plan, and make sure you have A players around you to hold you accountable? How do you decrease your time with the C players in your life, without hurting or insulting them, while continuing to keep them as friends?

If I am to succeed, I know that I need to be with people who build me up and who give me energy. I designed my personal Go Forward plan around the A players in my life. And to make sure that I've properly aligned my decisions about the people in my life with my Go Forward plan, I also analyze my relationships with them.

Respect from my wife, Ronda, means the world to me. I doubt a wife can give her husband anything more important than respect. And a husband can't give his wife anything more important than love. While we all need both things, I think Dr. Emerson Eggerichs had the emphasis right in his 2004 book, *Love and Respect: The Love She Most Desires, the Respect He Desperately Needs.* In order to generate that respect from Ronda, therefore, I make her my first priority and desire.

We love spending time together, especially now that we're empty nesters. When we still had children living in our home, I remember hearing all kinds of people talk about how hard the adjustment was for them when their children left the nest. I find that hard to comprehend, frankly, because I think it took us all of fifteen minutes to get used to an empty nest. Now, I love my kids—Andrew and his wife, Nina; Bethany; and Aaron—but I also love the time I get to spend with Ronda, just her and me. After all, it was just us before our kids entered our lives. Although my frequent travel sometimes gets in the way of our time together, even when I'm away, I call her every night. Ronda likes to joke we've been married thirty-one years, and due to my travel, it's been the best two years of her life.

When I am home, I find one of Sean Delaney's concepts very useful: Be Here Now. His advice to "Practice doing one thing at a time" means I try hard not to talk to a family member while continuing to work on the computer, talk on the phone, or e-mail someone. No one does anything well while juggling five things at once.

Develop a ritual that says, both to you and to those around you, "I'm done with work." When you do work at home, develop specific blocks of time to perform that work and communicate that fact clearly to your family. Also tell them when you will be done. Don't let your work consume all your time at home.

We all have friends who consume our time unproductively. I've been able to address the problem by managing a small inner circle, a larger middle circle, and a very large outer circle. The inner circle includes my small group of three other guys with whom I meet weekly. It also includes members of my immediate family and my parents. My partners at CCMP are also part of the inner circle. These are the people to whom I am closest, the individuals with whom I live life on a weekly basis.

The middle circle features a few more fairly close friends, including the couples we mentor and those who mentor us. These are our "Pauls and Timothys." I've profiled many of the men who mentor me. I mentioned earlier that Ronda and I (along with Britt and Julia Harris) mentor seven couples every year over Memorial Day Weekend in Colorado. Nearly one hundred folks have gone through this program so far, and we really enjoy having dinner and spending time with them.

My middle circle also includes a small group of CEOs with whom I regularly interact, whether the leaders of companies owned by CCMP, CEOs and boards of the companies I serve, or CEOs whom I've met over time. I try to touch base with each of them every quarter. That might not sound like a lot, but it represents quite a lot of contact when you factor in the many individuals it includes.

In my outer circle are many others, including all those to whom we send books at Christmastime every year. This circle numbers around six hundred families, plus acquaintances who migrate in and out of our lives throughout the year. I try to touch base with each of them at least once a year.

My goal is to make each of these individuals know how

important they are to me, regardless of how often we speak. I wish I could bat 100 percent in doing so and am working hard at it. As Mitt Romney told me, in every interaction you either gain or lose share. Wouldn't it be great if we could always gain share?

When I identify individuals in my life who drain my energy (providing only 5 percent or less of the value in my life but taking up 70 to 80 percent of my time), I start moving them from an inner circle to a circle further out. Some individuals who used to be in my inner circle have moved to my middle circle, and some even to my outer circle. I try not to lose contact with them altogether, but decreasing the amount of contact I have with them frees up a lot of my time. If I'm not that close to them on a day-to-day basis, they can't easily consume large pieces of my schedule. Whenever we do talk, they can't make their minor problems mine because we tend to spend more time catching up than we do diving into unproductive issues. I do my very best to accomplish this with love and compassion and try to remain available if a true crisis does enter their lives.

Try to think win-win-win when you limit these unproductive relationships. I'd be willing to bet that if limiting the time is good for you, it's also good for the other person. It frees them up to pursue another relationship that can benefit a third person.

Think again about the men and women in your own life. Can you identify anyone in your smallest circle who consumes an enormous amount of your time without giving much back? If you can, gently move these individuals to your middle circle, and perhaps even to your outer circle. That will help you a great deal.

If such an approach seems too calculating, I should tell you that I have confidence in using it because even Jesus Himself employed something much like it. He had an inner circle of three (Peter, James, and John). He had a middle circle of a dozen (the twelve disciples, one of whom eventually got moved out), and an outer circle of seventy-two (see Luke 10). He spent more time with those in His inner circle than He did with those in His middle circle, and He spent more time with those in His middle circle than He did with those in His outer circle. Even so, He still had more intimate contact with those in the largest group than He did with the masses who constantly clamored for His time.

My bottom line is that I apply the same approach to my personal life that I use in my business life. At CCMP, I have an inner circle of individuals with whom I'm in weekly contact. This includes some of the CEOs executing turnarounds for us. I have monthly or quarterly contact with those in my middle circle, including CEOs we support and others with whom I have natural and ongoing business; most of the CEOs of our portfolio companies fit in this category. Finally, I have an outer circle of businesspeople with whom I try to touch base about once a year, using a tickler list. Of course, I see a lot of overlap between my friends and my business associates, but this just makes for an integrated life.

Such an approach can free up a lot of time without offending too many people.

Learn to Say No

If you want to save time for your close friends, family members, and business partners who give you energy, then you must learn how to say no. If you don't learn how to say no, you'll never have the time to do what you most need to do.

In fact, saying no when people ask you to do things—even good things, valuable things, important things—is often far more important than saying yes.

Before you say yes to anything, make sure you have your personal Go Forward plan in front of you and then run through the Five Fs (Faith, Family, Friends, Fitness and Finance) to make sure you make a good decision. Get used to doing this, because it's a crucial mental exercise. Why? Because without this discipline, most of us just keep saying yes to things until we discover we lack the time to do anything well. We spread ourselves too thin… and too late we discover we've picked up a whole bunch of white chips from our to-do list and no blue chips at all.

I've struggled with this problem over the years, and I've had to practice to get good at saying no. Consider, for example, our family giving strategy.

We used to keep expanding our number of charities without allowing any of them to drop off. That eventually became a problem, because every charity took not only the effort required to write the check, but also our time and our talent: individuals wanting to meet, wanting input, asking to come solicit us for more or bigger donations. We discovered that we were supporting thirty-two charities, with each of them taking a fair amount of our time.

To address the problem, we met as a family and decided together to focus our giving on the platform we had been given, which we loosely called Faith at Work. We pruned the number of charities down to twenty—the number we could realistically manage with our time, talent, and treasure.

Now, whenever a request for donations to a new charity comes in, we look at how that charity fits with our Faith at Work generosity statement. In about 75 percent of the cases we say no, even though the charities look perfectly good. We can say to them, "That isn't what our family is focused on now, so we're not going to waste your time by having you come to us just so we can send you a note later to say, 'We're not focused on it.' We can tell you that right now." Saying no saves an enormous amount of time for us and time and money for the charity. It frees up our time to spend with the charities and people in whom we're really invested.

Pruning Has Its Benefits

It takes time to align your interests with the interests of those in your various circles. It takes effort to weed and prune your relationships to make sure you're spending your life in ways that make a significant difference. It takes real work to create a well-oiled team that can win championships rather than continually hover at the bottom of the pack.

Do you want to enjoy some fine wine? Or do you want to settle for a box from Kroger?

The people mentioned at the beginning of this chapter, the folks who traveled to Sonoma County to help their friend tend his backyard vineyard, know that pruning and weeding costs them something in terms of their time, their effort, and their comfort. But they also know something about the rewards they can expect.

Despite the really hard work, the author of the blog reported that "most people who come once actually come again to toil away in the hot sun." Why? Why would they do that? The author describes the big payoff:

> *[Afterward they] relax by the pool with good food, wine and company, plus a little music provided live by Dave and some of his guitar and accordion playing compañeros.*

But then there's the pool and people jumping into its cool depths, fully clothed. And the cheese and biscuits and brownies, not to mention a glass or two of Dave's finest. As the sun gets lower in the sky, the music starts and dinner is served at the long table, the chatter gets louder and the sun sets on the newly tended vines and who, in their right mind, would ever want to leave?

Why would anyone spend so much time and effort in pruning and weeding and aligning? Maybe the better question is, who in their right mind wouldn't?

MY MENTORS

Howard Brenneman: Treat Everyone with Dignity and Respect

Aggressive entrepreneurs like my great-uncle Lyle Yost can sometimes overextend, which leads to a key lesson I learned from my dad, Howard Brenneman.

My dad had an amazing career at a young age. He grew up in Hesston as a Mennonite farm kid and married my mom at age nineteen. I was born two years later, so we had a very young family. Dad put himself through local Mennonite colleges while working at night as an accounting clerk at Hesston Corporation. He quickly worked his way up to become president and COO of Hesston Corporation in 1975, and then president and CEO in 1982. He didn't get those jobs through nepotism. My dad was just very good at what he did and legitimately worked his way up the ladder. He was the first professional manager I ever knew (my great-uncle Lyle was a classic entrepreneur).

My dad and my great-uncle worked together to turn Hesston Corporation into a global powerhouse, selling farm equipment all over the world. Dad would visit Europe, Russia, wherever they saw a viable market. I still fondly remember visiting farm equipment dealerships with him in the United States, and I continue to get a real kick out of seeing Hesston farm equipment as I travel across the nation. It brings back great memories.

My dad ran Hesston Corporation in the late seventies when the farm crisis hit. The Russian wheat embargo triggered a nosedive in demand even as wheat supply skyrocketed, a toxic combination that just crushed the average farmer. Farms started going broke right and left, agricultural operations began shutting down, and the money to buy Hesston hay balers and swathers simply disappeared. During that difficult time, the famed country singer Willie Nelson held a series of Farm Aid concerts to provide a little help to the embattled American farmer.

I remember looking out my dad's office window at Hesston Corporation and staring at hay balers as far as the eye could see, lined up in the field adjacent to the manufacturing facility. The company had vastly overextended its inventory and gotten way out ahead of itself. Hesston Corporation no longer had a fortress balance sheet.

Sales plummeted, and to save the company my dad had to lay off many friends and fellow church members. Many church sermons in those dark days got aimed directly at my dad, focusing on how unfair it was to lay off one's fellow Christians. Few people understood that to save the majority of jobs in a company you sometimes have to sacrifice a few. I've had to follow that hard path several times in my own business career.

My dad had to make those kinds of dreaded choices, and he caught a great deal of flak for doing so. It was a very rough time.

Hesston Corporation eventually was sold in a fire sale to Italy-based Fiat. Its new owners brought in an Italian manager, and my dad lost his own job in 1986, after spending more than twenty-five years building Hesston Corporation.

Through it all, Dad refused to get angry. He did what he knew he had to do, while continuing to treat everyone in a dignified and respectful way. He handled the painful situation with incredible grace. Over and over, he did the right thing. And quite frankly, the business survived because of his leadership. Today the company is part of J.I. Case, but all the manufacturing jobs remain in Hesston, largely because of how my dad handled a tough situation.

As a CEO and business owner, I've taken on a lot of business turnarounds. As I do, I always try to remember my dad's sense of the human element.

Let the Inmates Run the Asylum

> *As we look ahead into the future, leaders will be*
> *those who empower others.*
> BILL GATES

I LOST A CLOSE FRIEND this year. Many others would say the same thing of him. It's still hard for me to believe that he's gone.

James B. Lee—Jimmy Lee to just about everyone—was the vice chairman of JPMorgan Chase. He died unexpectedly on June 17, 2015, after working out on his treadmill at home. He worked at JPMC for nearly forty years and passed away far too early, at the age of sixty-two.

Jimmy Lee looked every bit the part of a Wall Street banker, complete with the suspenders, the two-tone shirt, and the slicked-back hair. Jimmy was confident, hardworking, and press-friendly. He did the very biggest deals of our time: the merger of United Airlines and Continental Airlines; the acquisition of Dow Jones (the *Wall Street Journal*) by Rupert Murdoch; the IPOs of Burger King, Facebook, and Alibaba; the go private of Dell, and many, many more. At the time of Jimmy's death, he was in the process of assisting GE's CEO, Jeff Immelt, in selling off all of GE's financial assets. In one way or another, Jimmy touched nearly every one of the companies we've discussed in this book.

Jimmy Lee was no ordinary banker.

Few players on Wall Street ever earn the title "beloved." In fact, many are demonized and looked down upon—but when Jimmy died, the outpouring of eulogies and kudos from every corner was overwhelming. Praise came from liberals and conservatives, businessmen and politicians, the press and bloggers alike. Basically, everyone had something exceptionally kind to say about Jimmy Lee. The *New York Post* called him "the Street's No. 1 investment banker." The *Wall Street Journal* called him "one of Wall Street's most formidable deal-makers."

Jamie Dimon, my friend and Jimmy's boss, declared, "Jimmy made an indelible and invaluable contribution to our company, our people, our clients, and our industry over his nearly forty years of dedicated and selfless service. Jimmy was a master of his craft, but he was so much more—he was an incomparable force of nature."

I'd like to tell you my own story about Jimmy Lee.

As a CEO, every time I did a debt or equity offering in which JPMorgan was involved (which was quite a lot, across several companies), Jimmy would show up at the kickoff, completely unannounced. He'd quickly take over the room, filled with hundreds of investors, and would spend the first five minutes telling everyone why I was the best CEO he'd ever seen and what a great company we were. By the time he finished, I actually believed him because *he* believed it. And I did so even though I knew he did the same thing several times a week for others.

Jimmy would call often, just to see how I was doing. He called at every major juncture of my life, and he was the first to reach out after my business partner Steve Murray passed away. Right after Rupert Murdock bought Dow Jones, Jimmy and I had lunch at the Four Seasons in New York City. Afterward, Jimmy introduced me to Rich Zannino, then Dow Jones's CEO. We got along so well that after the deal closed, Rich joined us at CCMP as a partner. We have worked together ever since.

Jimmy orchestrated all of that.

Jimmy and Jamie Dimon ran a conference every year that attracted the world's top CEOs. It didn't matter if you were Jack Welch of GE or Jack Ma of Alibaba, you would attend their annual "can't miss" event. I started attending them in the early 2000s, when Jimmy Lee held them in Deer Valley. Now they're held in the offices of JPMorgan Chase in New York.

Jimmy lit up the room wherever he went. He genuinely cared about you, regardless of your title or your job. Jimmy created an enormous amount of positive energy in the lives of everyone he touched. He had a special way of making everyone feel as if they were the most important person in the world. When you called, he had a habit of stopping whatever he'd been doing, focusing on you, and really Being Here Now. And he did that with everyone.

Jimmy Lee was what I'd call a culture carrier. He deeply understood and lived out the values and culture of his organization, making the bank a much better place just by his presence.

People want to follow that kind of exceptional leadership. They want to work in a place where the culture oozes genuine caring, one that strives to treat people honorably. The best companies intentionally create a culture that values far more than merely delivering business results. Organizations do best where everyone pulls in the same direction and works for a bigger purpose.

Part of your Go Forward plan has to identify the good things that you intend to deliver for your customers, the communities around you and your coworkers. How do you intend to build a culture that truly values people, that treats them as far more than cogs in a wheel? How can we each "Be Here

Now" as we deal with others? How will the culture of *your* business encourage and empower your coworkers?

Build a Winning Culture

You can't turn around a company or take a business from under-performing to its full potential without creating and maintaining a flourishing culture. If you want to win, you have no choice but to carefully think through how you and your coworkers can work together to create something special. A great business culture makes all the difference in the world, which is why the very best companies in the world always find a way to build a strong, healthy culture. What do I mean by this?

Your corporate culture is the blend of the values, beliefs, and unwritten rules that all companies develop over time. Whether the culture is written down or not, it encapsulates the way company managers and employees think and act. As a leader at any level of the organization, you are responsible for embracing the positive aspects of your corporate culture and changing those that are negative. If you are the CEO, you have a special responsibility to preserve the culture and create a winning organization.

Winning can mean different things to different people. For some, it means recognition and getting some public kudos for a job well done. For others, it might mean additional compensation. Or it might mean a promotion to a new job. In the very best companies, it means all three: recognition, compensation, and promotion. To build a winning company, you need to carefully think through how to create true teamwork. You will never succeed if your end of the canoe rides high in the water while your customers' or coworkers' sinks.

One thing I know for sure: if you want to win, you have to support and empower *all* of your associates and coworkers. They have to know, very clearly, what you expect of them. They have to know how they're doing against what you expect. They have to know that you care about them. And they have to know that if the company wins and the customers win, they win too.

Howard Shultz, chairman and CEO of Starbucks, said it best. He noted, "People want guidance, not rhetoric. They need to know what the plan of action is and how it will be implemented. They want to be given responsibility to help solve the problem and the authority to act on it."

If you really want to win, you can't hamstring your coworkers with a bunch of unnecessary rules. They must have the freedom to serve their customers. You'll notice I chose the word "coworkers," the term we used at Continental to refer to our fellow employees. Home Depot uses the word "associates" to communicate the same thing, namely, *everybody* has an important role to play in the company's success. It's never management versus employees. The best and most successful companies always create a culture that encourages a coworker/

associate mindset… and then the leaders of those companies turn 'em loose.

Take a look at two charts that Bernie Marcus and Arthur Blank used years ago to set the culture at Home Depot. The first (Figure 5) displays the value wheel; the second (Figure 6) features an inverted pyramid. I think they explain themselves. If you are starting to think about the culture of your own company, this is a great place to start.

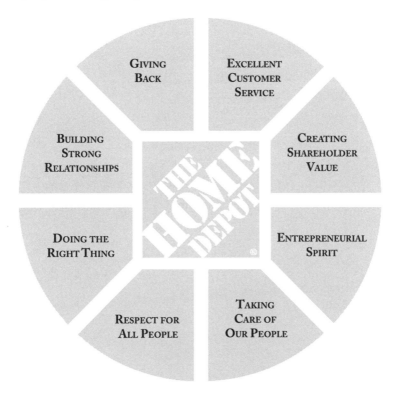

Figure 5: *Chart from the Home Depot annual meeting presentation.*

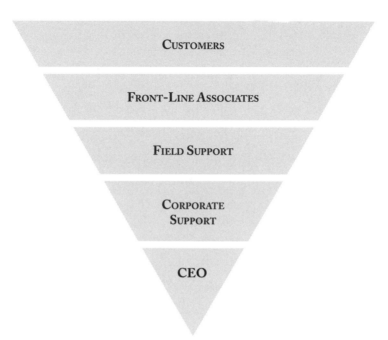

Figure 6: *Chart from the Home Depot annual meeting presentation.*

Better yet, Home Depot celebrates these values by publicly recognizing and rewarding employees who go out of their way to serve customers. These employees are not only given financial rewards and recognition at their stores, but they're often invited to the annual meeting to be celebrated by the Home Depot board and shareholders.

How to Turn 'Em Loose

You've created a Go Forward plan that shows everyone on your team the way to success. You've stopped doing things that lose you money. You've focused on growth and have put the right people in the right slots. Step Five is all about turning the asylum over to the inmates. Now you demonstrate your trust in the people you've hired, letting them execute their portion of the plan. Let me give you an example of empowering your coworkers.

When I served as president of Continental, one night I got awakened at 2:00 a.m. by a call on my unlisted number. Whenever you run an airline and the phone rings in the middle of the night, your mind immediately goes to the worst-case scenario. When I picked up the phone, however, I started hearing from an irate customer who somehow had found my number. Storms in Newark had forced his flight to be several hours late and controllers had changed his nonstop flight from Newark to Greensboro to stop first in Greenville before taking him home. He demanded to know why it happened and what I intended to do about it. I really started waking up only by the time he finished his story.

When I got off the phone with him, I called the head of Continental's system control, located on a fortified floor in our corporate offices that had so much technology it looked like a scene out of *Star Wars*. From this nerve center, Continental operated the airline 24/7/365. A very competent manager with complete decision-making authority headed each eight-hour shift.

I got the system control manager on the phone and explained the customer's call. He told me that due to the storms, air traffic control had limited departures, and he and his coworkers thought it best that, instead of canceling either the Greensboro or the Greenville flight, they should just get all our customers home. That sounded like a great solution to me too.

He then asked a question I'll never forget. "Greg," he said, laughing, "we make these decisions every night. Do you want me to wake you up and discuss them with you?"

"Never," I replied with a chuckle. "I have your back and the pilots' backs and the flight attendants' backs and the gate agents' backs and the mechanics' backs, every time."

News of that call spread quickly throughout the company. We proved over and over again that we wanted our talented coworkers to make decisions in their areas of responsibility.

And how can you empower your employees? Let me highlight six key practices that I have used.

1. Continually communicate your Go Forward plan.

Constantly, consistently communicate your Go Forward plan in speeches to coworkers, investors, the press, and your community. Every time you speak, you should describe the culture you are creating and talk about the Go Forward plan, over and over and over again. Do it until you think everyone gets it, and then do it a thousand more times. Drive it into the organization with a jackhammer. Ask them to repeat it back to you in casual conversations. When everyone can do so, you'll know they have it.

I often scheduled monthly open houses where our people could come in and ask whatever they had on their minds. If the company had multiple sites, we rotated the location of the open houses so that all of our people had a chance to attend. At Continental, for example, we held them in our three hubs (Houston, Newark, and Cleveland).

I'm dating myself here, but I learned from Gordon Bethune about the value of leaving a weekly voice mail with a 1-800 number that employees could dial to inform everyone in the company (and franchisees too), "Here's what we did on the Go Forward plan this week, and here's where we're headed next week."

Later, when e-mail and then social media became the tools of the time, I still found the voice mail approach valuable. I discovered that people wanted to hear my *voice* and that they'd especially listen for my tone—did the boss sound happy, confident, and positive? While e-mail and social media are wonderful tools that you should find ways to use, I believe that giving people the opportunity to hear your voice is worth a little extra. Use it to establish confidence in the direction of your company and to build expectation that good things are on the way. I strongly believe that you can accomplish some significant things verbally that you simply can't manage through e-mail or social media.

Consistency is the key thing here. I would leave my voice mail at the same time every Friday, so people would know that when they dialed in at the established time, they'd get the latest and greatest information. They never had to wonder, *Did he leave a new one this week? Can I hear it on Friday or will I have to wait until Saturday or Sunday? And if that happens, what would it mean? Do you think we're going under?*

I'll warn you right now: You'll get tired of doing these regular updates. You'll think you're communicating the same thing, repeatedly, without end. Frankly, you'll get a little bored with it. You may even daydream a bit as you record your messages; but the fact is, the only way to establish a healthy culture is by constant repetition. So find and use multiple communication channels to ingrain your Go Forward plan in the minds of all your coworkers. That's the best way of enabling them to execute it as required.

2. Open up direct lines of communication to you as the leader.

Stephen Covey once said, "Seek first to understand, then to be understood." That's doubly true in business. We discussed this in chapter eight, but it needs to be said again. While you want to empower your management teams to run their own divisions, you also want every coworker to have the ability to reach out to you. That can happen very easily through e-mail. Obviously, you'll need to set up some appropriate parameters so that a trickle doesn't become a perpetual flood. The key thing is to make sure your people know they can get in touch with you directly when the circumstances warrant it.

Make sure you respond to every single e-mail within twenty-four hours. When folks e-mail me with a suggestion, I always tell them that I will respond with one of three things:

> ⇨"We will do that right away!"
> ⇨"We will not do that, and here's why."
> ⇨"We need a little time to think about that and will get back to you (define the time)."

3. Identify the key elements of your desired culture.

As we've seen, culture is incredibly important to a healthy company or organization. You need to communicate your cultural expectations alongside your Go Forward plan.

What values will enable you to articulate the culture you want to build? Identify them and clearly spell them out. In addition, figure out ways to articulate your behavioral expectations. Let me give you two quick examples of the latter.

Don't tolerate nasty e-mails.

While e-mail is a great tool, people can hide behind it. E-mail encourages some individuals to say negative and even nasty things in messages that they'd never dare speak in person. I'm sure you can think of some egregious examples; we all can. In the companies I've run, I've always let our people know that nasty e-mails will not be tolerated. They are never appropriate.

I usually say, "If you have a problem or an issue with someone, never send your complaint in an e-mail. Always pick up the phone and call, or better yet, walk down the hallway and have a conversation, face-to-face. Let the person hear your voice so that you can relate to one another in a respectful and dignified way."

When nasty e-mails got sent out anyway—and they'd always make their way to me, because invariably the individuals who felt upset by them wanted me to see the outrage—I would go in person to correct the author of the offensive note. I would say, "We're not going to tolerate that kind of behavior. It's not part of our culture. It's not part of our company. It's not part of treating people with dignity and respect."

Once at Burger King and another time at Quiznos, after I tried to correct the guilty person a time or two, he or she continued to send nasty e-mails. So I fired them. If someone can't control his or her thoughts in an e-mail, then he or she can't work in our company. We insist that we treat each other well, and we back up that insistence with appropriate action.

The interesting thing about what I call these "culture dismissals" is that the news spreads throughout the company like wild-fire. And very quickly, the problem tends to take care of itself.

Reward positive behavior.

The most powerful way to reinforce a culture is to reward positive behavior. Home Depot, for example, has all kinds of rewards and recognition for associates who do a great job serving customers. Associates get patches to put on their aprons for providing great service, and after they accumulate a certain number of them, they earn cash or gift certificates. A book gets pulled together every year that details and celebrates the best customer service stories across the company. Because the company highly values customer service, it rewards it. Nearly every company I've worked with has learned to become very good at giving rewards. We have found the practice to be vitally important to our success.

4. Set up compensation systems to align with your Go Forward plan.

In our efforts to turn around Continental, we made the company into what we called "a pilot's airline." Since we wanted to run on time, we put in place several incentives to motivate our people to run the airline on time. We told the captains, "When it's time to go, you have the ability to make the call at the airport. You can tell your passengers you're going to leave.

Maybe you hear that one or two passengers are still coming but won't be there for a while. At the end of the day, it's your call. You can decide when to go. You can get the bags loaded and whatever else you need to do to get ready to take off." The whole system ran much more smoothly when we empowered our people and set up compensation systems to align with our Go Forward plan. That's a big part of building a thriving organizational culture.

Both executives and coworkers at Continental also had compensation systems tied to the Go Forward plan. Our coworkers, for example, had a profit sharing plan. Before shareholders ever touched the airline's profits, 15 percent went to our coworkers. We passed out profit sharing checks each Valentine's Day. We also paid monthly bonuses when we led the airline industry in on-time performance so that when customers won, our coworkers won. (We'll look at these programs in more detail in the appendix.) Our compensation systems got everyone in the company completely aligned with the Go Forward plan.

At Home Depot, every associate is part of a success-sharing program based on the performance of their respective stores, tied to sales versus budget. Every six months, in January and July, every associate gets a payment according to how well the associate's store has done. The success-sharing checks get passed out on the same day system-wide, at big celebrations in the break rooms at each of the approximately 2,200 Home Depot stores. When customers win, Home Depot associates win.

The same principle applies in the financial services world. At CCMP, we're all completely aligned with our Go Forward plan. We give our folks base pay and a bonus every year, but the vast majority of our compensation comes only if/when we deliver results for our investors. The investors appropriately receive the first fruits of our efforts; after that, we get a percent of the gains. We all get paid from the same pool, from the same results, at the same time. We all win together or we all lose together.

5. Communicate the Five Fs.

This may be the most important aspect of building a thriving culture. I realized its critical importance in 2008 when the fallout from the financial crisis hit, stretching the finances of many people in ways they'd never experienced. As person after person came into my office, describing their family's financial difficulties, it really struck me: *as the leader, I have a chance to communicate the crucial importance of the Five Fs.* And so I would often say, "The most important thing in my life is Faith, Family, Friends, Fitness, and Finance—in that order."

You have to communicate this conviction in more than mere words, of course. Let your people know that you care about them, that you care about their families. Tell them, as one small example, that you want them to take their vacations. I just sent a note yesterday to two of our really talented coworkers who have been laboring incredibly hard on a project nearing its completion. "Make sure you spend some time now with your family," I wrote. "We'll cover for you on anything that needs to be done here, but you need to go back and invest in your Faith, Family, and Friends for a little while. You've worked really hard and done a great job." Let your people know that you want them to have a whole life, not just a work life.

Frank Blake, the former CEO of Home Depot, did a terrific job at this. When he first took the company's top spot, he had to deal with abysmal associate morale. Associates didn't feel valued as individuals, and their former leader hadn't chosen to get close to many of them. He spent a ton of time in individual stores with associates, talking to them and listening to them and answering their e-mails.

Frank's handwritten notes also were legendary. Every Sunday, in fact, Frank handwrote about two hundred notes to associates, customers, or those who had helped him, whether bankers or businesspeople. I've also received and kept several of Frank's handwritten notes. They mean a great deal to me.

From my perspective, this practice of sending out a ton of handwritten notes is the most impressive thing Frank Blake did during his highly successful tenure at Home Depot. Frank is yet another high-powered leader who always makes you feel as though you're the most important person in the world. He defined the culture of Home Depot by regularly doing this, and the company continues to succeed because of it.

6. Have some fun with your coworkers.

Maybe the best part of creating a great culture is that you can enjoy each other and laugh together. I'll never forget one day in the pilots' lounge at Houston Intercontinental Airport. I stopped by just to say hello to the pilots who had come to kill time between flights. Before long, a group of pilots stood around me. One had wound up at the bottom of the seniority list a decade earlier when Frontier merged into Continental.

"Greg," he asked, "why can't you review the seniority list and improve my seniority?"

Now, anyone in the airline business knows that to change the seniority list would trigger World War III. Seniority dictates whether a pilot is a captain or first officer, what type of equipment they fly, who picks the routes they fly first, and a host of other things. It's also a zero-sum game, so if someone moves up, someone else moves down.

"I have a question for you guys," I responded. "How many of you are on your first wife?" Several hands went up.

"How about your second?" Eight or nine more.

"Your third?" Four hands went up.

"Your fourth?" Two hands.

"Okay, for those of you who are on your fourth wife, do you ever blame her for what your first wife did? And if you do, does it work?"

The room got fairly quiet. I think the pilots were trying to figure out *What is this guy talking about? What does this have to do with our seniority?*

"Guys," I continued, "I am your fourth wife. I don't care what your first wife did with the seniority list a decade ago."

The whole place busted out laughing. Maybe not the answer that the pilot wanted, but we were having fun.

An Incredible Man, a Praiseworthy Career

I'd like to begin wrapping up this chapter the way I began it, by focusing on the kind of leader who builds a thriving culture. Leaders who win make it a point to empower their people to do the jobs for which they were hired. And one of the ways they empower them is by letting them know how much they care about them. One incredible man comes immediately to mind in this regard, a key member of the Greatest Generation.

George H.W. Bush served as US vice president from 1981–1989 and as president from 1989–1993. I had the great pleasure of spending a significant amount of time with the president after he left office and moved back to Houston.

I'll never forget participating in a gala event in 1997, when the city of Houston officially changed the name of Houston Intercontinental Airport to the George Bush Intercontinental Airport. I served as host for a ceremonial dinner held at a huge Continental Airlines maintenance hangar, with fireworks overhead spelling out in the sky "George Bush Intercontinental Airport." After the ceremony, about 250 of us climbed aboard a DC-10-30, had dessert, flew down to Galveston, and immediately returned to Houston, where we did the first official landing in the newly renamed airport.

President Bush would call me occasionally during my time at Continental to see if he could borrow our restored DC-3, a civilian version of the military plane he had flown during his military service. "Greg," he'd say, "I'd like to take the DC-3 down to College Station," home of the George Bush Presidential Library and Museum and where the president held his leadership summits. Our own pilots, of course, flew the airplane. I joked he could take the DC-3 under one condition.

"What's that?" he asked.

"No jumping."

(You may recall that Bush 41 has a longtime love of skydiving. He even marked his ninetieth birthday, in 2014, with his eighth career skydive.)

A very famous local boot maker named Rocky gave both President Bush and me a pair of custom-made boots to commemorate the renaming of the airport. To get fitted for them,

I had to visit Rocky's shop, a nondescript place in an older part of Houston. Rocky sat me down, pulled out a manila folder, traced the pattern of my feet, and asked, "What kind of boots do you want?"

"What did the president get?" I inquired.

"Well, he has about twenty pair of my boots. For this pair, he asked for black ostrich on the bottom, cherry red uppers on the top, his initials, GB, on the side, and the presidential seal in the middle," Rocky answered.

"Rocky," I said, "why don't you do the same thing for me? Except use the Continental Airlines logo instead of the presidential seal."

That's what he did, and every time I wear those boots, I think of President Bush.

President Bush also bailed me out during my first year at Burger King. Shortly after I started running the company, angry franchisees began protesting right in front of our Miami corporate headquarters. The members of our franchise association had been mistreated for a long time, and I didn't blame them for feeling so upset.

In response, the franchisees had taken control of the annual convention. Normally, that's something the franchisor does. In fact, it's one of the big things a franchisor does, since that's where the corporate agenda for the coming year gets laid out. We wanted to take back the convention, but almost 100 percent of the funding for the franchise association came from convention profits. When we moved to retake control of the convention, therefore, an uproar ensued—hence the protestors outside of my office.

We needed an ace in the hole. We needed something magical to happen so the franchisees would realize the convention would improve when it became our responsibility rather than theirs. We didn't have to persuade the leaders of the franchise association, because we knew it would be hard to convince them. We had to reach the average franchisee, the guys working hard to do a good job of running their restaurants. If we could convince them, then everything would quiet down, because the association would lose their support base.

So I called President Bush. "Mr. President," I said, "I really need a favor."

"Greg, what do you need?" he asked.

"I need you to come and do a speech for me," I answered.

He hesitated. "You know I don't do that anymore," he stated.

"Yeah, I know."

"I'm supposed to go up to Maine to my house in Kennebunkport," he continued.

"I'd heard that," I said, but then I explained the situation. "I really need this," I pleaded, knowing that the convention would take place in Las Vegas, nowhere close to Maine.

"Can you send me a plane?" he asked.

"I'll send you whatever you want," I replied. "I just really need this."

"Okay," he declared, "I'll do it."

I didn't tell any of the franchisees that the president was coming. The meeting started out fine, and we had just begun to describe some of the positive changes coming, when out walked President Bush. The whole place went silent. Jaws dropped, and then everyone in the audience stood up and gave him a standing ovation. His arrival radically changed the tone and tenor of that convention.

After the president gave an amazing talk, I interviewed him onstage. I started to ask him about his son, Jeb, at the time the governor of Florida. Jeb lives in Miami, and I'd met him a number of times.

The president started tearing up. "Greg," he said, "don't ask me any questions about Jeb or any of my kids. I'm an old man. I get emotional really easy when I'm talking about my kids." I've never seen a more endearing moment.

For our company, the president's appearance had the desired effect. It turned around that whole convention and contributed greatly to our ability to turn around the company. What happened that day taught me some further lessons about what makes people tick and how to get sick companies well.

The thing I'll remember the most about President Bush, however, is that whenever he traveled on Continental, he would make a point to spend time with our pilots, our flight attendants, our mechanics, and our gate agents. He'd take pictures with them, sign items for them, and greet them in ways you just didn't expect of a former president of the United States. He really cared about my coworkers.

The president also loved to send out personal notes. I saved several of his notes to me, personal messages he wrote simply to thank me for this or that. As you might guess by now, I think sending out personal notes is one of the great lost arts, something that many of us could get much better at doing. Face it, we all have a drawer full of the encouraging notes others have sent to us. Affirmation is a powerful tool. It works, so why don't we affirm people more by writing them notes of encouragement and thanks?

There's a bigger question here, however. Why do powerful and influential men like President George H.W. Bush take the time to treat "ordinary" people with such care, dignity, and respect? "It's just part of their personal makeup," someone says, and no doubt that's true. But I'm certain it's more than that. A *lot* more.

Such incredible leaders know by long experience what it takes to build a thriving culture. They know that to motivate individuals to do their best, men and women need to know that their leaders care for them, are interested in them, and want them to succeed. These leaders don't try to do everything themselves, because they know that's impossible. To accomplish some worthy goal, they know an effective leader has to empower others to do the tasks assigned to them, and that they need encouragement and recognition to do their jobs well.

It's More Fun to Win

I love my job. It's really, *really* fun to work at CCMP, running a firm in which everyone pulls in the same direction, win or lose.

But obviously, it's more fun to win.

A big part of winning requires that you get everybody on the same team and that you let them do their jobs. Your co-workers have to know that you trust them, will empower them, really care about them, and that you have their backs. You need to create a place where it's fun to come to work every day—but the only way you'll ever get there is to let the inmates run the asylum.

My Mentors

Frank Blake: True Servant Leader

Frank Blake had a very unusual path to the CEO role at Home Depot. He got his bachelor's degree from Harvard and juris doctor from Columbia, and then spent some time as a law clerk and working as general counsel for GE and as deputy secretary in the Department of Energy. He joined Home Depot in 2002 as head of business development. Harvard, Columbia law, GE lawyer, Washington—an unusual path to Home Depot CEO/servant leader, don't you think?

Frank took over as CEO after the resignation of his longtime boss, a battlefield promotion. While on the surface the company looked fine financially, in fact it was in disarray. Frank's predecessor did many good things, including the centralization of many tasks that had to become consistent across the store base. By the time he finished, however, the whole culture had changed, and not for the better.

Home Depot was built around the store associates, the orange-aproned employees who greet customers and ask how they can help. You still hear legendary stories about how these associates, many of them skilled electricians or plumbers or handymen, would help customers figure out how to fix their problems, even to the point of volunteering to visit a customer's home. The "orange-blooded associate" *is* the Home Depot.

Unfortunately, before Frank took over as CEO, the associates lost their standing in the company and customer service suffered dramatically. Foot traffic in the stores dropped. The board gave Frank the task of turning things around. Boy, did he, initially with two simple moves and later with some recognition programs.

The first thing Frank did was to embrace all three founders, Bernie Marcus, Arthur Blank, and Ken Langone. When Frank showed up at the store manager meeting with the legendary Bernie Marcus at his side, everyone knew things were about to change.

Second, in the middle of the housing downturn, Frank declared, "We're going to take a bunch of money that Wall Street doesn't think we have and use it to invest in our associates. We are going to add back skilled tradesmen, we are going to continue to give annual merit increases when almost no one else does, and we are going to double down on success sharing." And with that simple but daring decision, Frank began to flip around the entire culture. He again instilled in the company the critical importance of its orange-blooded associates.

Frank also built on the example of the three founders, who had spent a lot of money to help associates in need through what they called the Homer Fund. This nonprofit charity's sole purpose is to "take care of the 300,000+ associates that make the Home Depot a success," according to the fund's website.

Funds are awarded by a committee of associates for disaster relief, health emergencies, and other unique issues that associates face from time to time. Each month, the fund awards more than a million dollars. Since its creation in 1999, it has provided more than $113 million to more than 90,000 associates.

The critical turnaround at Home Depot began with Frank's humility. He put up Bernie and Arthur's chart in the form of an inverted pyramid, with customers at the top, then the line associates, then store managers, then other management personnel, and finally him.

"This is how Home Depot works," he said. "This is what matters." And he didn't just say it, he lived it.

More than any other person I've ever worked with, Frank Blake exhibits true servant leadership.

Invest in Family and Friends

> *Truly great friends are hard to find, difficult to leave and impossible to forget.*
>
> UNKNOWN

I'D NEVER MET ANYONE like Dr. Walt James, a professor at Washburn University. Without question, Dr. James was the most intimidating person I'd ever known. He stood six foot two and weighed 240 pounds. He taught Intermediate Accounting I, the "weed out" class on the way to the CPA. Only about 50 percent of the students who started his class ended up finishing it.

On the first day of class, Walt would say, "Turn to your left. Now turn to your right. Only half of you are going to be here

by the end of this class, so figure out which half you're in."
Only the survivors came out smiling on the other side.

Walking into Walt's class was like going to war. He expected
you to be prepared and would grill you mercilessly if he suspected you were goofing off or just hadn't studied the assigned
homework. He would grab an eraser off the chalkboard ledge
and chuck it at you (ah, the good old days). He aimed it right
at your head. I learned later he did it for effect, but at the time,
it didn't seem like it. He demanded excellence. As a result, his
students consistently earned some of the highest first-time
pass rates on the CPA exam in the country.

I too passed the CPA exam on my first try, with high
marks. One hundred percent of the credit for that goes to Dr.
Walt James. In those days, we took the exam over three days,
with no calculators allowed. We had to do the math by hand.
Dr. James had prepared us well. He gave us odd tasks to do, for
example, as we drove down the road. "Add up the license plate
of the car in front of you," he commanded. He had us doing
crazy stuff to improve our calculating speed, to prepare us for
the strictly timed test. He just grilled us. And it all paid off.

I think he may have felt a little disappointed when I worked
as a CPA for only two years. But he got over it once I told him
that Harvard Business School had accepted me into its MBA
program.

After my graduation from Washburn, Dr. James became

Walt, and Walt has never missed a single speech I have given anywhere in the state of Kansas. He was there when Ronda and I got married. He was there when I got my honorary doctorate from Washburn. He was there when I got inducted into the Kansas Business Hall of Fame. He never tells you he's coming; he just shows up. He has been doing this for thirty years, long after he retired. And he does this not just for me, but for all his former students. He makes Washburn a very special place. He is always there, a very faithful guy.

So what can we learn from observing individuals like Dr. Walt James? Like Jimmy Lee? I see four primary takeaways:

⇨ Know your platform
⇨ Invest over a long period of time
⇨ Know the enemies and be prepared to deal with them
⇨ Have fun

Know Your Platform

God has given us all some platform of influence in this world. Dr. Walt James's platform was the students he invested in and encouraged throughout his life. Jimmy Lee's platform was his clients, for whom he cared deeply for more than forty years.

Have you discovered your platform? Who do you care about? Who would you like to invest in? This should fly right off the pages of your personal Go Forward plan.

Years ago, a man had heard the story of Mother Teresa and her incredible work with the poorest of the poor orphans in Calcutta, India. He felt so moved by the work that he sold all of his possessions and left for Calcutta to serve in her ministry. When he got to Calcutta, he couldn't meet with Mother Teresa right away, so he immediately went to work in her ministry.

Several weeks went by, and one day as he cleaned up after some orphans, Mother Teresa walked into the room. I never met Mother Teresa, but I've spoken with some who did. Despite being less than five feet tall, I understand that her presence completely filled any room. The man told Mother Teresa about hearing of her work, selling all his possessions, and coming to India to serve with her.

Mother Teresa had an interesting response. She looked at the man and said, "I know your story and have been watching you work for the last several weeks. Son, you are terrible at this ministry. God called me to this ministry, to the orphans in Calcutta. Son, you need to go and find your own Calcutta."

What is your own Calcutta? What is your unique platform? For many of us, our Calcutta is in the marketplace, working with others in secular endeavors. So what platform has God given you to influence others? Find it and pursue it with everything in you.

The fun part of this is fully integrating this platform into our lives so that we don't have a marketplace life on Monday through Friday and another life on Sunday. Rather, we have a fully integrated life, seven days a week, working in whatever platform God has given us.

Maybe you've already discovered your platform. Great! Most of us are not called to be preachers or para–church leaders, but rather to be leaders in the marketplace or in the home. We would be terrible at doing anything else. And what if you haven't yet identified your platform? While I believe that will be revealed to you over time, don't wait for God to give you all the answers. Work hard wherever you are employed and He will show you your own Calcutta at the right time.

You can tell from my personal Go Forward plan that I have identified my platform. It includes my family, the three businessmen I share life with, my partners at CCMP, the couples who have been through the couple's retreat Ronda and I have hosted over the past eight years, the charities we support, and the six hundred board members and CEOs on our annual Christmas book list.

Am I where I want to be? Not completely, although I've come a long way.

Does everyone with whom I have regular contact know that I care about them, like Jimmy Lee's friends did? Honestly, I believe I have some work to do there.

Do I have some relationship work to do with a few individuals who have disappeared altogether from my friends circle?

Should I spend some time figuring out how to repair and reinstate those relationships, even if at only a cordial level? Most certainly.

The guys in our small group challenge each other to think about any relationships from which we may have disconnected, or to identify the individuals we may have harmed in some way. We try to hold each other accountable to go back and repair at least some of those relationships. We remind ourselves of a verse from the New Testament: "If it is possible, as far as it depends on you, live at peace with everyone" (Romans 12:18). It's not always possible, but when it is, part of a commitment to investing in the lives of family members and friends is to "live at peace" with them.

What about you? Have you unintentionally disconnected from any formerly close relationships? Who might you have harmed in some way that, just maybe, you should approach and try to seek reconciliation? No, it won't be easy. But turnarounds never are, whether in business or in life. The key questions are: "What do I really care about? And how can I best invest in the lives of my family and friends?"

Invest Over a Long Period of Time

When I think of those who consistently invest in others over time, my close friend Britt Harris comes to mind. Britt has a highly impressive résumé, but perhaps the thing that impresses me most about him is what he does in a mega-popular class he teaches every semester at Texas A&M.

You may remember that Britt serves as the CEO/CIO of the Teacher Retirement System of Texas (usually called Texas Teachers), the third-largest pension fund in the country. He's been named one of the top ten investors in the nation. And so when he offers a class called Titans of Investing, you can believe me when I say that he has no trouble finding students to sit in every available seat. In fact, the class has become so popular that hundreds of students apply each semester for only about twenty available slots.

Britt teaches the course as a combination of investment strategies and key life skills. He's created a real legacy, even in how students get selected for the class. He leaves the selection up to his students; graduates from each class pick the students for the following class.

At the beginning of the term, Britt requires his twenty students to write extensive reports on recently published books, which are sent to Britt's contacts, a group of top businesspeople nationwide. Each report gives a terrific ten-page summary of one of twenty new books each semester. That's the equivalent of reading forty books a year, without having to digest every word. If you especially like a particular summary, you can read the whole book.

Britt has contacts with every major consulting firm, every

major investment bank, every major private equity firm, every major investor, and many industrial companies in the nation, and he uses those contacts to relentlessly promote his Titans. As a result, he now has hundreds of young people under age thirty-two operating in the highest places of government, business, consulting, and investment banking. Britt tracks every one of his former students. He follows where they are, who they're working for, and what they're doing.

But he doesn't stop there. He makes annual visits to every major city where his former students now work: Houston, Dallas, New York, San Francisco, LA, London. In each city, he throws a dinner for the alumni Titans in that city. He brings in a terrific speaker, and at some point during every event, he hands out a list that details for the group life and contact information on every Titan, so they can stay in contact with one another.

Britt Harris cares deeply about every one of his former students. He has made a personal commitment to getting them the best jobs and mentoring them over the course of their careers. When they get married, he knows it. When they change jobs, he knows it. All the major events in their lives, he tracks. He has been doing this for more than a decade— hundreds and hundreds of students. What a phenomenal example of faithful presence! It staggers me, really, to see how much he cares about those young professionals.

If you look at anyone who has had an outsize impact, who has left a legacy of eulogy virtues, almost always the individual has done it over an extended period of time. These leaders know their platforms and have consistently leveraged them.

In your business, letting the inmates run the asylum means that you invest in them the authority they need to accomplish your Go Forward plan. That includes equipping them with the proper resources, making clear their responsibilities, and finding ways to encourage them and support them.

On the personal side of the ledger, with your family and friends, you need to do essentially the same thing. You must find ways to invest and empower them. The only difference is that you need to do it over a much longer period of time.

Watching men like Senator Lloyd Bentsen, President George H.W. Bush, Jimmy Lee, Dr. Walt James, Britt Harris, my great-uncle Lyle Yost, and Paul Friesen has convinced me to become consistent over time.

Have you identified your platform? Are you focused on it for the long haul?

Know the Enemies and Be Prepared to Deal with Them

We live in a broken world. In that world, life throws us a lot of curveballs. We have to lead through the difficult times, just as we do in the easier times.

Think about your favorite college football team. When it plays at home, the crowd grows quiet when the team's offense takes the field but gets loud and rowdy when the opposing offense takes over, which makes it really tough for opposing players to hear. It is *much* tougher to play away than at home!

In the marketplace, nearly all of our games are away games. We have lots of fierce competitors and many hurdles to overcome. As I lead through tough times, I try always to ask myself several questions.

To use the language of my boyhood, I ask, "Am I being holy?"

"Am I doing the right thing for the right reasons here?"

"Am I being just?"

"Does the punishment fit the crime?"

"Am I meting out justice, as leaders often must do, in a fair, loving, and compassionate way?"

Holy. Just. Compassionate. That's my acid test for when the tough times hit, whether with family, with friends, or with business associates.

When you're the leader, whether you lead at home, with your friends, or in the marketplace, you have to deal with all kinds of "people issues." Certain categories of those issues come up repeatedly. I've identified three big curveball issues in the lives of those closest to me.

1. Friends who fall into infidelity

I have several friends who have fallen into this hole, and I've done what I can to help them put their families back together again. Psychologists tell us it takes about seven years for the offended marital partner to really allow forgiveness to heal the relationship, but in my experience, it's taken anywhere from seven to eleven years. In any event, it takes a *long* time to bring healing to broken marriages and families.

In order to help several friends work through the pain of infidelity, I've seen the need to speak to them in a holy, just, and compassionate way. Some of these friends have managed to put their lives back together again and some haven't. The process is never easy or smooth. The ones who have managed it will tell you it's definitely worth the effort and pain.

But how much better if they never had to go through the pain at all?

I strongly advise my executives to have their antennae up when spending time with the opposite sex on business trips, at business meals, or during one-on-one office conversations. It doesn't mean you shouldn't mentor others, but keep the focus on business issues and make sure any friendships formed don't spill over into romance. If there is any hint of flirtation or attraction, beware. If possible, find a plausible way not to deal with the person yourself, perhaps by having an associate handle communication in your place. Whatever happens, don't give in to temptation. It is not worth the pain that is sure to follow.

You may consider me a little prude, but I've found three basic rules that can help to avoid falling into infidelity.

First, nothing good happens after nine p.m. on a business trip, so make sure you're in your hotel room, by yourself, after nine p.m. Second, avoid one-on-one meals with members of the opposite sex, except in well-lit, very public places. That may sound quaint, but over the years I've observed how infidelity usually occurs. It almost always starts with, "Hey, let's go to lunch together"—nothing formal, just casual. That often leads to dinner, which all too often leads to breakfast. I don't need to explain what that means. Third, if you're spending one-on-one time in a business setting with a member of the opposite sex, to the extent that you're not talking about anything super-confidential—such as people's performance reviews—always leave the office door open. Just following these simple guidelines would have prevented most of the trouble I've seen.

2. Friends who fall into depression

It might surprise you to discover how many Americans suffer from one form or degree of clinical depression. In 2010, the Centers for Disease Control estimated that about 10 percent of the US population suffered from occasional bouts of depression, while 3.4 percent suffered from major depression.

Some of these individuals have learned how to keep it pretty well hidden.

Maybe a friend is quietly going through a midlife crisis. Maybe things aren't working out the way she or he wanted them to. Whatever the cause, he or she has fallen into depression, and that can be a dangerous and even deadly place to be.

One successful business guy who's fought his own battles with depression recently wrote, "We live in a world of perception, of *what* you are, not *whose* you are. As servant leaders, we need to be able to address the undercurrent of pain below the surface, hidden behind the windshield of the Lexus and under the Armani suit."[10] The author, Isaac Manning, described how rediscovering his faith has enabled him to cope with the darkness when it descends, but he cautions, "Don't think for a moment, however, that Christ is a silver bullet for all the problems of modern life. Last time I checked, all of us are still humans, deeply fallen and prone to do foolish things. When we come to faith in Christ, what gets removed, through God's grace and forgiveness, is the crushing weight of our inadequacy."

Don't be afraid to have a conversation with someone close to you who seems to have withdrawn a bit, who seems not quite himself or herself, who might be struggling with depression. Have the conversation! And do whatever you can to help your friends and family members go wherever they need to go to get the counseling or treatment they may require.

3. Friends who fall into addiction

Addiction doesn't care whether you're a CEO or a line worker, a four-star general or a buck private. And it doesn't care what your particular addiction might happen to be, whether alcohol or drugs or even gambling. I've seen all of them and watched each of them take down a lot of strong, confident, talented men and women. Down doesn't necessarily mean out, of course. Some of these folks have recovered; but I've also watched helplessly as others fell down and stayed down.

I hate addiction. But I also know it doesn't always have to win. I recently heard of a CEO who lost his sixteen-year-old daughter in a fatal crash caused by a drunk driver.[11] The businessman had just hired an executive coach to help him find ways to have more fun in his life, even as he expanded his business. But after the accident, the CEO's relationship with his coach changed. The two men started having long discussions about how to find meaning beyond the task of building a growing company.

The CEO soon decided to change the way he operated. Rather than allowing himself to descend into a pit of despair, shaking his fist at heaven and demanding, "Why me?" he asked instead, "What good can come from this tragedy?"

Not long afterward, one of his employees landed in jail after getting convicted of dealing drugs. The CEO visited his former coworker in prison every week for one year, bringing him fresh reading material and going out of his way to maintain a personal connection. After the young man had served his time and left prison, the CEO rehired him.

Happily, the young man made the best of his second chance. He gave up the drugs, turned around his life, and became not only a model employee, but a leader at work. Around the same time, the company's whole culture significantly improved, and not because everyone felt moved by the story, because neither man made it broadly known. Rather, in the aftermath of his personal tragedy, the CEO started looking beyond the financial success of his business to see how he could invest in the lives of his coworkers. As a result, he built an intensely loyal workforce that to this day looks forward to coming to work. Not surprisingly, his company is thriving.

Our society loves stories of redemption, of a turnaround, of a recovery. Forgiveness and redemption are extremely potent tools. The recovering addict may have to change jobs and deal with unpleasant consequences caused by what he or she has done. But most people are willing to forgive in this kind of scenario, and there's always a chance for redemption.

One of the best ways to make sure that addiction doesn't steal your life is by paying careful attention to the moral compass that tells you the right direction to follow. Some of us find that compass in our faith, through the rules, guidelines, commandments, or principles of Scripture. Others find it in a long family heritage or a strong cultural background. When we think back to the environment in which we grew up, most of us see that our parents or guardians did their best to teach us ethical behavior; and even if they didn't, somewhere along the way, each of us found some kind of moral compass.

Sometimes, unfortunately, those who know what is morally right stray from it and wander off onto all kinds of illicit and hurtful paths. Many of those paths lead to addiction. I would encourage anyone in that situation to remember that there *is* a path back. You have to be willing to change, but there's always a path back.

Have Fun!

Do you know what I love about my family? About the three guys I meet with every week? About my partners at CCMP? About the CEOs we know, the couples we mentor, our friends, or the guys who hang out at NCS (the men's gathering I referred to earlier)?

We live life together. We joke around and laugh. We enjoy each other's company and fully enjoy life *together*.

We have talked about many serious things in this book, both business and personal, but none of it is worth much if you can't laugh with others and at yourself. Make your time with others *fun*.

Caleb, My Personal Hero

I grew up hearing a lot of Bible stories, but my favorite is the one about Caleb. Maybe I like it because Caleb wasn't a priest, a pastor, a king, a prince, or a prophet. He was just a guy, a faithful, courageous man who left an amazing legacy. This man knew how to lead, and he did so in a way that invested heavily into the lives of his family members and friends.

Perhaps more than any other character in the Bible, Caleb's story really challenges me today, even though he lived about 3,400 years ago. This was a guy who posted for God.

We first meet him in Numbers 13, where he's listed among twelve "spies" sent by Moses to do some reconnaissance of the Promised Land. The dozen Hebrew scouts see a rich country with abundant crops and plenty of natural resources—but they also see strong enemies in well-fortified towns. Ten of the spies say, "We need to turn around! The people we saw would just *crush* us. Compared to them, we're grasshoppers. Better to live in a low-rent neighborhood than die in a gated community!"

When the people heard this alarming report, they nearly started a riot. Caleb silenced the crowd and declared, "Don't listen to these guys! We can take this land!" He spoke out even before Joshua, who fully agreed with him. But the doom-and-gloom speech carried the day, and the people refused to cross the Jordan River to begin their conquest of the Promised Land. As a result, God told the people that they would wander around in the desert for forty years, until all the men over the age of twenty (except for Caleb and Joshua) had died.

At that point, Caleb disappears from the Bible… for forty-five *years*. The Scripture doesn't mention him in the rest of the book of Numbers, or at all in the book of Deuteronomy. After Moses's death, Joshua takes over as leader. I've always wondered if Caleb felt a little disappointment in that. Forty years before, *he'd* been the one to take the lead in urging the people to follow God's call, and now his friend Joshua gets the top position instead of him. Caleb followed Joshua anyway, and about five years later, when the time came to take the most difficult part of the Promised Land—the portion allotted to him—Caleb suddenly reappeared, in spectacular fashion.

"Joshua," he says, "you and I were the only ones there when Moses agreed that this land was mine. I am now eighty-five years old, but I'm just as strong and vigorous as I ever was. With God helping me, I'm going to take it!"

What could Joshua say?

Caleb knew he couldn't do this by himself, of course. I wonder if he realized, *Hey, I'm eighty-five years old. I need help. I have this beautiful daughter, Achsah, so I think I'll promise her in marriage to whoever helps me take the land.* A young man named Othniel took the challenge, captured the most heavily fortified city in the area, married Achsah, and became the first judge of Israel.

Caleb set an unbelievable tone and left an amazing legacy. He was a stud on so many levels. Who wouldn't want to be like him? He faithfully stuck around in the shadows for forty-five years. He had the humility to support Joshua's leadership. He lived out his faith and stood up for what he considered to be right. At age eighty-five, he was still working hard for God. And he kept his promise about rewarding whoever would help him to claim his inheritance, thus setting up Othniel as the first judge of Israel, leading to forty years of national peace and prosperity.

Caleb had an incredible, intentional, faithful presence—and through it, he changed the course of history. Which brings me to a series of questions and a simple challenge.

What will you do from age forty to eighty-five? Will you waste your life, or will you choose to be a Caleb? Will you leave behind a strong legacy, as he did? How are you investing in the lives of your family and friends? How will your actions today impact our own nation? How will your investments be remembered ten years after you're gone?

Choose to be a Caleb.

Résumé Virtues or Legacy Virtues?

Way back in the introduction, I mentioned David Brooks and his fine book *The Road to Character*. Brooks makes a crucial distinction between "résumé virtues," or the list of your career achievements and successes, and "legacy virtues," the character qualities and achievements mentioned at your funeral.

At this very moment, which is the longer list for you? Have your legacy virtues gotten trumped by your résumé virtues?

To make sure my own legacy virtues rise to the top, I know I have to remain committed to investing in the lives of my family and friends. I have to take the long view, like Caleb did. And I have to take great pride in watching those family members and friends succeed.

Fortunately, that last bit is the easy part.

Reflected Glory Is the Best Kind

I've learned over time that if you can help others find fulfillment through faith, family, and friends, a kind of glory comes back to you that exceeds anything else. The joy that returns to you, the aura generated from them doing well, feels better than anything you can do for yourself.

In other words, the best kind of glory is reflected glory.

If you're helping someone or leading a team and that individual or team does well, the very best celebration is knowing that you played a key role in encouraging that person to succeed or helping that team to win. That's absolutely the best kind of credit, the greatest reward, and the most thrilling kind of glory.

Reflected glory really is the best kind. So invest in it.

My Mentors

Senator Bob Dole: Faithful Presence

Senator Bob Dole grew up in Russell, Kansas. Like me, he attended Washburn University in Topeka, Kansas. Senator Dole never forgot that he grew up in America's heartland. In the eyes of a lot of us who grew up in Kansas, he is a real American hero. Senator Dole, a World War II vet, also never forgot the American troops who had served their country so well. To this day, you hear stories of Senator Dole frequently visiting various memorials in Washington, DC, several times a week to greet the troops.

Whenever you spend time with Senator Dole, you feel like the most important person in the world. Senator Dole has accomplished a tremendous amount of good in his life—as I write, he's ninety-one years old and still going strong—largely because of his commitment to serving people and honoring their service. I'm proud to say that the two of us are from the same home state and the same great university.

Right Away and All At Once

Y OU MIGHT THINK A title like "Right Away and All At Once" would better describe a chapter at the beginning of a book instead of at its end. Wouldn't that be more logical?

You might be right. But in this case, the title really comes from two sources. First, it was the title chosen for the *Harvard Business Review* article referred to throughout this book, reprinted in the appendix. But more importantly, it comes from questions I get all the time from individuals at all levels of organizations after they hear me speak about turnarounds. They ask me things like:

> ⇨"What's the single most important thing you did to turn around Continental?"
>
> ⇨"What should I do first in my business?"
>
> ⇨"What can I ignore until later?"
>
> ⇨"Shouldn't I focus on culture first?"
>
> ⇨"Can't I just work really hard in my twenties and thirties to get my life established, and *then* focus on faith, family, and friends?"

Do you see the common thread in all these questions? All of them, in one way or another, want to rank the five steps in order of priority, or at least in order of execution. They want to know if they can hold off on this or that step while they focus on another step.

But do you want to know the truth? In fact, there is no "one most important step." There is no one thing we did in any of the companies we turned around that sparked the transformation. If you want to know the *real* "secret sauce" to turning around a company, to driving a business to its full potential (and even to living a fully integrated life), I'd be glad to give you the recipe. But I should tell you beforehand that you may not like it much. Here it is:

> *You create by far the most momentum and deliver the best results if you do all five steps* **right away and all at once.**

Sorry, but there really is no other way.

Beware the Paralysis of Analysis

Most big companies, and some small ones as well, get caught up in what I call "analysis paralysis." It takes them months to process and make a single simple decision. Often this happens because they have created a culture where the coworkers, including management, have not been empowered and so feel *deathly* afraid of making mistakes. They end up killing their business by getting bogged down in analysis, everyone protecting themselves from a bad decision by making no decision.

But you do realize that by making no decision, you're actually deciding, don't you?

I tell all of my colleagues at CCMP, and all of the CEOs and managers of our portfolio companies, "We're better off if you make twenty decisions a day, get two wrong, and fix those two, than if you take a month to make the 'perfect' decision." The problem is, we'll still make mistakes, even if we take months in a wrongheaded attempt to achieve perfection. And in the meanwhile, the fifteen other decisions that really should have been made yesterday will still be waiting in the queue.

To make a turnaround work, you have to make lots, and lots, and lots of decisions, and you have to do so quickly. It's the only way I know to develop your 10,000 hours in decision making. This is where growing up and working in a farming community helped me tremendously. There, you had to make decisive decisions. Something breaks? Fix it; debating why it broke costs time and money when there is wheat to be harvested or a crop to get in. Rain in the forecast? Then work all night to get the crop in. We simply never debated these issues. It was unheard of.

I first realized the benefit of my upbringing, my ability to make lots of decisions quickly and not get caught up in analysis paralysis, when I worked at Bain & Company. Some Bain partners were outstanding at applying the 80/20 rule (80 percent of the value gets added from 20 percent of the actions) while others weren't. Early in my career it used to drive me crazy, as it did a lot of others at Bain who also worked long hours, when a partner asked for *yet another* piece of analysis to prove a point, although the answer already had made itself abundantly clear. I always thought that one big value of being a partner was your long experience—you needed only one data point to draw a trend line. If you knew the right answer, and the client agreed, you just moved on to execution.

Perhaps now you know why I like turnarounds so much. I truly believe that, in business, velocity and the momentum it creates are next to godliness.

Does that mean that I never make mistakes? Of course not. When I make my twenty quick decisions, I fully expect that I might get two of them wrong. But I also commit to quickly fixing whatever I missed.

Do you think we always selected the right routes to fly at

Continental? Of course we didn't. Despite our best efforts, a percentage of the new routes we selected always lost money. We didn't dwell on the mistakes or cut someone's head off because of an incorrect route analysis. We just learned from our mistakes, either fixed the route or canceled it, and moved on.

Do you think we always select the right deals at CCMP or always pick the right CEO? Of course we don't. Sometimes we fail to properly analyze the situation or we pick the wrong team. Do we denigrate the person who made the error? No; we have the operators necessary inside of our firm to address the problem. Twice in the past year, my partner Doug Cahill has stepped in to stabilize some stressed investments for us.

Don't get stuck in analysis paralysis. Quickly make your twenty decisions, expect that you might get a couple of them wrong, and then fix what you missed.

Make Your Mistakes Early

We've managed over a hundred companies at CCMP, and along with that comes a huge database of experience. All that history tells us, categorically, that we deliver the highest returns for our investors on the companies in which we have identified a quick, clear path to success. We tend to win big when we create a one-page plan that we use to make all the key decisions that must be made within the first twelve months of our investment.

Do we need to hire a new management team? If so, who? Do we have to make major capital investments, like plant moves or new IT systems? Do we need to fix or shut down money-losing operations? When we answer those questions quickly and then move to execution, we tend to get really high returns.

By doing the heavy lifting early, we also have time to recover from any missteps we may have made, which allows us to profitably grow the business much faster. When we don't do this, we get more meager returns. We're not perfect at making decisions early in an investment, but we're getting better all the time.

One of the competitive advantages I have is that I'm very good at simplifying complex problems and making decisions very quickly. Sometimes when you do this, you can leave others behind. Make sure you *use all five steps* to get full buy-in for where you want to lead others.

Most people hate change. In general, change frightens them. They don't like change in their business lives or in their personal lives. But I love change. So I have to take special care to take enough time to bring people along with me. No doubt that has been the biggest learning challenge of my career. I had to learn to take the extra time and effort it takes to rally the whole organization around the Go Forward plan.

If you don't do this, you won't succeed. It really is that simple. But when you do take the time and effort necessary to engage everyone around the Go Forward plan, you equip yourself to do everything right away and all at once.

It Can Happen Quickly

We've looked at a number of companies over the course of this book, and now I'd like to go back and quickly review the time lines of several of these turnarounds. I want to highlight just how fast the critical changes took place.

We bought Francesca's in March of 2010, took out half of the money we'd invested in November of 2010, and took the company public in July of 2011—just fifteen months after we bought it. We sold all our shares within about eighteen months post-IPO at a big gain for our investors—about four times their money.

We bought Generac in 2006 and made some key decisions early on, after the housing market crashed and demand for home standby generators plummeted. We decided first to move into portable generators and soon afterward decided to expand into other products, such as light towers for construction sites. We also acquired a number of compatible companies. We took Generac public in early 2010 and allowed the company to appreciate. Then, over time, we sold out our shares. We completed the whole turnaround in three years, even in the middle of a housing crisis, and sold the last of our shares in 2013.

The investment generated a terrific return for our investors—nearly three times their money.

Milacron is a really interesting example. We bought the company in the spring of 2012 when it had about $80 million dollars of EBITDA. We completely revamped the strategy and the team. In 2013, we added about the same amount of EBITDA from another company we acquired and then made three or four other acquisitions. We combined the companies and brought in a whole new management team, including a new CEO, two new COOs to run different parts of the business, a new CFO, and a new head of sales. We made substantial investments in R&D and in our plant infrastructure all over the world. In June 2015, we successfully took Milacron public. This turnaround of a company that barely avoided extinction during the great recession took a little over three years.

I arrived at Continental in November of 1994. Within three years, the company went from a $640 million loss to a $770 million profit, its stock price had gone through the roof, and we made about twenty times our money.

We started the PwCC turnaround in early June of 2002, quickly made two major moves, and in two months, we took earnings from 4 percent of sales to 12 percent of sales. IBM then bought the business for $4 billion, just four months after we started.

These are just a few examples of what can happen when

you do things right away and all at once. I can't promise that you'll generate the same kinds of results, but I can tell you that by doing things this way, you set yourself up for comparable success.

A Cautionary Note

Speed, of course, is not the only factor in a successful turnaround. Yes, you need to move right away and all at once, but you have to get things *right*. If you're not good at determining the right value drivers, you can destroy a company by going too fast. Remember the infamous example of JCPenney.

To be able to pull off a speedy, successful turnaround, you do have to be *right* in your decision making. Once you know what you need to do—after you have your plan and you know the right levers to pull—the turnaround or initiative to reaching your full potential can happen very quickly when you move "right away and all at once."

But you have to be right!

That's the benefit of making twenty decisions a day and quickly correcting the few choices you get wrong.

A Finite But Unknown Time Line

We're all on this earth for a finite period of time. That much we know for sure. What we don't know is the time line, how many years each of us has. And that's why, on the personal side, it's imperative to implement the five steps right away and all at once.

In the first half of 2015, I unexpectedly lost three business friends I knew very well. Jimmy Lee died at age sixty-two. Ed Gilligan, the number two guy at American Express and the heir apparent to Ken Chenault, died on a plane on his way back from China. He was fifty-five. I was not as close to Ed in recent years as I had been when I worked at Continental and Burger King, but Ed was a terrific guy—like Jimmy, always mentoring people and taking time for others. He spent his entire career of more than thirty years at American Express. Many people loved him, as they did Jimmy. His death was a heartbreaking loss for the company, his friends, and family.

My business partner at CCMP Steve Murray died in the spring of 2015 at age fifty-two. Steve is the guy who brought me into CCMP in the first place. We successfully ran the company together for seven years. Steve was a very good investor.

All three of these men essentially spent their entire careers at one company. They all had very close relationships with their family and with their friends. They all were outstanding business executives and even better people. And as they went into 2015, none of them knew it would be their last year on earth.

Forgive me if this sounds morbid, but I think it's necessary to mention, because *this* is the world we live in. None of us is guaranteed a long life, so we have to ask the question: *What do I want my family and friends to remember about me?*

Do you have your personal Go Forward plan? Have you left your family financially secure? What changes do you want to help instigate in the world? Have you invested in others? Have you thought about where you'll go when you die? Have you reconciled yourself to it? Are you focused on résumé virtues or eulogy virtues?

In your personal life, doing things right away and all at once is really the only option.

A Surprising Response

I do quite a bit of public speaking, often related to turnarounds and how they work. And especially in the past few years, I've noticed a consistent pattern in audience response, one that might surprise you. I wonder if the same pattern might not apply to you.

When I speak, I know that the vast majority of audience members have come out to hear something about the business side of turnarounds, hoping to glean some insight into how to turn around or improve their own companies. But by the time I finish and a line starts forming of individuals who want to talk to me about something mentioned in my talk, I know that maybe 80 percent of them won't want to talk about business.

They want to open up about their personal lives. They chose to attend the speech in order to hear about business turnarounds, but they felt compelled after the talk to speak with me about some personal turnaround. I see this pattern nearly every time I speak publicly.

What about you?

It might be that, while you picked up *Right Away and All At Once* hoping to get some helpful tips on how to transform your business, you have realized by now that what your heart really craves is improvement in your personal life. Now, I know that books differ from talks, and so the same phenomenon may not hold here as it does with public speaking. Still, people are people, and in my informal discussions with CEOs and board members across the country and the world, I can't tell you how often the conversation eventually turns to personal issues rather than business ones. Most of these execs, of course, would never publicly admit that their personal lives could use a turnaround; but in private, just between the two of us, they want to know how the five steps could enrich their lives at home, away from the office.

In many ways, this only makes sense. We spend a large portion of our lives "doing business." When people look at us, they don't see our souls, the central core of who we are, but rather the accoutrements of a successful corporate career. They see the résumé, the travel, the cars or homes or whatever material part of the job impresses them the most. And truthfully, all of us like to be thought of as successful and prosperous; it sure beats being known for failure and being broke!

But you can't live on pride and accomplishments alone. Accomplishments are just a veneer, what people see on the outside. Through a lot of work, one can rack up accomplishments… but without changing the reality inside, it all seems to go for naught.

Alfred Nobel certainly managed to change his worldwide reputation through the Nobel Peace Prize, given annually to individuals in five categories (physical science, medical science or physiology, literature, and international fraternity). Most of us have forgotten that the lifelong bachelor made his fortune largely through the establishment of ninety armaments factories and his invention of dynamite. When his brother, Ludvig, died while visiting Cannes, France, in 1888, a French newspaper incorrectly reported that Alfred had died, using harsh words that captured the wealthy inventor's attention: "*La marchand de la mort est mort*," or, "The merchant of death is dead." The newspaper also reported, "Dr. Alfred Nobel, who became rich by finding ways to kill more people faster than ever before, died yesterday."

Historians believe that this unsympathetic article so shook Nobel that he decided to find a way to repair his reputation. In November 1895, he established a will in which he left 94 percent of his estate to establish the Nobel Prizes. He died the following year.

Nobel knew how to create thriving businesses. He became fabulously rich as a result. But what he really needed was a personal turnaround, one that would have allowed him to live to the end of his days with a sense of significance, not shame or regret. His money gained him a better reputation posthumously. But how much greater to gain a better life before you die?

It is possible. For you too. I hope this book—and its advice to apply the five steps right away and all at once—has shown you how.

Epilogue: Act Now

Y OU NOW HAVE THE tools you need to transform your business and enrich your life. Whether you're in a turnaround or simply trying to enable your company (or yourself) to reach your full potential, these five steps will provide you with an excellent path to get there.

So what are you waiting for? Dream your dreams!

Before I sign off, let me leave you with one final thought, an important reminder. I believe that God put businesspeople on earth to create jobs, because He means for men and women to work. Therefore, if someone can figure out how to create jobs, then he or she has made one of the highest forms of contribution possible on this earth, not only economically and socially but spiritually as well.

When human beings find themselves out of work, all kinds of bad things happen. They take devastating hits to their self-confidence, to their self-worth, and to their sense of purpose. But if a talented businessperson can create jobs and grow companies, then apathy and discouragement give way to energy, excitement, and fulfillment. The change is simply amazing.

As I've said, I like the saying, "Sales cures all ills." If you can increase sales and spur growth and expand opportunity and improve many individuals' chances for advancement, then you create a positive loop in human lives... and the whole ecosystem thrives.

As businesses mature and stop growing, it's our responsibility to figure out how to get them growing again. Growth leads to self-fulfillment and healthy, lasting change. One of the very best ways to give back is to encourage growth. We can talk about success and achievement until we're blue in the face, but if somebody lacks a job or is seriously underemployed, it's hard for that individual to feel fulfilled, productive, and happy.

Maybe you can see now why I have such a passion to help businesspeople engineer successful turnarounds. For me, it's a calling—one that benefits just about everyone.

MY MENTORS

David Bonderman: Willing to Bet on Capability Over Age

Most people know David Bonderman as the ubersuccessful founder of the private equity firm TPG, one of the largest private equity firms in the world. Before that, he was a University of Washington and Harvard Law School graduate, a lawyer at Arnold & Porter, and chief operating officer at the Robert M. Bass Group in Fort Worth. David is also very generous with his time and resources.

But I like to say I knew David when he still "flew coach," before he became famous. David took a huge risk in leaving the Bass brothers to buy Continental Airlines, his only deal at the time, which was funded by a small number of wealthy individuals. David took an even bigger risk when his only investment seemed ready to file for its third bankruptcy, and in response he named a thirty-three-year-old Bain consultant (me) as president and COO. I'm still not sure why David picked me. Perhaps he saw something promising in my partnership with Gordon. Maybe he just didn't have another choice. But he received a rich reward. The success of Continental (a twenty-fold return on investment) allowed David and his partners to form TPG and raise its first fund.

I'll always be grateful to David for giving a thirty-three-year-old consultant a chance to run an airline. It changed my career.

Appendix: An Airline Learns to Fly Right

> *Being a consultant is like flying first class. The food is good and the drinks are cold but all you can do is walk up to the cockpit and ask the pilot to bank left. If you are management, you have the controls. It is your leg.*
>
> GREG BRENNEMAN

W HAT A DIFFERENCE A few years can make.
        I arrived at Continental Airlines in 1994 to find the most dysfunctional company I'd ever seen. Just four years later, the *Harvard Business Review* asked me to write an article describing how we'd pulled off one of the greatest turnarounds in American business history. It really is one of those classic, "Can you believe *this*?" stories that continues to captivate people.

First, it clearly illustrates how anyone can use the five steps to breathe new life into a dying organization. When you identify and pull the key value drivers, even businesses that look hopeless can regain their footing and start sprinting again (or in Continental's case, flying profitably again).

Second, it demonstrates how long lasting and powerful the five-step approach can be. The five steps drove extraordinary success for more than fifteen years until Continental merged with United, while positioning the company to help consolidate the industry from a position of strength. While times certainly have changed since 1994, the essential strategy we used back then to turn around Continental works just as well now. Yes, I've enhanced the five steps since my Continental adventure—but that only highlights the rock-solid foundation on which the five steps are built.

Step Four, Build a Team, reminds me that I need to thank my coworkers at Continental for the key role they played in this turnaround. It could not have happened without them. While it's impossible for me to personally thank all 40,000 team members, I'm glad to say that whenever I fly United, I do still occasionally get the chance to tell many of them—pilots, flight attendants, and gate agents, in particular—how much I appreciate them.

Still, a few team members deserve special mention. Gordon Bethune, our great CEO, retired in 2004 after spending an incredible decade leading Continental. I mention him frequently in the upcoming story. Larry Kellner served as our

CFO during my tenure as president and COO. Larry became president after I left in May 2001 and chairman and CEO after Gordon left in 2004. Larry is one of the smartest leaders I have ever met. He assisted Gordon through the tragedy of 9-11 and then led the airline through the difficult financial crisis of 2008. Larry left the airline in a powerful position. Jeff Smisek served as our general counsel during my time at Continental; he became president in 2004 when Larry was named CEO, and then he took over as chairman and CEO after Larry left. Jeff saw the need to consolidate the airline industry and led the merger of Continental and United. That consolidation has led to a much more stable industry structure that benefits both employees and shareholders. Much of the original, outstanding Continental management team we had continued to work with Jeff at United.

A few more team members also deserve special mention. C.D. McLean retired as one of the best EVP operations I have ever seen. David Grizzle did all our important alliance partnerships at Continental and left to become the COO of the FAA. Dave Siegel ran scheduling and then Continental Express, then went on to run US Airways and Frontier. Glen Hauenstein ran scheduling and network for Continental and now does the same at Delta. Our Continental management team made it possible for us to succeed, and many of them went on to even greater success.

So now, let me take you back to a time not so long ago and to a scenario not so far away from where many of us live at this very moment....

Right Away and All At Once
How We Saved Continental
by Greg Brenneman

From the September–October 1998 issue of the
Harvard Business Review

I WILL NEVER FORGET MY first flight from Dallas to
Houston on Continental Airlines. It was a hot, humid day
in May 1993. At the time, I was a partner specializing in corporate turnarounds in Bain & Company's Dallas office. My goal
that day was to sell Bain's consulting services to Continental's
CEO and new owner, a leveraged buyout firm that had just
rescued the airline from its second bankruptcy in nine years.

Although I was a frequent flier with literally millions of miles
racked up on other airlines, I had always avoided Continental
because of its reputation for lousy service. In fact, back in 1990,
when we were deciding where to locate Bain's Texas office, we

specifically chose Dallas instead of Houston so we could use American rather than Continental for our constant business travel.

Continental lived up—or perhaps I should say down—to my expectations that day in May. Because I was not a frequent flier on Continental, I was seated in the last row of an unattractive and dirty DC-9. The airplane's interior had seven different color schemes, which I later found out was not uncommon. After all, Continental was the product of mergers among seven airlines; when a seat needed to be replaced, the company used whatever was in stock. Worse, no one had hooked up the plane's air-conditioning. Departure time came and went, and people continued to trickle on board for another 40 minutes. I found this remarkable given that the flight time was only 36 minutes. There were no announcements about our delay, and none of the crew seemed particularly concerned.

Finally, probably to prevent a riot, the captain turned on the DC-9's auxiliary power unit. This cooled down the airplane all right, but it also caused condensation to build up on the inside roof of the aircraft. When we took off at last—50 minutes late—the accumulated condensation flowed like a waterfall along the top of the baggage bins to the back of the airplane. It came pouring out above the center seat in the last row of coach—directly onto my head. My best suit and I were soaked.

To make a long story short—and it was a long day—Bain got

the job. I wasn't sure if I should celebrate or commiserate with my colleagues. My first assignment was to help Continental lower its maintenance costs and improve its dispatch reliability—in other words, figure out a way to fix planes that were breaking down when they needed to be flying. Drastic changes were made: within a year we had reduced the annual maintenance budget from $777 million to $495 million, and the airline jumped from worst to first in the industry in dispatch reliability. But the company was still sinking fast. By the fall of 1994, Continental had blown much of the $766 million in cash that it had when it emerged from bankruptcy in April 1993.

In my six-odd years of working on turnarounds at Bain, I had never seen a company as dysfunctional as Continental. There was next to no strategy in place. Managers were paralyzed by anxiety. The company had gone through ten presidents in ten years, so standard operating procedure was to do nothing while awaiting new management. The product, in a word, was terrible. And the company's results showed it. Continental ranked tenth out of the ten largest U.S. airlines in all key customer-service areas as measured by the Department of Transportation: on-time arrivals, baggage handling, customer complaints, and involuntary denied boardings. And the company hadn't posted a profit outside of bankruptcy since 1978.

But even with all these obstacles, Continental pulled out of its nosedive, just before it hit the ground, and it soared. (For

CLIMBING AGAIN

Continental Airlines has undergone a dramatic and profitable turnaround in the past several years.

REVENUE

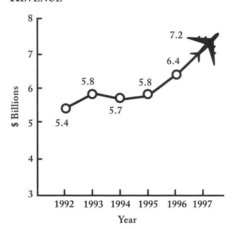

NET INCOME

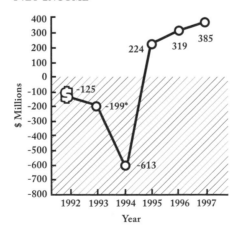

* *This figure excludes bankruptcy-related items.*

more on Continental's performance, see the exhibit "Climbing Again.") How did the reversal of fortunes happen? Looking back, I can see we were guided by five operating principles. Probably none of them will knock your socks off. In fact, sometimes when I talk to people about the lessons the turnaround taught us, they say, "Well, Greg, those seem simple enough. Maybe things were a bit dicey while it was happening, but it sure doesn't sound like brain surgery."

And they are right: saving Continental wasn't brain surgery. The actions required to revive a moribund company usually aren't. In Continental's case, we simply needed to fly to places people wanted to go, when they wanted to go, in clean, attractive airplanes; get them there on time with their bags; and serve food at mealtimes. The tough part—like in most turnarounds—was getting all that done fast, right away, and all at once.

The fact is, you can't afford to think too much during a turnaround. Time is tight; money is tighter. If you sit around devising elegant and complex strategies and then try to execute them through a series of flawless decisions, you're doomed. We saved Continental because we acted and we never looked back. We didn't say to the patient—if you can call a dying company that—"Now, just hold on a while so we can run a lot of tests and then perhaps perform an extremely delicate 12-hour procedure." No, we just took out the scalpel and went to work. We gave the patient little or no anesthesia, and it hurt like hell. Then again, the patient is cured now, right?

One last thing before we get to the lessons. You will see the word *we* a lot as you read this article. In the broadest sense, *we* refers to my 40,000 coworkers at Continental. The airline could not have been saved if everyone in the company, and I mean everyone, had not pulled together. But in a narrower sense, *we* refers to myself and Gordon Bethune, Continental's chairman and CEO.

Gordon and I met in February 1994. I was still with Bain, in the midst of my first assignment for Continental. Gordon had just left a cushy job, or at least one where he could sleep soundly at night, at the Boeing Company to become president and COO of Continental. In me, Gordon found a frustrated consultant who bristled at the slow pace of change in most companies. In Gordon, I found an extraordinary leader who knew the airline business inside and out, and who managed the men and women of Continental with great heart. We hit it off from the start.

That was a good thing, because we were in a big mess together—bigger than either of us knew at first. Sure, we were able to fix some problems, such as an incredibly slow reservations system and a substandard customer-response policy. But those fixes were like trying to bail out the *Titanic* with a coffee can. Continental was losing an incredible amount of money and, more important, burning through cash at an astonishing rate. We were on our way to a third bankruptcy.

In October 1994, Continental's CEO resigned. That left Gordon nominally in charge, and he asked me to help. He moved into the CEO's office, and I moved into his old office. We had a week to put together a turnaround plan for Continental and develop a pitch to the board to name Gordon the CEO.

Throughout that week, Gordon and I held several dinner meetings—dubbed our "Last Suppers"—at his house. We knew a major ending was on the horizon—either the old Continental was going to be entirely reinvented or it was going to go bankrupt for an unprecedented third time and would probably be liquidated. Over several bottles of wine, we wrote down everything that was wrong with Continental. It was a very long list. We organized our solutions to those problems into a strategy that we called the *Go Forward Plan*. We named it that because we knew our history was not going to help us. Did you know that there are no rearview mirrors on an airplane? The runway behind is irrelevant.

Our Go Forward Plan had four cornerstones. *Fly to Win* was the market plan: we were going to build up our Houston, Newark, and Cleveland hubs, for instance, and expand our customer mix from backpacks and flip-flops to suits and briefcases. *Fund the Future* was the financial plan: we were going to gain liquidity by restructuring our balance sheet and selling off nonstrategic assets. *Make Reliability a Reality* was the product plan: we were going to transform the customer's experience with us. And finally, *Working Together* was the people plan: we were going to change Continental's culture to one of fun and action and restore employees' trust. It was my opinion then, and remains today, that every company should have a strategy that covers these four elements—market, financial, product, and people—whether it is in a severe crisis or not.

Gordon and I weren't totally convinced that Continental could be saved, even with our plan. But we had to try—40,000 jobs were at stake. It was scary. And for me, it was a defining moment. I was thinking, "Greg, this is one of those times in life when you step up to the plate or you chicken out." I had spent the last six years making recommendations that my clients sometimes took and sometimes ignored. I wanted to make things happen. It was going to take hard work, but that didn't worry me. I'm from a little farming town in Kansas where hard work is a way of life. I held a paying job when I was in third grade, and no one even blinked. In the summer of my junior year in high school, I mowed lawns from 6:30 a.m. until noon, delivered office furniture from noon until 6:00 p.m., and then baled and stacked hay until midnight. Frankly, I'd rather be working than not any day of the week.

Most important, even with all the work ahead, turning Continental around seemed like it was going to be fun. Grueling

—without a doubt. Painful—certainly. Embarrassing—maybe, if we failed. But fun— yes. It's thrilling to lead people to do something no one thinks can be done. In fact, when we went before the board, we told them Continental could earn about $40 million in 1995. I know most of them thought we were on drugs. But who else was there volunteering to save Continental? The board approved the plan, and we were on our way.

Believe it or not, at this point I still wasn't on Continental's payroll. But both David Bonderman of Air Partners (the LBO firm that owned the airline) and Gordon were pushing me to join. They kept telling me I could be the only 33-year-old to run a $6 billion company. I kept telling them it was the world's worst $6 billion company. In spite of my reservations, I signed on. I truly believed the men and women of Continental could make the airline great again. We just had to get in there and do it.

Pulling Out of a Nosedive: Five Turnaround Lessons

File your flight plan and track your progress.

Strategic direction is never more crucial than during a crisis. Leaders must find the most leveraged plan of action, stick with it, and continually monitor the company's performance against it.

Clean house.

The same team that leads a company into a crisis is rarely able to get it back on track. The hard news about a turnaround is that you have no choice but to sweep out the old to make way for the new.

Think "money in," not "money out."

Companies that are headed for disaster try to cut costs, but that can sabotage the product, which lowers revenues more. Break the *doom loop* by apologizing for your mistakes and focus on delivering a better product.

Ask the customer in seat 9C the right question.

There is a huge gap between what customers want and what they are willing to pay for. Make sure you know the difference.

Let the inmates run the asylum.

Strong leadership, firm parameters, and clear direction are necessary in a turnaround situation, but the workplace needn't be repressive. In fact, if employees aren't having fun at work—that is, if they aren't engaged in the process and treated with respect—your turnaround will not succeed.

File Your Flight Plan and Track Your Progress

The foundation of any successfully run business is a strategy everyone understands coupled with a few key measures that are routinely tracked. Now, strategic direction is always important, but I would make the case that it is particularly important during a turnaround. In crisis situations, managers usually have limited time and financial resources. If you have very little money to spend and you have to spend it very quickly, you had better have a clear idea of the most leveraged plan of action. Moreover, pressure and fear often make managers do erratic, inconsistent, even irrational things. Companies may veer from one "strategy" to another just to make payroll or keep a client. Continental was a case in point. When we took over, you probably couldn't find a single employee, even among senior management, who could tell you the company's strategy. There had been so many over the past decade that they'd stopped keeping track.

Oh sure, people paid lip service to strategy. Here's a classic example. When I first arrived at Continental as a consultant, 18% of the flights were cash negative. I knew the fastest way to make money was to stop doing things that lose it. I sat the scheduling team down and started asking questions. "Why are we going from Greensboro to Greenville six times a day when both customers who want to fly that route are on the first flight?"

"It's strategic," someone told me.

"When did it last make money?"

"It never did," was the reply.

"How strategic can that be?"

There was silence. I asked, "Does someone's boyfriend or girlfriend live there? Why don't we just charter you a Lear jet?

It would be cheaper." That route, along with other cash-draining flights, was soon eliminated, and 7,000 employees were let go.

To put an end to Continental's strategic wandering, Gordon and I introduced the Go Forward Plan to our coworkers. It was our story and we were sticking to it (to borrow a line from a country-and-western song). The Go Forward Plan wasn't complex. It was pure common sense. We needed to stop flying 120-seat planes with only 30 passengers on them. We needed to get people to their destinations on time with their bags. We needed to start serving food when people were hungry. We needed to create an atmosphere where people liked coming to work. (For details of the strategy, see the exhibit "Continental's New Flight Plan.")

Continental's New Flight Plan

With little time and even less money to save the airline in 1994, Continental's leaders devised the *Go Forward Plan*, a four-part strategy focused on the fundamentals.

Fly to Win was the airline's marketplace plan; *Fund the Future* was the financial plan; *Make Reliability a Reality* was the formula to improve the product; and *Working Together* was the blueprint for improving the company's culture.

There was nothing complex about the Go Forward Plan:

CONTINENTAL'S GO FORWARD PLAN

FLY TO WIN

Focus on core assets:
⇨ Stop scheduling flights that lose money
⇨ Take out cost as we take out capacity.
⇨ Eliminate CALite.
⇨ Build up Houston, Newark, and Cleveland hubs.

Expand customer mix from backpacks and flip-flops to suits and briefcases.

Revise marketing policies to enhance relationships with travel agents, corporations and frequent fliers.

GOAL: *Increase revenues and deliver a profit.*

FUND THE FUTURE

Restructure the fleet:
⇨ Reduce the number of fleet types from 13 to 4.
⇨ Match airplane size with market size.
⇨ Eliminate above-market leases on airplanes.

Restructure the balance sheet.

Track cash.

Sell nonstrategic assets.

GOAL: *Secure liquidity.*

MAKE RELIABILITY A REALITY

Perform in the top 50% of the industry on key DOT metrics:
⇨ On-time performance.
⇨ Baggage mishandles.
⇨ Customer complaints.
⇨ Involuntary denied boardings.

Improve the image of the fleet:
⇨ Paint interiors and exteriors.
⇨ Add phones.
⇨ Offer first-class seats.

Improve aircraft cleanliness.

Improve food service.

GOAL: *Improve the product to become an airline of preference.*

WORKING TOGETHER

Restore employee confidence in management:
⇨ Offer on-time incentives.
⇨ Establish a consistent and reliable flight schedule.
⇨ Improve communication.
⇨ Deliver a profit and introduce profit sharing.

Maintain peace among the work groups.

Establish a results-oriented culture:
⇨ Let people do their jobs without interference.
⇨ Treat one another with dignity and respect.

GOAL: *Build a new corporate culture.*

it was just a matter of logic and common sense. It remains the backbone of the company's strategy today.

To implement the plan immediately and in its entirety, we sold it to our coworkers with energetic zeal. We knew that the two of us could not save Continental on our own. But if we could get every employee headed in the same direction, we had a chance. At the same time, we chose 15 or so key performance measures to track relentlessly and to compare against our competitors. We didn't pick randomly; we chose measures that could be verified by the Department of Transportation. Moreover, the measures had to be aligned with the Go Forward Plan. To monitor our performance in the marketplace, we decided to track our monthly load factor, revenue per available seat mile, and quarterly cost and profit margins. To monitor our product, we decided to track our monthly on-time performance, mishandled bags, customer complaints, and the rate of involuntary denied boardings. And to monitor the progress of our people plan, we decided to track turnover, sick leave, attrition, and on-the-job injuries.

Finally, and perhaps most important, to monitor our financial progress, we announced we were going to track cash. Let me tell you why. On Thanksgiving Day in 1994, I discovered that we were going to run out of cash on January 17, 1995—payday—and no one even knew it. I mean, no one had a clue. As you all know, cash is the lifeblood of any business. Without it, all your great plans to have a product you are proud of and people who like coming to work every day are meaningless. The buzzer will go off before you attempt the last shot, and you will lose.

You may be wondering why Continental's cash situation came as such a surprise. The reason tells you a lot about how people act when their companies are in a self-destructive mode. Some of the finance people had regularly been inflating our profit projections by plugging in overoptimistic revenue estimates. They felt pressured to do so, they said. In our business, revenue comes from credit card receipts. Naturally, our cashflow forecasts always came in lower than projected because revenue (and thus, credit card receipts) was overstated. To this day, I can't understand why anyone would try to hide an impending cash shortage. Sure, it's bound to make the shareholders very unhappy, but hiding the fact that you are about to run out of money is like resetting the fuel gauge when you're low on gas. Will things suddenly look okay in the cockpit? Yes. Will you land short of your destination? You bet.

When I discovered Continental's real cash situation, I called Gordon. "I have some bad news for you," I told him. "Unless we restructure our obligations, we will not be able to make payroll in mid-January." While both our hearts were beating a million times an hour, we had a remarkably calm conversation. We could either declare bankruptcy or we could try to convince our creditors that the Go Forward Plan was going to work and then craft a very quiet restructuring. It had to be quiet because if the press caught on, the headlines would send more customers running, taking our revenues with them.

A couple of days later, I found myself in a room with our largest creditors. They represented approximately $3.5 billion of our $5 billion in debt and capitalized aircraft leases. I took them through the current situation, what we were doing to fix it, and the help we needed from them. They began ranting and raving. After a while, when it became apparent we were going nowhere, I got up to leave the room.

"Where are you going?" they shouted.

"I'm going home to watch TV," I answered.

"How can you drop all this on us and then leave?" they demanded.

"Do you know what the first step in problem solving is?" I asked. After a moment of dead silence, I continued, "The first step in problem solving is asking, Who has got the problem? As near as I can tell, if you take the share price times the number of shares outstanding, this entire company is worth $175 million and you are in hock for $3.5 billion. You run the company." Then I walked out.

I'll never know what possessed me to say that. Maybe it was the 20-hour days I was working. Maybe it was the fact that I had seen a client of mine do largely the same thing during a real estate restructuring, to great effect. Maybe I was just fed up with the fact that everyone seemed to have a problem but no one had any solutions. But a few minutes later, the creditors came to my office and asked me to come back in. Things were much calmer. With the help of some talented financial experts, within a few weeks we had worked out a plan to restructure our debt. We made payroll on January 17 with the help of a $29 million wire transfer Gordon arranged from Boeing.

After that crisis was over, we knew we would never lose track of our cash again. It's all part of knowing our flight plan and monitoring our progress every mile of the way.

Clean House

I have never seen the team that managed a company into a crisis get it back on track. Oh, I'm sure it has happened some time in the history of business, but I can't believe it has happened very often. Instead, managers who have gotten a company into a mess are usually mired in a puddle of overbrained solutions. They can't see any way out either. In fact, they have many ways of saying, "If the solution were simple, we would have already thought of it." On top of that, they usually have trouble accepting responsibility for and reversing the poor decisions they made in the past. It's an ego thing. And there's one more problem with existing management teams sticking around for a turnaround. No one in the company trusts them anymore. They got us into this hole, the thinking goes, how are they going to have the sense to get us out of it?

Those are the main reasons we decided to clean house when we took over at Continental. But there were others. People want to be led, not managed, in a time of crisis. Members of Continental's existing management team were not up to this challenge. They were too busy trying to knock each other off. In fact, for 15 years, the way to get ahead at Continental was to torpedo someone and then take his or her job.

Gordon and I were determined to present a united front. No one was going to come between us; if they tried, they were out. I will always remember my first meeting with all the officers at Continental. Gordon started the meeting by saying, "Greg is going to take you through our plan to get this company back on track. I want you to listen to what he has to say, and when he tells you to do something, you assume it is coming from me, and do it."

In the span of a couple of months, we replaced 50 of our 61 officers with about 20 individuals. We were cutting bureaucracy and costs but also putting important stuff—like the right culture—back in. All new hires had to have three qualities. First, they had to pass what we called the "raw IQ test"—there is no substitute for smarts. Second, they had to be driven to get things done. Finally, they had to be team players, willing to treat everyone with dignity and respect in an extremely collaborative environment.

Speaking of dignity and respect, cleaning house needn't be a brutal or humiliating experience. Every turnaround involves creating a new culture. If you fire people inhumanely, you'll be left with a bunch of employees who don't trust the company or their coworkers. We needed to create a culture at Continental where people liked coming to work. We couldn't afford to have people hoarding ideas or sapping enthusiasm as we built our new organization. So when we let people go, we went out of our way to be fair by honoring their contracts and letting them resign with dignity.

We are often asked how we got such great people in the span of only a couple of months, especially at a company that appeared to be going down the tubes. The answer is, we started by hiring people we knew, many of whom were our friends. That expedited the process of screening candidates and greatly reduced our hiring mistakes. Some of these managers had spent their careers in the airline business and some hadn't worked a day at an airline. One of our techniques was to find people who were in a number two position in their current job and ask them to join Continental in the number one spot. For instance, we'd ask the number two person in pricing at another airline to come run our pricing department. We promised them full control of their domains.

And we sold Continental as if it were already a winner. At the time, our stock was trading at about $7, but I told people we wanted to hire that we were going to drive it up to $80 or higher. We offered them options along the way, so if the shareholders won, they would win. Most of them thought I was nuts, but as one of them later told me, "I figured if you were even half right, I was still going to be worth a lot of money." (And, in fact, the turnaround created many millionaires.)

It's important to point out that we didn't just clean house on the top floor of Continental. We went through the entire organization—from the highest supervisors to the baggage handlers. Many companies in crisis mode will change the CEO or president and leave it at that. In my opinion, that approach is like changing only the lead husky on a sled-dog team. Four dogs back, the look and smell stays the same. When you want real change, you can't do it partway. You have to do it fast, right away, and all at once.

Think "Money In," Not "Money Out"

Every turnaround involves cost reduction, and Continental was no exception. Most companies that are in trouble, however, tend to develop a myopic focus on cost. They forget to ask simple questions like, Do we have a product people want to buy? Will our distributors sell our product? and, Are we taking care of our best customers? In short, they forget to think about money in, or good old revenues.

Of course, when you are bleeding cash, it's hard to think about anything but tourniquets. But Continental had been cutting costs in ways that sabotaged its product. For instance, in the early 1990s, pilots earned bonuses if the fuel burn rate on their airplanes fell below a specified amount. The program did decrease fuel costs, but it motivated many pilots to skimp on air-conditioning. (Indeed, the program may have been the reason behind my first "refreshing" experience with Continental.) It also motivated them to fly more slowly. That made our customers late and angry and ruined the lives of our employees who had to work overtime because of tardy arrivals. It also forced the airline to pay more to accommodate customers who had to take other airlines because of missed connections.

Perhaps the ultimate manifestation of Continental's low-cost approach was CALite, the company's doomed low-cost airline-within-an-airline. For CALite, Continental removed all first-class seats in some airplanes. That lowered the cost per seat mile by adding more seats, but it alienated Continental's best business customers and often resulted in an all-coach airplane on long flights when airplanes were swapped during adverse weather conditions. CALite eliminated all food on its flights, and it also eliminated travel agent commissions and corporate discounts, which infuriated some very important customers.

All told, after 15 years of a low-cost approach, Continental had created what I call a *doom loop*. By focusing only on costs, the airline had created a product no one wanted to buy. Many customers, particularly business customers with a choice, selected other airlines, reducing revenues enough to create huge losses. Those losses made it impossible to borrow money at reasonable rates. Management then had to borrow from "pawn shops" to keep the company afloat, which increased interest expenses. In order to make up for these increased expenses, management cut costs further. Since the costs of the aircraft and fuel were fixed, and costs such as food had already been cut, the only way to reduce costs was to take back wages from employees. That ticked them off (to put it in language this publication will permit), which caused further reductions in service. As a result, more customers left, revenues continued to drop, and costs had to be cut more and more.

You might think the first step in breaking the doom loop is to fix the product, but that's actually the second step. The first is to beg forgiveness from all the customers you have wronged. Sure, you can skip this step, but you'll miss out on the goodwill it fosters and the relationships it spawns. Confession is good for everyone's soul, and often for the pocketbook as well.

Our forgiveness campaign had a couple of parts. First, we

divided the angry letters from customers among our officers—executives through the rank of vice president—and started making phone calls. Our goal was not only to apologize but also to explain what we were doing to fix the company. Gordon and I each took our share of the letters. It was a humbling experience. The calls would often last half an hour or more. People were incredibly frustrated and wanted to let us know how badly they had been treated. By the end of the call, however, they were usually appreciative that an officer of the company had taken the time to seek them out.

We also assigned one city in our system to each officer and asked them to go through the same process of apologizing to travel agents and corporate customers. Gordon and I took the largest of those accounts. Again, we heard our share of shouting—there was a lot of venom out there. But at the same time, people couldn't believe that we were coming around to say we were sorry and to thank them for their business. I never denied that Continental had been a terrible airline. In fact, I usually agreed with everything they said. But I also wanted them to know that a new beginning was under way.

The third step in breaking the doom loop was to cut our advertising budget in half. It is offensive and insulting to customers to advertise a product that they know is crummy. Until the time came when we could offer them something great, I didn't want to promote a product that we couldn't deliver.

So advertising less—lying less—was another way of saying we were sorry.

Begging for forgiveness can be unpleasant, that's for sure. But it's indispensable if you want to break the doom loop. Only after that has begun can you move on to making money—the subject of the next principle.

Ask the Customer in Seat 9C the Right Question

Deciding to focus more on customers' desires rather than on cutting costs is actually the easy part. The hard part is figuring out how to improve the customer's experience so that revenues increase faster than costs. Any first-year marketing student can tell you that to make more money, you have to listen to your best, most lucrative customers. In our case, that meant listening to the customers in seat 9C, the business travelers who book the aisle seats near the front of the plane. They pay full fare, and they travel a lot.

But we knew we couldn't listen to everything the customers in seat 9C had to say. If you ask customers what they really want, they will write you an epistle a foot thick. If you ask them what they want *and will pay extra for*, you will get a single sheet of paper with requests. That's where our focus was, and it's a good rule for any turnaround.

Relying mostly on our own experience as business travelers, we knew that the customer in seat 9C would pay extra for a few things: airplanes and terminals that are safe, comfortable, and attractive; on-time flights and reliable baggage handling; and good food at mealtimes. With the exception of safety, where Continental had always had a strong record, we were failing miserably on all counts.

We went to work at full speed. We asked the maintenance department to paint the exterior of every airplane the same and to match all the interiors. We also ordered new carpeting for all the airport terminals, and we launched a campaign to "retire the meatball"—that is, replace the old Continental logo, which was round, red, and ugly, with a blue globe with gold lettering. And we wanted it all done in six months.

The maintenance department was not amused. "Greg," I was told, "You have just proven you don't know anything about the airline business. You're asking for a four-year project." My response: "If you can't get it done, we'll find someone who will." Lo and behold, within six months, every plane was painted the same color inside and out, and all of the terminals had new carpeting. Our maintenance team worked their fannies off, and Continental's handsome new image was everywhere. Chalk one up for the power of persuasion.

Our customers loved Continental's new look. Who wouldn't after flying on the old Continental? In March 1995, I boarded a 737-100, which at 27 years was the oldest airplane in our fleet. The gentleman sitting next to me looked at me and said,

"Isn't it great that Continental is getting all these new airplanes?" I just smiled.

The new image had an even bigger impact on our employees. They could see senior management finally taking the actions they knew had been needed for years. They could come to work in airports and on airplanes that looked clean and new. One of our MD-80 captains called me and said, "Greg, I knew we would be a good airline again once our airplanes were the same color."

We also started an aircraft appearance department to make sure our airplanes would continue to look great day after day. We learned that in one of the early cost-reduction programs, management had decided to clean the airplanes less frequently and to have the pilots clean their own cockpits. We quickly set up a cleaning schedule that tripled the number of times the airplanes are cleaned, cockpits included.

As for improving reliability, we had to get two sets of folks talking to each other: those that wrote the flight schedules and those that ran the flight and airport operations. In the past, the scheduling department had simply written a flight schedule and given it to operations, often only days before they were to fly it, because it was "confidential." As a result, the operating departments were frequently stuck with a schedule they had no hope of following: they had mechanics, parts, and crews in the wrong locations. Very quickly, we required the scheduling and operating departments to review and sign off on the flight schedules before they were loaded to be flown. Presto, now people were in control of their own destiny, and the finger-pointing stopped.

Once Continental had a flight schedule that could be operated on time, we made an offer to our employees. For every month we finished in the top five out of ten airlines in on-time performance as measured by the DOT, we would give each employee $65. Incentives were now aligned; when the customers won, the employees did, too. Within months, we were regularly finishing first.

The offer sounds pretty bold for a company almost in bankruptcy, doesn't it? Truth is, the on-time incentive program is self-funding. When we made the offer, we were paying about $6 million per month to reaccommodate our customers on our competitors' flights. We were taking in approximately $750,000 per month. Since reaccommodation expenses showed up in a contra-revenue account rather than as a cost on the general ledger, they escaped the eyes of the cost reduction program. As an on-time airline, we pay out only $750,000 in reaccommodation expenses while taking in $4 million. Our balance of payments has changed by $8 million to $9 million per month. The on-time bonus costs only $3 million per month.

We also immediately started fixing our idiotic food policy. I don't know about you, but to me, a two-hour flight that leaves at 7:00 a.m. (after I have gotten up at 5:00 a.m. to get to the airport and haven't eaten breakfast) is a lot different from a two-hour flight at 2:00 p.m., which falls after lunch but before dinner. Customers told us they wanted and would pay for breakfast at 7:00 a.m. They may want food at 2:00 p.m., but they won't pay for it. We changed our meal service with an eye toward what our competitors were doing. Now our service reflects time of day, length of haul, and class of service.

In addition to changing *when* we served food, we also changed the food itself. Gone are the days when Continental put the meat, potato, and vegetable in a little ceramic dish and heated it until they all tasted the same. Nowadays, Gordon and I personally select the food we serve on our planes, and we test it ourselves every three months. You will find items like fresh pasta, soup and sandwiches, and freshly baked cinnamon rolls in first class, and Subway sandwiches and jelly beans in coach. We try to give everyone some brand quality with gourmet coffees and microbrewery beers. We're not trying to be a four-star restaurant, just an airline that gives its customers something they'd be happy to pay for.

And that's the whole point of asking the customer in seat 9C the right question. In a turnaround situation—or any business situation, for that matter—you can't afford to ask anything else.

Let the Inmates Run the Asylum

I'm not going to tell you that all the employees at Continental are "empowered." We fly airplanes, after all. When people's lives are at stake, certain rules and procedures are not open to interpretation or reinvention on a daily basis. And when you are an airline in a do-or-die situation, you don't exactly let your employees sort out strategy. It would take too long, and it's no way to act when strong leadership is imperative.

But within the parameters set for safety and those we set with the Go Forward Plan, we decided that at the new Continental, the employees were going to be liberated—to be able to do the right thing by the customer and to have fun at work.

Now, fun at work isn't about dancing on the tarmac. In fact, I think the word *fun* scares a lot of executives. They picture productivity plummeting, and profits along with it. But I would argue that people have fun at work when they are engaged, when their opinions are respected. People are happy when they feel they are making a difference.

When I arrived at Continental, it was a mean and lousy place to work. For years, different groups of employees had been pitted against one another in the effort to drive down labor costs. Management's implicit communication policy had been, Don't tell anybody anything unless absolutely required. As a result, most employees learned of the company's activities, plans, and performance through the press. Talk about sending a message about who matters and who doesn't.

On top of that, employees had no place to go with ideas

or questions. There were forms for employees' suggestions on how to improve the operations, but the suggestions disappeared into a black hole. Add to that the fact that corporate headquarters was locked up like Fort Knox: the president's secretary had a buzzer under her desk that she could use to summon the police.

Needless to say, morale was terrible. A couple of weeks after I arrived, I was walking the ramp in Houston saying hello to our mechanics and baggage handlers, and helping to throw a bag or two, when I noticed that almost all the employees had torn the Continental logos from their shirts. When I asked one mechanic why he had done this, he explained, "When I go to Walmart tonight, I don't want anyone to know that I work for Continental." His response still sends chills down my spine.

Now, how to create a new culture is the topic of hundreds, if not thousands, of books and articles. But Gordon and I didn't bother with them. We agreed that a healthy culture is simply a function of several factors, namely: honesty, trust, dignity, and respect. They all go together; they reinforce one another. When they are constants in a business, people become engaged in their work. They care; they talk; they laugh. And then fun happens pretty naturally. But honesty and the rest don't just sprout up like weeds in a cornfield, especially when there has been a long drought. In a turnaround situation, people are tense and suspicious for good reason. They've been lied to. They've seen their friends get fired. They fear they will be next.

So cultivating honesty, trust, dignity, and respect becomes the job of the leaders. It may even be their most important job; Gordon and I certainly considered it our top priority. That's why when we took over, we started talking with employees at every opportunity. We got out there in the airports and on the planes. We loaded bags; we stood alongside the agents at ticket counters. We just talked at every opportunity about our plans for the airline and how we were going to accomplish them. In general, our communication policy changed from, Don't tell anybody anything unless absolutely required, to Tell everybody everything.

We also told our employees we believed in them. They knew how to treat customers right, and we moved quickly to let them do just that. In the past, any time an employee provided a benefit for a customer that was considered unacceptable, the bankers and lawyers running Continental would write a rule documenting the proper action. Over the years, these rules were accumulated into a book about nine inches thick known as the Thou Shalt Not book. Employees couldn't possibly know the entire contents of the book. When in doubt, everyone knew it was advised just to let the customers fend for themselves. In early 1995, we took the Thou Shalt Not book to a company parking lot. We got a 55-gallon drum, tossed the book inside, and poured gasoline all over it. In front of a crowd of employees, we lit a match to it. Our message was this: Continental is your company to make great. Go do it—now.

Because it is critical to get everyone working together, we aligned employees' compensation with the company's objectives. The on-time bonus I mentioned earlier made it clear that our employees would win when our customers did. We also put in several programs to ensure that our coworkers would win when our investors did. For most of our employees, one incentive is profit sharing. Our workers receive 15% of Continental's profits—which has worked out to be approximately 7% of their pay over the last two years. We have a great time riding in Brink's trucks distributing profit-sharing checks every Valentine's Day.

To involve our employees even more in the turnaround, we put up 650 bulletin boards throughout the system. These boards contain everything an employee needs to know about the company, from a daily news update to Continental's operating results over the last 24 hours. In addition, Gordon records a voice mail each Friday that summarizes the activities of the week. Every month, Gordon and I hold an open house where employees can ask us questions, and we publish a newspaper describing what's happening in the company. Every quarter, we send a *Continental Quarterly* magazine to employees' homes, and twice a year we do the same with a state-of-the-company video and recent press clippings. The video is produced for our semiannual employee meetings, when we travel to nine locations to update everyone on our progress. By the way, sending select material to the home is one of the smartest things you can do. The support you get from each employee's family when they become part of the team is incredible. Finally, each corporate officer is assigned a city on the system. It is his or her responsibility to visit the city once per quarter to update employees, get their feedback, and fix their problems.

Of course, we'd be fools if all we did was talk *at* our employees. We listen, too. We set up a toll-free hotline that operates around the clock to handle employees' suggestions. Pilots, flight attendants, mechanics, and gate agents manage the hotline. They are required to research each suggestion and get back to the employee within 48 hours with one of three responses: we fixed it; we are not going to fix it, and here is why; or, we need to study it a little more, and we will get back to you by such and such date. We have taken more than 200 calls per week in the three years the hotline has been open.

We don't implement all of the suggestions—I'd say about one in ten is implemented—but we take each one seriously. A group of baggage handlers came to me a little more than a year ago and asked if we could tag the bags of our best customers "priority" and deliver them first off the baggage belt. It sounded like a great idea, but I was worried we would raise expectations and then not be able to deliver. They explained that the process was easy: as you pull the bags off the airplane, the ones marked priority go in the first baggage cart, which is the first to be unloaded. Priority bags are a big hit. The program didn't cost anything, but it added value to the customer. Today the plan is in place across our entire system.

The kind of talking and listening I've described goes a long way toward creating an atmosphere of honesty, trust, dignity, and respect. But to go the full distance, we knew that we would also have to communicate openly when the message was tough. Let me tell you, for instance, about the day I had to shut down our operations in Greensboro, North Carolina.

The historical norm for delivering bad news at Continental was for a senior manager to dump the news in the local airport manager's lap and then hide in our corporate office building. But I decided to go to Greensboro myself, make the announcement to the employees, and take my punches publicly.

When I arrived the night before the meeting, I found several messages waiting for me from the head of our pilots' union. He wanted to meet for breakfast the next morning, and I quickly agreed. When we met, he said that the Greensboro pilots were not angry that we were closing the airport—they could see that there were no customers on the flights. But they did not feel that the compensation package was fair. I said I was surprised; we had just finished negotiating the first pilots' contract in 12 years, and it had been ratified by a large margin. More-over, I had taken the financial relocation package called for in the contract and doubled it. I then offered it to all employees, not just pilots. Not mollified, the union president asked me to come to a meeting the pilots were having before my meeting with the entire airport staff.

That meeting was hostile, to put it mildly. But it would have been dishonest to back down or to fudge a reaction of sympathy I did not feel. I believed the pilots were getting a fair deal, and I said so. About an hour later, I met with the rest of the employees and their families—about 600 people in all. Along with explaining the details of the closing and relocation plans, I also shared with them my vision for Continental and how far we had come. I then opened the floor to questions and answers.

For about five minutes, employees expressed appreciation that I had personally come to give them the news and had developed a financial package to meet their needs. But then the pilots walked in—in full uniform—with their families. They surrounded the room and refused to sit down. A pilot came to the microphone to express how incompetent he felt man-agement was and how Continental was once again making the wrong decision. The rest of the pilots applauded.

Do you know what happened? The rest of the employees, led by a baggage handler who was also being relocated, stood up and defended me, one after another, for 20 minutes. They told the pilots that they should feel lucky that Continental finally had a senior management team that treated them with enough respect to deliver the bad news—as well as a good relocation package—in person. I left to a standing ovation.

Closing Greensboro was one of the toughest days of my life. It is a heavy responsibility to make decisions that affect the lives of so many coworkers. But it was a tough and emotional time for everyone. The pilots weren't bad folks; in fact, many of them are good friends of mine now. They were just frustrated with 15 years of poor decisions and were taking it out on me— like blaming your third wife for all of your problems with the first two. So I tell this story not to vilify them but to demonstrate the kind of trust that starts to emerge when a company's leaders neither hide nor mince words in bad times. It's easy to make everyone happy when things are going well. But real trust is a 365-days-a-year commitment.

Continental is a fun place to work today. Lots of statistics prove that fact, such as the huge reductions in turnover, sick leave, on-the-job injuries, and worker's compensation claims. But my favorite measure is the sale of Continental logo merchandise at our company stores. The same employees who used to tear the patches from their shirts so no one would know they worked at Continental have increased their purchases of hats, caps, T-shirts, and the like for themselves and their friends by more than 400%.

That's the kind of thing that happens when you let the inmates run the asylum. You may feel as if you've lost a bit of your authority and control over every last detail—because you have—but that's okay. You can't run a company from the executive suite of an office building anyway. When the employees are happy, everyone is happy—from the customers to the shareholders.

The Power of Momentum

Sometimes people ask me, "Did anything about the turnaround surprise you?" My answer is, "The fact that it didn't fail."

That's an exaggeration, because as I've said, I had enormous faith in my coworkers at Continental and the powerful logic of the Go Forward Plan. But at the beginning of the turnaround, there was so much wrong with the company—so many parts of it to fix—I really felt as if one little misstep could have brought us down. A single creditor could have blocked our restructuring. The economy could have been in a downswing. The pilots could have rejected their contract. We were working hard, yes—but we had great luck, too.

When I look back now, I realize the biggest factor in our favor was momentum. The rallying cry of our turnaround was, "Do it fast, do it right away, do it all at once. Do it now!" We lit a fire of urgency beneath Continental; we rotated quickly and picked up speed as we climbed to 41,000 feet. Pretty soon, we were unstoppable. What a ride it has been. Of course, the ride isn't over. We have big plans for Continental and mustn't lose our momentum. Even though the turnaround is over, we won't forget the lessons we learned from it. In fact, we're putting them to practice every day.

Notes

1. Brian Grow, Bloomberg Business, "Burger King's Whopper-Size Woes," July 6, 2004

2. Brad Tuttle, "The 5 Big Mistakes That Led to Ron Johnson's Ouster at JCPenney." *Time* magazine, April 9, 2013. http://business.time.com/2013/04/09/the-5-big-mistakes-that-led-to-ron-johnsons-ouster-at-jc-penney/

3. Ibid.

4. See, for example, http://www.quickmba.com/strategy/porter.shtml

5. Earnings before interest, taxes, depreciation, and amortization

6. C.S. Lewis, *Mere Christianity* (New York: Macmillan Publishing Co., Inc., 1952), p. 82

7. Senn Delaney suggests four tips for putting into practice Be Here Now:

   1. *Practice doing one thing at a time.*
   2. *Prioritize better so you are less overloaded and less over-scheduled.*
   3. *Find a way to "draw the line" to separate work life from the rest of your life.*
   4. *Let people around you know when you are distracted and you can't be there for them.*

8. Senn Delaney lists thirteen moods for its Mood Elevator, with curiosity in the middle. From top to bottom, they are: grateful, wise, creative, optimistic, appreciative, understanding, curious, frustrated, irritated, anxious, defensive, judgmental, depressed.

    It also suggests four tips for using the Mood Elevator:

    1. *Be aware of your moods.*
    2. *Take better care of yourself.*
    3. *Create a pattern interrupt. (Go for a walk, have a coffee, etc.)*
    4. *Be grateful for what you have and don't sweat the small stuff.*

9. KathyRM, "Tending the Vines in California," June 2, 2015. http://www.infobarrel.com/Tending_The_Vines_In_California

10. Isaac Manning, *It's Whose You Are, Not Who You Are*, self-published, 2015

11. Larry Briggs, *Sticky Leadership*, self-published, 2015